THE EUROPEAN UNION SERIES

General Editors: Neill Nugent, William E. Paterson

The European Union series provides an authoritative library on the European Union, ranging from general introductory texts to definitive assessments of key institutions and actors, issues, policies and policy processes, and the role of member states.

Books in the series are written by leading scholars in their fields and reflect the most up-to-date research and debate. Particular attention is paid to accessibility and clear presentation for a wide audience of students, practitioners and interested general readers.

The series editors are **Neill Nugent**, Professor of Politics and Jean Monnet Professor of European Integration, Manchester Metropolitan University, and **William E. Paterson**, Honourary Professor in German and European Studies, University of Aston. Their co-editor until his death in July 1999, **Vincent Wright**, was a Fellow of Nuffield College, Oxford University.

Feedback on the series and book proposals are always welcome and should be sent to Steven Kennedy, Palgrave Macmillan, Houndmills, Basingstoke, Hampshire RG21 6XS, UK, or by e-mail to s.kennedy@palgrave.com

---

General textbooks

Published

Desmond Dinan **Encyclopedia of the European Union**
[Rights: Europe only]

Desmond Dinan **Europe Recast: A History of European Union**
[Rights: Europe only]

Desmond Dinan **Ever Closer Union: An Introduction to European Integration** (4th edn)
[Rights: Europe only]

Mette Eilstrup Sangiovanni (ed.) **Debates on European Integration: A Reader**

Simon Hix and Bjørn Høyland **The Political System of the European Union** (3rd edn)

Paul Magnette **What is the European Union? Nature and Prospects**

John McCormick **Understanding the European Union: A Concise Introduction** (4th edn)

Brent F. Nelsen and Alexander Stubb **The European Union: Readings on the Theory and Practice of European Integration** (3rd edn)
[Rights: Europe only]

Neill Nugent (ed.) **European Union Enlargement**

Neill Nugent **The Government and Politics of the European Union** (7th edn)

John Peterson and Elizabeth Bomberg **Decision-Making in the European Union**

Ben Rosamond **Theories of European Integration**

Esther Versluis, Mendeltje van Keulen and Paul Stephenson **Analyzing the European Union Policy Process**

Forthcoming

Laurie Buonanno and Neill Nugent **Policies and Policy Processes of the European Union**

Dirk Leuffen, Berthold Rittberger and Frank Schimmelfennig **Differentiated Integration**

Sabine Saurugger **Theoretical Approaches to European Integration**

Also Planned

The Political Economy of European Integration

Series Standing Order (outside North America only)
ISBN 0–333–71695–7 hardback
ISBN 0–333–69352–3 paperback
Full details from www.palgrave.com

Visit Palgrave Macmillan's
EU Resource area at
www.palgrave.com/politics/eu/

The major institutions and actors

Published

Renaud Dehousse **The European Court of Justice**
Justin Greenwood **Interest Representation in the European Union** (2nd edn)
Fiona Hayes-Renshaw and Helen Wallace **The Council of Ministers** (2nd edn)
Simon Hix and Christopher Lord **Political Parties in the European Union**
David Judge and David Earnshaw **The European Parliament** (2nd edn)
Neill Nugent **The European Commission**
Anne Stevens with Handley Stevens **Brussels Bureaucrats? The Administration of the European Union**

Forthcoming

Wolfgang Wessels **The European Council**

The main areas of policy

Published

Michele Chang **Monetary Integration in the European Union**
Michelle Cini and Lee McGowan **Competition Policy in the European Union** (2nd edn)
Wyn Grant **The Common Agricultural Policy**
Sieglinde Gstöhl and Dirk de Bièvre **The Trade Policy of the European Union**
Martin Holland **The European Union and the Third World**
Jolyon Howorth **Security and Defence Policy in the European Union**
Johanna Kantola **Gender and the European Union**
Stephan Keukeleire and Jennifer MacNaughtan **The Foreign Policy of the European Union**
Brigid Laffan **The Finances of the European Union**
Malcolm Levitt and Christopher Lord **The Political Economy of Monetary Union**
Janne Haaland Matláry **Energy Policy in the European Union**
John McCormick **Environmental Policy in the European Union**
John Peterson and Margaret Sharp **Technology Policy in the European Union**
Handley Stevens **Transport Policy in the European Union**

Forthcoming

Karen Anderson **Social Policy in the European Union**

Hans Bruyninckx and Tom Delreux **Environmental Policy and Politics in the European Union**
Jörg Monar **Justice and Home Affairs in the European Union**

Also planned

Political Union
The External Policies of the European Union

The member states and the Union

Published

Carlos Closa and Paul Heywood **Spain and the European Union**
Alain Guyomarch, Howard Machin and Ella Ritchie **France in the European Union**
Brigid Laffan and Jane O'Mahoney **Ireland and the European Union**

Forthcoming

Simon Bulmer and William E. Paterson **Germany and the European Union**
Brigid Laffan **The European Union and its Member States**
Baldur Thórhallsson **Small States in the European Union**

Also planned

Britain and the European Union

Issues

Published

Derek Beach **The Dynamics of European Integration: Why and When EU Institutions Matter**
Christina Boswell and Andrew Geddes **Migration and Mobility in the European Union**
Thomas Christiansen and Christine Reh **Constitutionalizing the European Union**
Robert Ladrech **Europeanization and National Politics**
Cécile Leconte **Understanding Euroscepticism**
Steven McGuire and Michael Smith **The European Union and the United States**
Wyn Rees **The US-EU Security Relationship: The Tensions between a European and a Global Agenda**

The US–EU Security Relationship

The Tensions between a European and a Global Agenda

Wyn Rees

First published 2011 by
PALGRAVE MACMILLAN

Palgrave Macmillan in the UK is an imprint of Macmillan Publishers Limited,
registered in England, company number 785998, of Houndmills, Basingstoke,
Hampshire RG21 6XS.

Palgrave Macmillan in the US is a division of St Martin's Press LLC,
175 Fifth Avenue, New York, NY 10010.

Palgrave Macmillan is the global academic imprint of the above companies
and has companies and representatives throughout the world.

Palgrave® and Macmillan® are registered trademarks in the United States,
the United Kingdom, Europe and other countries

ISBN 978–0–230–22184–0 hardback
ISBN 978–0–230–22185–7 paperback

This book is printed on paper suitable for recycling and made from fully
managed and sustained forest sources. Logging, pulping and manufacturing
processes are expected to conform to the environmental regulations of the
country of origin.

A catalogue record for this book is available from the British Library.

A catalog record for this book is available from the Library of Congress.

10   9   8   7   6   5   4   3   2   1
20   19   18   17   16   15   14   13   12   11

Printed in China

This book is dedicated to two very special people,
Marcus and Sophie

Contents

Acknowledgements

I would like to thank Professors Simon Duke (Maastricht) and Michael Smith (Loughborough), as well as anonymous reviewers for Palgrave Macmillan, for their helpful comments on an early draft of this manuscript. They bear no responsibilities for any shortcomings within the book. I am grateful to Professors Willie Paterson and Neill Nugent for including this book within their series. Thanks are also due to Steven Kennedy of Palgrave Macmillan and Keith Povey Editorial Services Ltd for their work in bringing this book to publication.

WYN REES

List of Abbreviations

ABM	Anti-Ballistic Missile Treaty
BAE	British Aerospace
CAP	Common Agricultural Policy
CEECs	central and east European countries
CFE	Conventional Forces in Europe
CFSP	Common Foreign and Security Policy
CIA	Central Intelligence Agency
CJTF	Combined Joint Task Forces
CPI	Counter-Proliferation Initiative
CSDP	Common Security and Defence Policy
CSI	Container Security Initiative
CTBT	Comprehensive Test Ban Treaty
CTRP	Nunn–Lugar Cooperative Threat Reduction Programme
DHS	United States Department of Homeland Security
DRC	Democratic Republic of Congo
EAW	European Arrest Warrant
EC	European Community
EDC	European Defence Community
ENP	European Neighbourhood Policy
ESDI	European Security and Defence Identity
ESDP	European Security and Defence Policy
ESS	European Security Strategy
IAEA	International Atomic Energy Agency
ILSA	Iran–Libya Sanctions Act
JHA	Justice and Home Affairs
JLS	Justice, Liberty and Security
LIBERTAD	Cuban Liberty and Democratic Solidarity Act
MAP	Membership Action Plan
NAFTA	North American Free Trade Agreement
NATO	North Atlantic Treaty Organisation
NIE	United States National Intelligence Estimate
NMD	National Missile Defense
NNWS	non-nuclear weapon states
NPT	Non-Proliferation Treaty

NRF	NATO Response Force
NSG	Nuclear Suppliers Group
NSS	United States National Security Strategy
NTA	New Transatlantic Agenda
NWS	nuclear weapon states
OECD	Organisation for Economic Co-operation and Development
OSCE	Organisation for Security and Co-operation in Europe
PDBTS	High Level Policy Dialogue on Borders and Transport Security
PNR	Passenger Name Records
PSI	Proliferation Security Initiative
RMA	Revolution in Military Affairs
UN	United Nations
UNMOVIC	United Nations Monitoring, Verification and Inspection Commission
UNSCOM	United Nations Special Commission
UNSCR	United Nations Security Council Resolution
WEU	Western European Union
WMD	Weapon(s) of mass destruction
WTO	World Trade Organization

Introduction

The US, the EU and security

In the post-Cold War period, the United States (US) security relationship with the European Union (EU) is an important subject for analysis. Books on the transatlantic security relationship traditionally focus on the North Atlantic Treaty Organisation (NATO), the formal alliance arrangement that has guaranteed the defence of Europe. NATO includes amongst its members the states of the EU, but the two organizations are not coterminous and NATO includes non-EU members such as Canada and Turkey. Conversely, books on the US–EU relationship have tended to concentrate on economics because the EU and its forerunner, the European Community (EC), was principally a trading actor. This book is therefore somewhat unusual in its approach, raising the question: can security really be regarded as vital to America's relationship with the EU?

Justifying the investigation of the US half of the equation is relatively straightforward. Since 1991 the US has been the acknowledged sole superpower – indeed, in the words of former French Foreign Minister Hubert Vedrine, it has stood out as a 'hyper-power'. US interests are defined globally and the country possesses allies all over the world. None of these allies are as close as those in Europe; countries to whom the US tied its fate during the Cold War. The transatlantic relationship is the most closely integrated and interdependent relationship in the world, fashioned from a shared history and culture (Kennedy, 1962). The US has built its standing in the world partly on its leadership of a group of democratic states in Europe.

As for the EU, it has gradually become the centre of gravity for the European continent. McGuire and Smith (2008, 37) refer to a 'Euro-American system' that has evolved with its patterns of behaviour and argue that this has become synonymous with an 'EU–US system'. From its birth as an economic and trade actor, the EC/EU has come to assert its competences over a wide range of issues. It was first a trading power, before progressing to economic and monetary union and taking steps towards political union. Efforts have focused subsequently on giving it the capacity to act in international affairs

1

and according it a defence dimension. Its main value has been to mitigate the collective action problem inherent in all international organizations (Kirchner and Sperling, 2007, 238). Although the Union does not always speak with one voice, there has been a trend amongst its members to try to coordinate their positions. This has stemmed from individual states recognizing that they can achieve little alone, but that as a group of (now 27) states they can wield much more influence.

The pattern of interaction between the US and the EU is neither harmonious nor a stranger to tension. Brimmer (2007, 8) describes the US relationship with the EU as one in which 'amity [is] tinged with ambivalence'. In reality it is a complex relationship characterized by competition as well as cooperation. There is rivalry between the two that stems from their stature as global economic powers. This rivalry is managed by mutually agreed rules and regulations, but it sometimes breaks out into trade wars, such as happened in the cases of bananas and passenger aircraft. The Europeans have demonstrated a tendency to envy America's strength and act as a critic of its policies. America expresses exasperation with Europe's perceived failure to live up to its international responsibilities and act like a world power. In short, the US–EU relationship is tetchy and subject to occasional rounds of mutual recrimination.

The history of the relationship

Security has always infused the US relationship with the EC/EU, alongside economics, politics and culture. In the aftermath of World War II, there was a fear on both sides of the Atlantic that Soviet influence would spread. A particular source of concern was that it would feed off and exploit the economic dislocation of Europe. A reluctant US, that had envisaged the rapid withdrawal and repatriation of its forces, was drawn inexorably into the role of protector of the continent. These efforts resulted in the signing of the Washington Treaty in April 1949 and the formation of NATO (De Porte, 1979). A grand bargain emerged: in return for its protection, Europe would support US attempts to contain and deter the advance of the Soviet Union. The security interests of the two sides became intertwined and inseparable, resulting in debates during the 1950s and 1960s about the possibility of creating an institutionalised and permanent relationship between them, an 'Atlantic Union'.

NATO grew into a two-pillar concept, with Europe and the US on either side. US troops and strategic assets were placed on the territories of European states, joint planning was undertaken and force goals were negotiated. An American Supreme Allied Commander was appointed with control over both US forces in Europe and allied forces in NATO's central region. The very survival of European nations became dependent on the decision of an American President to release nuclear weapons in the event of war with the Soviets. Germany's allies were reassured that it no longer presented a threat to their security. Similarly, Greek and Turkish membership within NATO was used as a means to calm the enmity between these two rivals.

A challenge to the pivotal role of NATO arose with the concept of a European Defence Community (EDC) in 1950. This envisaged a supranational defence structure with a European Minister of Defence and a European army of over 100,000 men (Dockrill, 1991, 42–4). It enjoyed US support as a way to facilitate the rearmament of Germany and to provide for a more cohesive European contribution to the common defence. The EDC failed in 1954, as a result of the UK's decision to stand aloof and France's fear of inadequately supervised German rearmament. This led to an agreement by which German rearmament was overseen by the Western European Union (WEU) and the Federal Republic was admitted to NATO. The Alliance became the foundation stone for European security, and independent efforts by Europe to provide for its own defence were shelved. US protection allowed Europe to embark on a protracted process of economic regeneration, but it also ensured that defence would remain firmly within a transatlantic framework.

The Treaty of Rome, signed in 1957 by six founding states, had an explicitly non-military purpose. Its forerunner, the European Coal and Steel Community, was designed to control the war-making industries of the major powers and to promote reconciliation through fostering free trade. The US was a supporter of European integration, viewing it as an indispensable contribution to Western strength, an opportunity to build European unity in the face of the Soviet threat and as a means to escape the continent's destructive past (Winand, 1993, 190). However, there were times when US administrations were equivocal about the path of European integration as they feared it could become a way of keeping the US outside the continent (Peterson, 2004, 616). The Nixon administration, for instance, came to see the US leadership of the Atlantic Alliance on the one hand and European integration on the other as potentially in conflict with each other.

Some analysts have accused the US of behaving in an imperial manner towards its European allies, in the sense of subordinating their views to American interests. In a similar way to European powers in the past, the US could be said to have used its economic and political power to control its allies (Ferguson, 2004). But such an analysis does more to obfuscate rather than clarify the nature of the transatlantic relationship. If it was an imperial relationship then, in the words of a leading commentator, it was an 'empire by consent' in which the Europeans invited the US to serve as their protector (Lundestad, 2003). European countries relied upon American aid to rebuild their economies and assist their balance of payments. They bandwagoned on America's ability to deter aggression by the Warsaw Treaty Organization. European states also enjoyed the luxury of dissenting from US policies without fear of retribution.

Nevertheless, there were sources of friction within the transatlantic relationship. One major issue was over the relative burdens that each side was carrying. As European economies grew more prosperous, the US expressed resentment that it was spending proportionately more on defence and was carrying a higher degree of risk. The US economy was put under pressure in the early 1970s by the quadrupling in the price of oil and President Nixon took the dramatic step of suspending the convertibility of the dollar. In the light of this situation, America felt more aggrieved that it was bearing a heavier share of the burden. Secretary of State Henry Kissinger noted the paradox of America defending Europe, on the one hand, juxtaposed with political and economic competition between the allies, on the other (ibid., 180). Thus began one of the long-term strains across the Atlantic over Europe's willingness to contribute more to the common defence effort.

The burden-sharing debate was also manifested in relations outside of Europe. The US had tended to take responsibility for security issues beyond the continent and had expected a degree of solidarity from its allies in return. But as détente between the superpowers reduced European fears of the USSR in the late 1960s and 1970s, EC countries became reluctant to provide unqualified support for Washington (Bowker and Williams, 1988). Differences of view arose over US policy towards Vietnam and Cambodia and the Middle East, with European states outlining their own independent positions.

America came to perceive that its allies were unwilling to provide material support for its global security policies yet were eager to criticize and undermine its efforts.

With the ending of the Cold War, the transatlantic community entered uncharted waters. The threat that had underpinned this confluence of American and European interests disappeared. During the Cold War, Europe was the cockpit of superpower confrontation but now, with its demise, there was less reason for the two sides to remain together. The continent was safer than it had been since the end of World War II with no likelihood of territorial aggression against any west European country. Maintaining the transatlantic relationship around past concerns was no longer possible. Generations of people on both sides of the Atlantic could not be expected to feel the same sense of common ties that their forebears had done.

Theorists of International Relations envisaged two possible outcomes. One group, led by realist and neo-realist theorists, foresaw that, in the absence of an external threat, national interests would re-emerge amongst the key European states as well as between the US and Europe. According to this view, a sense of shared threat had enabled the Western allies to overcome the natural tendency to balance power amongst themselves: 'realist hegemony theory holds that American power created and maintained the order in the West by offering incentives to the other Western democracies to participate' (Deudney and Ikenberry, 1999, 180). Once this external threat was removed, interstate rivalries and competition would resume.

According to neo-realists, institutions represent temporary manifestations of congruent state interests. Organizations such as NATO and the EC had resulted from unique configurations of power within the West and, once these changed, the organizations themselves would be undermined. It was judged that the end of the Cold War would promote centrifugal forces that would undermine NATO and the EU. The result would be the withering away of the bonds that kept the transatlantic allies together and a return to the old balance of power politics that preceded the Cold War (Walt, 1987; Mearsheimer, 1990). According to this view, countries such as Germany, France and the UK could be expected to return to a policy of interstate competition as a multipolar international system re-emerged.

This bleak assessment of the future of US–European relations was counterbalanced by various strands of liberal, neo-liberal and social constructivist thought. Liberal institutionalists (Ikenberry, 2001) argued that the strands that had tied the transatlantic allies together during the Cold War would prove more durable. Both sides of the Atlantic had invested heavily in creating an institutional order in security, trade and finance. It was expected that this institutional relationship, 'or practice of co-binding constraint' (Deudney and Ikenberry, 1999, 182), would not unravel and that it would continue to hold them together. It would be more costly for them to disengage than to maintain their relationship (Keohane and Nye, 2001). Organizations such as NATO, that had been created to regulate the relationship, had developed a momentum of their own and would not be dissolved in the new, more uncertain environment. The routine ways of developing policy within an institutional relationship would continue to constrain the members and would not just break apart once the Soviet menace had been removed.

Constructivists argue that the interests of actors are not immutable; rather they are socially constructed and interpreted according to the circumstances in which they find themselves. Thus a shared sense of meaning between actors is vitally important, and constructivists contend that the transatlantic relationship is impregnated with shared ideas and common values (Risse-Kappen, 1995). These common ideas and values cannot be quickly undone even amidst a changing external environment and act as a glue keeping the two sides together. The sense of a shared identity had taken time to emerge but, once established, it could not easily be dissolved. Thus the relationship would be likely to weather the storms of the ending of the Cold War and would have the capacity to adapt itself to new tasks.

The breadth of security challenges

The end of the Cold War did not terminate all former security concerns immediately. There were no longer any overt threats to national territory and the military confrontation between east and west, that had been conducted on a knife-edge and risked escalation to thermonuclear exchange, was gone. Yet some of the underlying issues remained. For example, Russian forces remained forward deployed on the territory of the former German Democratic Republic and were not removed until 1994. The 1990 Conventional Forces in Europe (CFE) Treaty had been negotiated to provide a framework for disarmament but there was a long process of dismantling military

units and verifying their removal. The prospect of German unifica-
tion stirred deep-seated fears amongst its neighbours, as demonstrated by the hostile responses of both the Thatcher and Mitterrand
governments (Stares, 1992). The Alliance legitimized the continuation of allied and particularly American forces on German soil and
reassured both Russia and France about Germany's future orientation. NATO's Article V defence guarantee continued to provide
stability after 1990. The US was able to remain as a vital power
balancer amongst the various European states as well as a country
that could galvanize those states around its leadership.

There were security problems that arose as a consequence of the
demise of the Cold War. One of the great ironies was that instead of
heralding a period of peace and stability, the post-Cold War era
marked the drawing of America and Europe into a series of
conflicts. The Balkans was to preoccupy the attention of the transatlantic allies for most of the 1990s. The former Yugoslavia, that had
been held together artificially, began to break apart as first Slovenia
and then Croatia announced their intention to secede from the
Federation. Whilst these presented crises in their own right, fears
were concentrated on the precedent that could be set for the seces-
sion of the multiethnic Bosnia, that contained Muslims, Croats and
Serbs. In 1992 Bosnia duly announced its decision to break away
from Serbia and there followed a vicious and protracted ethnic
conflict. In 1999 the secessionist demands of Kosovo ignited a
further conflagration in which NATO found itself in a fight against
Serbia. After the conflict was over, Macedonia was only kept from
internal strife by skilful NATO intervention.

These experiences illustrated the changing nature of conflict.
Unlike the mass mobilization, interstate wars of the twentieth
century, the conflicts in the Balkans were intrastate in nature, with
ill-defined protagonists and objectives. The conflict zones were situated amidst the civilian population and there was a deliberate
targeting of non-combatants and the practice of ethnic cleansing to
drive communities out of a region. In the words of General Rupert
Smith, this has represented 'a new era of conflict – in fact a new
paradigm ... [of] "war amongst the peoples": in which political and
military developments go hand in hand' (Smith, 2007, xiii). Western
militaries have found themselves fighting not on battlefields against
opposing military formations, but in urban areas and villages
against paramilitaries or insurgents that present no easily identifi-
able target.

The adversaries of Western countries have recognized the superiority of US and European armies in conventional conflicts. In terms of firepower and manoeuvre, no force can stand up to a Western army on the battlefield. The result has been that enemies have chosen to engage the US and European countries asymmetrically, using insurgency and terrorist tactics. These have been designed to inflict casualties and sap the will to fight, whilst avoiding set-piece encounters. Western forces have found themselves unable to bring their military superiority to bear and have been forced to modify their tactics and fight in ways dictated by their enemies.

Such conflicts have been labelled 'Wars of Choice' because Western countries have enjoyed the option of deciding whether to intervene. The objective of intervention has been to improve the security of the citizens of the countries involved: only indirectly do these operations contribute to the security of Western citizens. They have taken the form of complex emergencies in which there are multiple ethnic groups and a lack of clarity about whom to blame for the aggression (Duffield, 2002). Such conflicts test military forces to the utmost because of the sensitive political environment in which they occur and because the intervening nations have no vital interests at stake. They carry with them the risk of escalation, as a small intervention may lead to a larger engagement that can risk entrapment.

Outside forces have struggled over the issue of who grants the legitimacy to intervene. United Nations (UN) Secretary General Kofi Annan (1999, 82) asserted that in cases of humanitarian intervention, the UN charter 'requires the (Security) Council to be the defender of "common interest"'. A UN mandate would be required before violating a country's sovereignty. But in 2004 a UN appointed panel discussed the idea of 'a responsibility to protect' amongst states who were witnesses to the abuse of human rights in a third country (United Nations High Level Panel on Threats, 2004). This placed the onus on countries to intervene if they saw large-scale abuses of human rights or genocide. The panel also took issue with the concept of sovereignty, arguing that states had obligations to their own people which, if not upheld, could justify outside intervention.

What is clear is that such situations present the militaries of America and European countries with a range of problems. First is the issue of who intervenes and under what organizational mandate. In the early 1990s, NATO and the US put themselves at the disposal of the UN in the cases of Bosnia and Somalia. But acting as a military subcontractor proved to be harrowing and the US decided not to repeat the experience. In the case of Kosovo, NATO knew that it would not obtain UN authorization for the use of force against Belgrade for the expulsion of the Kosovar Albanians as this would be vetoed by Russia and China. Instead, it chose to act under its own authority, on the grounds that its legitimacy derived from the democratic nature of its membership. This failure to secure a UN Security Council Resolution remained a source of controversy after the conflict.

Second, the purpose of conflict becomes less the defeat of an adversary and more the cessation of hostilities and the restoration of stability. Because Western countries are not fighting for their own survival, their objectives have become more limited. At one end of the spectrum, the goal may be to prevent hostilities breaking out in the first place. A document drawn up to crystallize EU thinking towards the use of force, the European Security Strategy, discusses the need for 'preventive engagements' (European Council, 2003b). A military force might be positioned between rival groups, during a period of high political tension, or protagonists supervised and disarmed. Humanitarian assistance may be provided to civilians caught up within a conflict zone, ensuring that they have access to food, water and medical supplies. At the other end of the spectrum, conflicts already underway may require outside intervention to break the will of one of the warring factions to bring a cessation of hostilities.

Third, if a peace agreement is signed then it may need to be enforced and policed by Western forces. In the case of the 1995 Dayton Agreement, the Implementation Force commander made a point of conducting firepower demonstrations to show the various factions that NATO would not hesitate to enforce the peace agreement (Jackson, 2007, 199). Tasks can vary along a spectrum, ranging from peacekeeping and peace enforcement to post-conflict stabilization. These roles can extend beyond the remit of the military, particularly if the aim includes the reconstruction of a war-torn society. Rebuilding the infrastructure, creating a functioning judicial system and holding elections – 'nation-building' – demands a range of skills that necessitates the involvement of civil agencies and non-governmental organizations. This has been illustrated in numerous situations such as Bosnia and Kosovo, as well as the use of Provincial Reconstruction Teams operating alongside the military in Afghanistan. Not only are these complex tasks but they are also protracted ones that may absorb Western efforts over a period of many years. Their frequency has been increasing, commensurate with the greater number of interventions that Western states have been conducting.

In addition to these hybrid emergencies, the US and the EU have found themselves confronting security challenges from outside of Europe. Some of these have been military in nature, such as the risk of interstate conflict. Even though major interstate war has been rare in recent decades, it would be imprudent to discount its future possibility. Such a war is unlikely to occur as a result of a deliberate attack upon a Western country but could result after an assault upon a Western ally. Examples include the potential for war between China and Taiwan over the Taiwan Straits or between India and Pakistan over Kashmir. The possibility of interstate conflict needs to figure in the planning assumptions, as well as the equipment procurement programmes, of all Western countries.

Weak or 'failed' states are countries that constitute poorly governed spaces. This may result from civil war or the breakdown of government control. Examples of such failed states include Liberia, Sierra Leone, the Democratic Republic of Congo and Afghanistan. Because they are places of internal disorder, they can provide nefarious groups, such as organized criminals, drug traffickers and terrorists, with sanctuaries from which to operate with impunity (Byman, 2005). The problem of pirates seizing and ransoming ships off the Horn of Africa stems from the lawlessness and lack of control exercised by Somalia. The realities of globalization and increasing interdependence mean that such zones of instability can constitute a danger to the security of the wider world (Singer and Wildavsky, 1993).

Nuclear proliferation has been an additional preoccupation in transatlantic security relations. The spread of weapon technologies, including nuclear, bacteriological and chemical know-how, has brought highly destructive capabilities within reach of a larger number of international actors. The US has been perturbed by two sorts of scenarios. The first is one in which a country opposed to the prevailing international order could develop such technologies and threaten to use them against the US or one of its allies. The vulnerability of allies such as Israel and South Korea have been particular sources of concern to America. Another scenario is one in which a state determined to damage the West indirectly could give or sell its weapons to a terrorist organization (United Nations High Level Panel on Threats, 2004). The potential acquisition of a weapon of mass destruction (WMD) raises the spectre of catastrophic terrorism in which casualties could run into the hundreds of thousands.

International terrorism has become one of the foremost concerns of the Western community following the 9/11 attacks in New York and Washington DC. Although terrorism itself is far from new, its contemporary manifestation is deemed to be different because it is religiously inspired, global in coverage and networked in structure (Copeland, 2001). Bobbitt (2008b) argues that what he calls Western 'market states' are particularly vulnerable to this new phenomenon because it deprives them of the ability to deliver security to their citizens and thereby robs them of their legitimacy. Terrorism does indeed prey upon many of the characteristics of democratic forms of government: open borders, freedom of movement and unrestricted forms of communication. Terrorism has been able to exploit Western progress in globalization and turn it into a weapon against these societies. Governments have been forced to tread a delicate line between enhancing security but at the same time preserving the freedoms that they claim to uphold.

In sum, the security agenda since the end of the Cold War has broadened and diversified. Although the transatlantic allies are no longer existentially threatened, the variety of dangers has made the situation more complex. This complexity contributes to the way in which the two sides interpret and prioritize threats in different ways. It also demands a wider range of capabilities and greater flexibility of international institutions to address these challenges.

The focus of this book

Security has become a highly contested subject and there has been considerable debate within the academic literature about the extent of the issues that it should encapsulate. It ranges from the potential for armed conflict between states to the sources of threats to individual human beings. Security can include all manner of issues: from economic problems to societal identity and environmental challenges to mass migrations. I have chosen to focus upon a narrow definition of security: namely, issues that involve questions of force. I will adopt Walt's (1991, 212) understanding of security as 'the study of the threat, use and control of military force'. This is not to ignore the importance of other types of human security issues such as the spread of pandemic diseases. Nor is it to deny that the US–EU relationship is becoming engaged in new sorts of security issues such as environmental degradation. Rather, it is because managing the threat of force remains a central feature of the transatlantic relationship and has increasingly involved the US and the EU. Focusing upon this narrow interpretation of security also represents an attempt to limit the scope of the issues considered within this book.

The central argument is that a paradox has been evident in post-Cold War transatlantic security relations. This paradox derives from the fact that there have been a number of issues leading to security divergence between the US and Europe. Some of these were structural issues that resulted from the changing situations in which the actors found themselves. Others were the historical predispositions that led the two sides to react differently to the new challenges that they faced.

Amongst the factors promoting transatlantic security divergence has been the diminishing need for the collective defence of Europe. This was traditionally the ballast of the relationship, a core of shared interests that kept the US and Europe thinking and acting together. NATO was the organizational relationship that enacted these shared interests. It provided a framework for security cooperation and sustained a regular dialogue between the two sides. As the issue of continental defence has declined in importance, the US–European relationship and NATO itself has been subject to instability and prone to sharp criticisms from both sides. Residual security concerns about Europe have continued to be a part of transatlantic relations, but the centre of gravity has shifted. The need to find a new organizational focus, to supplement NATO, is a manifestation of these issues. Since 1990, the transatlantic allies have argued over the appropriate institutional framework in which to discuss security matters. In the words of Daalder (2003, 148), 'the changing structure of relations between the United States and Europe means that a new basis for the relationship must be found'.

A second argument is that the US has been less and less preoccupied with security matters pertaining to the European continent. Europe was the focal point for US efforts during the Cold War but as the memories of that confrontation have receded, so America no longer looks at security issues through this prism. This change began soon after the demise of the Warsaw Pact but has been exacerbated by 9/11 and the US 'War on Terror'. Europe dropped down America's list of priorities once it became apparent that the threats to the continent had receded. This is not to argue that Europe is unimportant in US security considerations. It still links America to relations with Russia as well as to the security of recently independent, pro-Atlanticist countries in central Europe. But the US no longer regards the continent as under imminent threat and it has reduced significantly the size of its military forces stationed there.

A third argument is that the US has prioritized attention on global security issues such as 'States of Concern', nuclear non-proliferation and the global 'War on Terror'. States and substate actors that reject or threaten the prevailing international order have come to absorb a growing part of Washington's consideration. Extra-European issues were relatively peripheral to US–European relations during the Cold War and, when they did appear on the agenda, they were often a source of tension. The two sides never attempted to generate common analyses of these problems and this resulted in them having relatively few foundations on which to build their cooperation. The US has complained that the EU has remained preoccupied with regional concerns and has failed to raise its sights to matters of global concern. The increasing prominence of this extra-European agenda has exposed fault lines in transatlantic priorities. The Middle East has figured centrally in this revised list of US–EU issues, whereas regions such as Asia and Africa have been much less important to the relationship.

A fourth argument is that the EU and America have disagreed about the most appropriate instruments for addressing the main security challenges (Kagan, 2004). The status of the US as a global hegemon, with unchallengeable military resources, has given it the confidence to confront potential adversaries. America has been intolerant of threats and it has proved resolute in tackling weapons proliferators and terrorist organizations. It has been dissatisfied with the prevailing multilateral security system that concerts activity amongst leading countries (Drezner, 2008, 195). Washington has strained against what it has perceived as the externally imposed limits upon its power. The EU, with its lesser power capabilities, has been reluctant to sanction the use of force and has sought other instruments to address security challenges. Differences amongst member states of the EU have persisted and the Union's capability and will to act has evolved slowly. In light of such factors it has been a staunch supporter of multilateral frameworks.

A fifth argument is that although many factors have promoted security divergences between the US and the EU, at the same time there have been factors promoting convergence. The post-Cold War environment has brought with it a broader range of security threats that are more diffuse in nature. These threats cross the traditional boundaries between internal and external security and they have tended to be less state-centric. They have presented complex challenges that have required new patterns of response. Few have been susceptible to large-scale military solutions. Instead they have necessitated cooperative and multilateral action so as to ensure the greatest degree of legitimacy. In the face of these demands the US and the EU have been obliged to find innovative ways of working together.

The EU has been well placed to adapt to this broader spectrum of threats. Its member states have come to realize that only by acting together, by coordinating their respective foreign policies, can they have any prospect of addressing these security challenges. Unlike NATO it has not been constrained by a narrow military remit. Instead, the Union's competences range from economic and diplomatic instruments to law enforcement and judicial powers. Since 1999 it has added a range of military capabilities to its toolbox. The EU has been able to respond to these demands and work towards a common set of strategic perspectives amongst its members.

As it has evolved as a more capable actor, the Union has found itself interacting increasingly with the US. For Washington, the EU has become a partner in a growing number of security issues, particularly in relation to issues where NATO's competences are not relevant. In the words of the former US Ambassador to NATO, Victoria Nuland (2008), 'as we in the United States look across the globe for partners in meeting [security] challenges ... our first stop is often at the European Union'.

In this book I seek to explore issues within the US–EU security relationship over the last two decades. By looking across a range of security concerns, I attempt to investigate how each side conceives of the problem and the factors that have influenced their approach to its resolution. An attempt is made to determine whether strategic divergences between the transatlantic allies are increasing or whether they have found ways of adapting their relationship to resolve the new challenges.

In Chapter 1 I try to conceptualize the very different natures of the US and the EU and the implications of these differences on their relationship. I seek to identify some of the important ideas that underpin both actors and how these have shaped their outlooks in the post-Cold War period. I proceed to assess the implications of these differences, especially the 'Martian' and 'Venusian' dichotomy that dominated discussions of transatlantic relations in the period after 2003.

In Chapter 2 I look at the principal ways in which the US interacts with its European allies: which is bilaterally, through the EU and through NATO. Whilst bilateral relations continue to be important, the US relationship with its partners in NATO has become relatively less important. This chapter assesses the extent to which the EU has taken over from NATO as the principal vehicle for US–European security interests. It proceeds to evaluate the different approaches that the US and EU have exhibited towards international organizations such as the UN.

Chapter 3 is about the defence arrangements for Europe and the increasingly important role played by the EU. Attention is devoted to how the post-Cold War security challenges evolved in Europe, changing from the expectation of high intensity, interstate warfare to Western intervention in intrastate, ethnic conflict. The focus of the chapter is on the debate about a stronger European identity in defence, that eventually culminated in the ESDP (subsequently CSDP) and a series of EU hybrid operations. I assess the reaction of the US to these developments in the light of the changing perceptions of warfare.

Chapter 4 investigates the enlargement of the EU. In the chapter I trace the complexity of the process of enlargement and the attitudes of the US towards the issue. It focuses on enlargement issues towards central and east European countries and on the planned enlargement to states in the western Balkans. It also investigates the way in which Russia and countries in the EU's neighbourhood have been treated.

Chapter 5 marks a switch in the focus of the book, away from European issues, to the global security agenda. This chapter looks at the issue of 'states of concern' that has been a tendentious matter between the Atlantic allies. Although this term has been applied to a variety of errant behaviours, for analytical purposes the issue of nuclear proliferation is dealt with in the subsequent chapter. I look in detail at the contrasting strategies of the US and EU towards these countries, ranging from diplomatic isolation to attempts at regime change. A case study is provided of the 2003 war against Iraq that witnessed a clash between the US and countries such as France and Germany.

In Chapter 6 I analyse the topic of nuclear proliferation and the contending approaches of the US and the EU towards managing the problem. I look at the various instruments that are available to prevent the spread of weapons of mass destruction, ranging from multilateral controls, through to economic sanctions and on to the possible use of force. The chapter looks at two principal case studies, North Korea and Iran.

In Chapter 7 I look at the field of transatlantic homeland security cooperation. I investigate how the two sides have been developing innovative patterns in counter-terrorism collaboration in judicial and law enforcement activity, in intelligence and data sharing, and in border security.

In the conclusion I try to draw these various threads relating to European security and global issues together. I seek to highlight where obstacles remain in the security relationship between the US and the EU and the ability of the two sides to sustain and build on their cooperation into the future.

Chapter 1

Conceptualizing the Transatlantic Relationship

Introduction

It is readily apparent that the US and the EU are dissimilar types of actors. The US is a single state with a federal political structure. Its size and power accords it the ability to act decisively in the world and to gather other states behind its leadership. The EU comprises a group of states, all with different histories. They have been brought together by shared interests, but the process of European integration is still evolving and remains a 'work in progress'. The EU is a unique experiment, a *sui generis* actor, in which there is no single vision about what it will eventually become. Prime Minister Tony Blair (2000) described the EU as an emerging superpower but not a super-state. Both the US and the EU are guided by the power of ideas. They possess a sense of legitimacy that they derive from their own political and economic systems. The power of these ideas differs in the case of the US and the EU and helps to explain their approaches to security.

In this chapter I will look at the different characters of the US and the EU, at the ideas and the experiences that have shaped them. In the light of those differences, I will seek to elucidate the implications that these have for the transatlantic security relationship. I will argue that their particular histories and capabilities have forged contrasting approaches to their use of force. This has made it difficult for the two sides to agree on the appropriate ways to deal with new security challenges.

American exceptionalism

America has always conceived of itself as special, a nation set apart from the rest of the international community. This derives first of all from the democratic nature of its domestic political system. Since its

17

founding, the US has been a country with a strong belief and pride in the power of its written constitution. This was seen as distinguishing it from the despotic regimes of Europe: a document carefully assembled by rational men, that created checks and balances between executive, legislative and judicial powers. These controls were designed to enshrine the rights of citizens, guarantee basic freedoms and build political structures that would be subject to the rule of law.

The confidence of the US in its political system has been translated into its overseas policies. America's opposition to the Soviet Union was predicated on a belief in the innate superiority of its democratic system. In the aftermath of the Cold War the goal of democratic enlargement became the cornerstone of US foreign policy. The US has believed that promoting its own model of political development will improve the governance of other countries and reduce the likelihood of conflict. A strong assumption in its policy-making has been that democratic countries are peaceful and refrain from armed conflict with each other.

The US democratic system has also provided an underlying sense of legitimacy for those occasions where America has intervened militarily abroad. Even in cases where no multilateral organization has sanctioned such action, the nature of America's own political system and its adherence to principles of freedom has been regarded as sufficient authorization. In the context of the 'War on Terror', President George W. Bush acknowledged that there would be occasions when allies would not support the US position and it would be necessary to act alone. This he considered acceptable, with the words 'after all, we are America' (quoted in Daalder, 2003). There has been a tendency to assume that the facilitation of elections will transform the situation of countries and there has been a failure to appreciate that America's own democratic story was a hard fought and difficult road (Hodgson, 2009, 16).

Another strand of America's uniqueness is perceived to arise from its capitalist economic system. This system extols the virtues of free enterprise and the accumulation of wealth by individual effort. The prospects for self-advancement are considered to be available to all citizens, depending upon their talents and willingness to work hard. This is the heart of the so-called 'American dream' that has led immigrants to flock to America to pursue individual prosperity and fulfilment regardless of their ethnicity or socio-economic backgrounds. According to this vision, America is the land of opportunity in which all can realize their ambitions providing that they have the determination to succeed.

The principles of free-market economics have been at the heart of American foreign policy. After World War II the US supported a liberal international order that was designed to keep countries out of the Soviet embrace. It funded this through Marshall Aid and was willing to suffer discriminatory trade policies in order to see the economic viability of its allies restored (Calleo, 1987). Washington also served as the architect of a network of global economic institutions. Successive administrations fashioned an economic order based on financial and trading institutions such as the International Monetary Fund, the World Bank and, later, the World Trade Organization (WTO). With the US as the lynchpin, these institutions regulated interaction between capitalist states, promoted international commerce and free trade, and helped to foster foreign direct investment. They also promulgated a set of American values, which gave the country huge amounts of influence outside its own territory through the positions its appointees enjoyed on the boards of these organizations. In the post-Cold War era, increasing the number of free-market countries became a central tenet of American policy as well as pressuring those countries still wedded to centralized control.

The success of its economic system and the domestic prosperity that it engendered made American culture widely known. The US film and television industries have helped to disseminate American values and ideas. Its music, clothing and food have all been enormously influential. There has been no evidence of a diminution in the attractiveness of US popular culture. Its technological prowess has made America a global leader in designs and industrial innovation. US multinational corporations, public servants, members of its armed forces and diplomats have successfully marketed this culture and these products overseas. As well as drawing admiration, this culture has excited hatred in those that fear the replacement or dilution of their own value systems by Western ideas.

A third and final strand of America's 'specialness' has been its sense of moral superiority (Hodgson, 2009, 10). This has arisen from its religiosity, its belief in its own virtue as a kind of 'New Jerusalem'. This is evidenced in the moralistic rhetoric of US politicians and it has underpinned the conduct of American foreign policy. In the latter part of the nineteenth century and the early part of the twentieth, US presidents kept their country from interference in European affairs because they feared America would become tainted. In the second half of the twentieth century it has found expression in America's sense of leadership of the West. It has lent itself to a good versus evil dichotomy in popular perceptions.

Walter Russell Mead identified four principal domestic schools of thought that have helped to mould US foreign policy by drawing upon the strands outlined above (Mead, 2001). The first school are 'Hamiltonians', who emphasize the importance of the US capitalist system and extol the need for a strong relationship between big business and government. This group of thinkers see trade and access to raw materials as the irreducible objectives of an enlightened foreign policy and have stressed the role that access to energy must have in strategic planning. The second school are 'Wilsonians', who seek to advance democratic values around the world because they believe that democracy promotes accountability and makes for more predictable and reliable allies. They also tend to uphold the concept of moral leadership by the US because its domestic values accord it a special role in international affairs. President Jimmy Carter's advocacy of human rights vis-à-vis the Soviet Union during the 1970s was an illustration of this approach. A third school are 'Jeffersonians', who concentrate on protecting American democracy at home rather than trying to spread it overseas. They fear that the very act of attempting to export US values will undermine the nature of American society. The last school are 'Jacksonians', who lay emphasis on the physical security of the US. They believe that the country should focus on its own national interests and should avoid being drawn into overseas actions on moral pretexts that easily become confused.

The ideas and values of these four schools of thought have been evident within all American administrations to a greater or lesser extent over the last sixty years. Particular strands of thinking have been uppermost at various times as influential figures within the executive have vied for the ear of the president. Not only have these strands been present within government, but also within other sectors of the body politic, such as Congress and a plethora of interest groups. Each school of thought has sought to advance its priorities in the key debates about America's role in the world: about the extent to which it can lead, engage with other countries or withdraw behind its own borders.

The presidency of Bill Clinton drew heavily on some of the principles embedded within Wilsonianism, including support for international organizations and the promotion of democracy around the world. He came to power at a time when the West was wrestling with the implications of the end of the Cold War. It led to a questioning of the willingness of the US to continue leading in the world and the price it was willing to pay. Clinton inherited an expanding US economy that was at the same time facing economic competition from countries such as China. He chose to adhere to free-trade policies, such as supporting the WTO and creating the North American Free Trade Agreement (NAFTA). America remained a promoter of liberal values and supported the work of international organizations, such as the UN. Clinton pursued a humanitarian agenda and this contributed to a series of costly interventions in areas that were not traditional American interests, such as Somalia, Kosovo and Haiti. A leading critic, Michael Mandelbaum (1996), was to characterize this approach as 'foreign policy as social work', namely the desire to try to improve the lives of people all over the world by the intervention of American military power. The implication was that America was neglecting its interests for ill-thought-out liberal ideas.

President Clinton was followed by the administration of George W. Bush, which was strongly influenced by Jacksonian ideas. This was manifest in the dismissive attitude towards global institutions and the sense of frustration with multilateralism. Bush was eager to pursue US national interests and was willing to ignore international structures that were not deemed to serve that end. Conservative nationalists within the higher reaches of the executive, such as Defense Secretary Donald Rumsfeld and Vice President Richard Cheney, saw the 1990s as 'a decade of neglect' of American interests and were determined to reassert the country's power. Drezner (2008, 205) observes that President Bush was the least travelled American President and Colin Powell the least travelled Secretary of State for thirty years, whilst Cheney only travelled abroad once during the first term.

Also within the administration was a particular strand of Wilsonianism that was evident in some of its leading neoconservative thinkers (Ikenberry, 2004, 10). These included figures such as Douglas Freith, Paul Wolfowitz and John Bolton inside the government, and Irving Kristol and Richard Perle outside (Mann, 2004). This group believed strongly in the moral rectitude of the US and its mission to confront states who threatened the US-led international order. They argued that democracy was sufficiently important to justify being actively exported. If necessary, America had to be prepared to export its values, including democracy, by force.

Commentators have tended to emphasize sharp differences between the presidencies of Bill Clinton and George W. Bush. In retrospect, however, the significance of the differences are questionable. There were undoubtedly variations in tone, not least because the Bush presidency was critical of, and determined to assert its distinctiveness from, its predecessor. Yet underneath there were many aspects of continuity, a factor true of successive post-war administrations. Both leaders shared the strategic objective of preserving America's position of primacy in the world (United States National Security Strategy, 2002). Sustaining a global order has taught the US that it must have the forces to police its interests and has created a perception of the fungibility of military power.

Both Clinton and Bush sought to manage the international system according to the vital interests of the US. They were prepared to engage multilaterally with other states and organizations only so far as those interests could be advanced. The values that they sought to promote were consistent in both cases: freedom and democracy. They both sought to maintain and extend America's ability to act. All US presidents jealously guard their country's independence from external influence. In the words of Bailes (2005a, 181), 'the US ideal stands out in clear contrast (to Europe) as one of intactness and immunity from intrusions of all kinds'.

What was different between the Clinton and Bush presidencies was the context in which they found themselves. The Clinton period was relatively benign and was faced with overseas conflicts in which the US could choose whether or not to intervene. But by the time of Bush the international situation was far darker as the shock of the 9/11 attacks had changed the environment in which American power was exercised. Not since Pearl Harbor had the US suffered an attack with such dramatic psychological consequences. It propelled the Bush administration into a fundamental reordering of American security policies.

Thus far the presidency of Barack Obama has represented a throwback to some of the ideas within Wilsonianism. Under his leadership, the US has endeavoured to rebuild international support for its policies and has moved away from the unilateralism of the Bush era. But there are also strong continuities in Obama's policies with those administrations that have gone before. For example, he has continued record levels of US defence spending in a bid to prevent the emergence of a strategic competitor. In addition, whilst Obama has emphasized his break with the past by drawing down American forces in Iraq, he has counterbalanced this by substantially increasing force levels in Afghanistan.

The EU: a new sort of power

In Europe, unlike the US, there has been no belief in the inherent goodness of the body politic. Rather the opposite: the states of Europe have tried to transcend the logic of balance of power politics that led to two self-destructive wars in the twentieth century. The aim has been to contain internecine quarrels and domesticate the relations between European countries. In this post-war endeavour Europe has been spectacularly successful. France and Germany have been reconciled and war has become an unthinkable way to resolve interstate differences. In the words of the European Security Strategy, 'European countries are committed to dealing peacefully with disputes and cooperating through common institutions' (European Council, 2003b).

The mechanism by which this was achieved was economic integration and the active pooling of sovereignty; first through the European Coal and Steel Community, then the EC and finally the EU. The EU has moved beyond the boundaries of the Westphalian states system into a system of multilevel governance that is unparalleled elsewhere in the world. Some policies are pursued on a supranational basis, others remain within the exclusive provenance of the member states, whilst a further category involves mixed competences. European integration has occurred through a process of agreeing norms and then building institutions around them. This complex system is underpinned by the rule of law and the Union has moved forward by the agreement of legal texts.

Power has been mediated through an institutional framework, thereby facilitating clarity of information and the reduction in potential transaction costs. Members large and small have been enabled to negotiate peacefully over their interests and the European Commission has been tasked with protecting the interests of the community as a whole. There has been criticism throughout its history that the EU is overly preoccupied with institutions and that it focuses on process to the neglect of outcomes. This view fails to understand the nature of the Union, that institutional relationships have actually been at its heart and have made the European project possible: 'for the EU ... grand strategy is the preservation and enhancement of the integration process' (Smith, 2009, 14).

Central to this evolution has been the development of a free-trade area in which the member states have dismantled their tariff barriers and moved towards the creation of a single market in goods and services. The European social market approach has differed from the more purist model of capitalism championed by the US, although individual countries stand at various points along a spectrum between a liberal model of capitalism and a social-market version. Countries such as the UK gravitate more to the American end of the model and countries such as Sweden gravitate towards the other. Whilst the US has traditionally placed more emphasis upon self-reliance and entrepreneurship, the European model has been more committed to social justice and welfare programmes. EU countries have tolerated a much larger role for the state in the economy and have supported key industries, such as agriculture, in order to protect the internal economic system from the chill winds of international competition.

Although the EC started in the economic realm, it has gradually extended its competences into foreign policy and security. This growth in competences, particularly as a result of the 1992 Treaty on European Union (or 'Maastricht Treaty') has meant that ministers from member states are drawn together regularly in a web of discussions. They meet with their counterparts from other member states to discuss matters of common interest. Parts of the EU are supranational in nature, such as the European Commission, the European Parliament and the Court of Justice, and the Commission has played a growing role in guiding relationships and instigating new initiatives. This has encouraged the development of common European views and has been described as 'transgovernmentalism' (Wallace and Wallace, 2000) in which actors in discrete sectors of national governments cooperate closely together.

This process by which an increasing range of issues are decided upon in EU institutions – 'Brusselisation' (Allen, 1998, 54) – has been counterbalanced by the fact that it is the member states, through the overarching European Council, who decide what powers and policies are pooled and which remain intergovernmental in nature. Nation states have remained the principal actors in European politics and there is still considerable diversity amongst states in the nature of their governments and the policies they adopt. These governments have been reluctant to cede additional competences to supranational bodies in Brussels, particularly in relation to foreign and security policy. The Common Foreign and Security Policy (CFSP) is not a common policy as such but resembles more of a mechanism by which the foreign policies of the key European states are discussed and reconciled with each other.

Francois Duchene (1972, 39) foresaw that the peculiar nature of the EC would shape the sort of power that it would want to project: namely 'civilian' power. By the term 'civilian power', Duchene was indicating that the EU would be non-military and non-coercive in nature. It represented a new type of actor in international relations: a 'power' whose influence derived from its trading strength and its attachment to legal processes. It is able to exert 'soft power'; namely, a power of attraction as a result of its own political system and the values that it represents (Nye, 2002). This resonated with the growing interdependence of European states in the post-war period as well as their relative lack of power in the face of super-power military rivalry.

The EC/EU not only pacified the bellicose intents amongst its members but also externalized these policies so that it presented no military challenge to neighbouring states. Exercising coercive power on a large scale would be contradictory to the EU's own sense of mission; namely to mitigate the anarchical nature of the international system. This has confronted the Union with a dilemma when addressing certain types of security concerns because of its reluctance to draw upon hard power resources. Formal civilian power status ended with the ratification of the Treaty on European Union, when the ambition of a security and defence policy was realized (Nuttall, 2000). It took a further step forward with the creation of an ESDP in 1999 as hard power instruments were formally acquired (Smith, 2005, 68). Nevertheless, the Union has continued to perceive itself as a power of a special nature within the international system. It represents a group of post-modern states that pursue significant interests through an institutional framework (Cooper, 2003, 50; Kirchner and Sperling, 2007, 221).

Manners (2002) developed the theme of 'civilian power' when he described the Union as a 'normative power' within the international system. By this he meant that the Union seeks deliberately to externalize the values that it contains within its own institutional nature. For example, the EU actively promotes democracy, human rights and the protection of the rights of minorities (Cameron and Balfour, 2006). It has incorporated these principles from its relationship with the Organisation for Security and Co-operation in Europe (OSCE). Such values are then pursued through its conflict prevention policies and the peaceful resolution of disputes (Smith, 2003). Unlike the Westphalian model in which states pursue selfish national interests, the EU sees itself as an ideological power. Tocci (2008, 2) argues that the EU should not only embody certain values but should also act consistently in terms of the means it employs and the results that it obtains.

Aggestam and Hill have built on the idea of the EU having a sense of its own exceptionalism and special mission. They see it as attempting to conduct a civilizing role by pursuing a notion of itself as an 'ethical power' (see Aggestam, 2008, 1). Its own internal value system leads the Union to act in certain ways: to strengthen international order by adherence to multilateralism and to exercise military power in principled ways. Its ethical dimension has been uppermost in its humanitarian operations when it has sought to act as a 'force for good' within the international system (Orbie, 2008, 28). This civilizing mission is exported to surrounding countries through the values it expects them to adopt prior to becoming EU members.

This idea that the EU, through its economic strength and its particular set of values, has come to embody a particular sort of power has gained widespread acceptance. Ortega (2007, 124) argues that 'the European Union contributes to the global order in two different ways: as a model and as an actor'. It is a model of political and economic integration and multilevel governance. It seeks to address the root causes of problems and to use economic incentives to influence the behaviour of others. McGuire and Smith (2008, 54) talk of the Union's power in terms of 'soft balancing': the influence that it derives from negotiation and persuasion. The EU engages with others using a variety of instruments ranging from aid through to commercial agreements. By doing so it aims to modify their behaviour. Its approach reflects the Union's own historical experience of trying to steer its members away from conflict through the mechanism of economic interdependence. Such policies are designed to channel energies into peaceful competition and to make countries so tied together as to make conflict unattractive.

The extent to which the EU is a 'global actor' is more open to contestation. In terms of trade and the regulation of financial interactions, the Union represents a partner equal to the US. In the disbursement of aid, the EU has become the world's largest provider. But its ability to exercise power remains open to question.

Biscop (2008, 16) differentiates between the EU as a global *player* – a reflection of its size, population and economic prowess – and as a global *power*, which it can only become through sustained effort. Niblett (2005, 49), borrowing from the idea of Commission President Romano Prodi, describes the EU as 'a global civilian power'. McCormick (2007) takes this a stage further by arguing that this civilian power status gives the Union a unique advantage in navigating the current and future international system and justifies its description as a new type of 'superpower'.

Critics of the civilian power model regarded it as a post hoc rationalization. In their view the EC/EU was making a virtue out of its own inadequacies. Hedley Bull (1982, 51) argued that the EC's status, particularly in relation to the threat from the Soviet Union, was made possible by the presence of American military power to guarantee its security. The inability of the EU to deploy 'hard' power led it to rely upon 'soft' power, such as economic and trade instruments. Critics contrast the EU model to that of the US which emphasizes its military power and sees its own interests and those of the international order as coterminous.

Most analysts agree that the EU is still less of a global actor than it could be. This is a reflection of the multiplicity of views amongst its members and its failure to build the necessary political will to face security challenges. There have been numerous attempts to address these weakness in reflection groups and at European Council meetings. They have led to: discussions about different speeds of integration within the Union; mechanisms by which states can abstain from involvement in foreign policy decisions without binding the rest; and the divisive idea of a foreign policy *directoire* of the most powerful states (Keukeleire, 2001, 77). A spectrum of opinions about these issues has been a feature of EU discussions about CFSP since the signing of the Maastricht Treaty.

Now that the Union possesses hard power capabilities through ESDP it has the full range of instruments of a global power. Yet in reality the CFSP is not truly a common policy because the member states tend to pursue their various national interests in moments of crisis (Gordon, 1997). This inadequacy has been reflected in two scholarly debates. One has been the so-called 'capabilities–expectations' gap between what some hope the Union should be capable of achieving and what it can actually deliver (Hill, 1993). The second has been the debate about EU 'actorness': namely the extent to which the EU can mobilize its resources and political will to achieve objectives. In the future, the EU will need to choose whether it wants to focus its energies on being a regional pacifier or whether it wants to devote itself to being a global actor (Gunilla Herof, quoted in Ortega, 2007, 60).

The implications of US–EU differences

The fact that the US and the EU are different sorts of actors has led many commentators to view post-Cold War transatlantic relations as exhibiting growing patterns of divergence. A relationship that was once regarded as the bedrock of the West has come to be seen as fractured. One element of this is a sense of a widening cultural gap between the two sides. Garton Ash (2005, 94) notes how the US no longer defers to European values and even appears to question whether European views are worth taking into consideration. A generation of American post-war leaders that looked to Europe as their natural allies has been dying out and being replaced by individuals with no discernible affiliation to Europe. President Barack Obama exemplifies that development. The demise of an east coast political elite has led to a shift in the centre of political gravity from a European orientation towards America's interests in the Pacific (Walt, 1998–99). This has been compounded by the greater proportion of American trade crossing the Pacific than the Atlantic. America's rapidly growing Hispanic community is pulling the orientation of the country in another direction, towards Mexico and south America.

There are important differences between the two sides in relation to domestic values. Attitudes towards crime and the treatment of offenders is an example of this, with the US incarcerating a much higher proportion of its population. The retention of the death penalty is linked to this and has been a source of concern in Europe. The provision of health and social security benefits is another feature that distinguishes European and US societies, although President Obama has moved the US closer to Europe by his health care reforms. Rising religiosity has been an aspect of the US, especially in the south. This has carried over into political discourse and results in national politicians invoking strong moral language in their speeches. The influence of the 'Christian Right' and its ability to mobilize opinion, on issues ranging from abortion to stem cell research, is widely remarked upon. This contrasts with the values of secular societies in Europe where religious vocabulary is rare. 'It is evident that in the spiritual realm the United States and Europe have grown far apart' (Pfaff, 2008, 51).

Other commentators dismiss the thesis of a growing cleavage in transatlantic values. They point out that on fundamental issues such as support for liberal democracy, market economics, the rule of law and human rights, the US and Europe are closely aligned. These shared values underpin the relationship and ensure that no group of states have more in common. Assistant Secretary for European and Eurasian Affairs Philip Gordon (2009, 1) states that 'the United States and the European Union form a community of shared values and a partnership of shared interests'. Nau (2008, 82) endorses this by arguing that 'transatlantic institutions and values are much stronger today than they were when communism prevailed in half of Europe'. Shared values continue to act as the glue in transatlantic relations in the sense that it preserves a security community and a sense of what puts them all at risk.

A second element in the thesis that Europe and America have been growing apart relates to the perception of Western decline (Harries, 1993). This is the argument that the rise of other powers is eclipsing the West. There is a wealth of evidence that the West is no longer in the driving seat of world affairs and is increasingly over-shadowed by the rise of other states. In particular, the post-Cold War hegemony of the US seems to be waning, and its position of unipolarity is giving way to the prospect of 'multipolarity' or 'non-polarity', in which the world is divided between many states possessing different sorts of power (Haass, 2008; Prodi and Verhofstadt, 2010). Critics point to overstretch in the American military brought on by the interventions in Afghanistan and Iraq. It is alleged that America has squandered its global dominance and paved the way for its own imperial decline.

The economic challenge presented by emerging powers is even more apparent, reflecting the huge populations that they represent. Due to their high rates of growth the economic dominance of the Group of Eight Leading Industrial Countries (G8) has been super-seded by the 'G20', led by countries such as Brazil, Russia, India and China ('BRICs'). If China continues to grow at its present rate, it will overtake the American economy within the next twenty years. Russia has been in the process of returning to the international stage, wielding the influence that it derives from its reserves of oil and gas. Such powers as these perceive themselves to have been marginalized by the Western-led order in the past and now reject the constraints imposed by its rules and norms. Countries such as India and Brazil demand radical change within the UN Security Council on the grounds that it no longer represents the distribution of power within the world. In the words of Zakaria (2008, 4–5), 'in every other dimension (than politico-military power) – industrial, financial, educational, social, cultural – the distribution of power is shifting, moving away from American dominance'.

These pressures can be interpreted as having provoked a crisis in transatlantic relations. Instead of encouraging the Atlantic allies to club together to preserve their ascendancy, these external challenges have compounded the divisions within the West. No longer willing to act as the obedient lieutenant of America in the face of its declining position, the EU has become more ambitious and assertive as a rival centre of power to that of Washington. European political and economic union spurred the emergence of a European foreign and security policy that can be argued to have unsettled the transatlantic relationship. According to this view, Europe has repudiated Atlanticism and has struck out on its own, trying to act as a second voice in the West and a counterweight to America (Gordon, 2003). The EU can be seen as unifying around its opposition to the US and seeking to become a new pole of power (McCormick, 2007).

This thesis contains some elements of truth, but it is easily exaggerated. There are echoes here of past debates about US decline (Kennedy, 1989). After expectations of a downward spiral in American power in the 1980s the country proceeded to experience long-term economic growth during the 1990s. Today the US is the foremost economic power in the world and it has proved many times its capacity to re-energize its economy and achieve remarkable innovation. The economic recession that began in 2008 was certainly a cause for concern and there remain long-term problems in terms of America's budget deficit. But its economy remains dynamic and in military terms it remains far more powerful than any of its potential competitors. The US spends on defence as much as the rest of the world put together and it possesses an unrivalled capacity to project power. By historical standards its proportion of gross domestic product spent on defence, at 4 per cent, is low, and there is every prospect that this will be preserved.

Furthermore, America continues to lead a Western world that exerts influence and control through global organizations. Within frameworks such as NATO, the Organisation for Economic Co-operation and Development (OECD) and the WTO, the West still dominates. The US and its allies have created systems of international trading, monetary exchange and regulation that provide the architecture for the entire international system. Voices calling for more representative international organizations have been unable to relinquish the vice-like grip exerted by Western countries.

As for the EU attempting to rival the US, the prospect is unconvincing in all except economic terms. In other indices of power, the EU is not the equal of America – its population is ageing and its level of economic growth relatively slow. Whilst the EU has been determined to assert its own identity and viewpoint, even when that has differed from the position of the US, the organization has not coalesced around an anti-American position. It has continued to need US leadership in strategic affairs. To expect the EU to unite against America is to misunderstand the breadth of opinion within the Union itself. Countries such as the UK, the Netherlands, Denmark and Portugal oppose such an orientation and would prevent a common European front from emerging in opposition to America. It is misguided to think that Europe can draw strength from opposing Washington: such a course would leave the EU paralysed and listless.

A third body of opinion has sought to explain transatlantic tensions as the result of growing disparities in power. Krauthammer (1990) described the period after 1990 as marking the 'unipolar era' in which the US was less dependent on the support of its allies and less beholden to multilateral cooperation to achieve its objectives. The end of confrontation with the former Soviet Union meant that the US was freed to focus on global security concerns. In contrast, Europe had neglected these issues in the past and relied upon the US to manage them. The EU has possessed insufficient means to address global challenges and has been unable to make a significant contribution.

Debates about disparities in power have led to a perception of divergence in the strategic cultures of the US and the EU. Strategic culture is based on the understanding that a country's approach to the use of force has been shaped by its history. Kagan (2003, 11) supports this, arguing that 'now that the US is powerful, it behaves as powerful nations do. When the European[s] ... were strong, they believed in strength. Now they see the world through the eyes of weaker powers.' Other factors that help to shape strategic culture include the nature of the political system, technological development and national values. Ziemke (2000, 88), one of the pioneers of this idea, has suggested that it revolves around a state's self-conception, mediated though its historical experience of past conflicts. Strategic cultures serve to determine what states identify as being in their interest and what they find threatening, as well as deciding how these threats will be addressed (Cornish and Edwards, 2005; Giegerich, 2006; Meyer, 2006b).

The US has a clear strategic culture shaped by its hegemonic status and based upon its vast material and technological power. In the 1990–91 Gulf War and the 2003 War against Iraq, the US used this power against a conventional adversary and demonstrated its awesome capabilities. Both Democratic and Republican administrations have increased levels of defence spending in order to ensure no state can become a competitor. The aim has been to ensure that the US can fight and prevail in multiple theatres simultaneously. American policymakers believe that their country inhabits an international system in which military threats emanate from a variety of sources and have therefore been predisposed towards a security culture that privileges a military response.

The impact of 9/11 was significant in two respects. In the first place it galvanized the US into using its military power offensively. It led the US to disregard the importance of its allies because it saw no value in including them in its operational tasks. Second, 9/11 exposed the vulnerabilities in US homeland security, something that had been overlooked for a long period of time. It led the American government to allocate significant spending to the field of domestic security and look for allies to work with in this field.

In contrast to the US, a European strategic culture and what it wants to achieve in the world has been unclear (Kirchner and Sperling, 2007, 243). Within the EU, a number of cultures have coexisted simultaneously, ranging from the muscular cultures espoused by the UK and France to the culture of constraint of Germany and the neutralist traditions of Ireland and Austria (Meyer, 2006b; Giegerich, 2006, 67–81; Toje, 2008, 19). There were attempts in the 1990s to bring the strategic cultures of EU states closer together, and there were even discussions of an EU White Paper on Defence. Nothing materialized from these debates and, until the Union developed competences in defence, a common culture was irrelevant (Heisbourg, 2000a, 9–10). Since the creation of an ESDP (renamed the Common Security and Defence Policy after the ratification of the Treaty of Lisbon) there has been a concerted effort to converge the strategic thinking of the member states in order that the EU can act with greater unity and maximize its potential.

Military power remains a secondary and relatively novel instrument for the EU. Instead, it uses its economic leverage to cajole adversaries towards its position. Whilst 54 per cent of Americans agreed that the best way to ensure peace was through the preservation of military strength, only 28 per cent of Europeans concurred (Transatlantic Trends, 2004). The EU has exhibited a distinct lack of ambition to play a strategic role on the international stage. In the words of Bertram (2006, 41), 'beyond the boundaries of their Union, European governments either have no strategic ambition at all or are content with things as they are'.

In 2003, under the leadership of Javier Solana, the European Security Strategy (ESS) was agreed at the European Council meeting in Thessaloniki. The ESS was an attempt to conduct systematic thought about challenges to the security of the EU, its soft and hard power capacities and the objectives it would like to attain (Missiroli, 2008, 2). The ESS represents more of a doctrinal statement, or system of shared beliefs, than a strategy because of the inherent heterogeneity within the EU (Dannreuther and Peterson, 2006, 5). The fact that the ESS exhorts its members to develop a common strategic culture is evidence that this was not felt to exist at the time. Whitman (2006, 8) argued that the ESS 'is part of a wider CFSP/ESDP "work in progress" and in this context ... [it] is part of the attempt to forge a consensus on what should guide the EU's international role'. In this sense it establishes a framework in which EU security policy can be developed. The ESS may help an EU strategic culture to develop but, if so, it will remain to be seen how compatible this would be with the prevailing strategic culture of the US.

Kagan (2003) castigated the EU for its apparent attachment to Kantian principles of international peace and security. He described Europe as 'Venusian', ignoring the multitude of threats to Western interests. This artificial sense of security was made possible, Kagan argued, because the US invested so heavily in military power and extended its protection to its allies. Europe is accused of having grown used to tolerating threats because it abdicated its responsibility for trying to counter them. According to this view, Europe is in long-term decline and has become susceptible to compromising with dangerous states because it lacks the political will to build up its coercive power. Kagan (2003, 4) proceeded to argue that 'they [the

US and Europe] do not share the same broad view of how the world should be governed, about the role of international institutions and international law'. Europe has allowed itself to believe that it can address threats without resorting to coercive power. This view has found an echo in no less than Robert Gates, the US Secretary of Defense. He described the 'demilitarization of Europe – where large swathes of the general public and the political class are averse to military force and the risks that go with it' (Gates, 2010).

Other commentators have reacted to these criticisms in different ways. Some, such as Espinosa, agreed, contending that 'while Europe developed a free-rider culture on security matters, the United States developed a superpower culture' (Espinosa, 2005, 46). It is undeniable that Europe has not invested in military capabilities to the same extent as the US: after the Cold War they reduced defence spending and sought to enjoy a 'peace dividend'. Their defence budgets have remained focused on national priorities. At the same time, they have failed to generate the necessary political will to act together. Even on matters that involve conflict between its own members, such as the Cyprus issue, the EU has been unable to resolve the problem itself. Asmus contributed a more nuanced point. He argued that a power gap had always existed between America and Europe but the main difference had become the purpose to which America was prepared to use its power (Asmus, 2003, 23).

Other European commentators have rebutted Kagan's allegations. Nicolaidis argues not that the EU is Kantian by default but by deliberate choice. It is not a lack of resources that causes the Europeans to invest relatively little in their armed forces but a result of how they see the world. Nicolaidis (2005, 98) contends that 'Europe is no longer Kantian because it is weak; it is weak because it is Kantian.' European states look back to the experience of twentieth-century wars that were catastrophic in terms of the numbers of lives lost and damage wrought. In the words of Cooper (2003, 85), 'the use of force is a failure of policy, rather than an instrument of policy'. According to this view, the EU comprises post-modern states that reject both coercion as a means to resolve disputes and the imposition of democracy upon those that do not seek it. In matters of security, the Union has been more sympathetic to issues such as humanitarian intervention and state building, where it can exercise its own strengths through the use of economic resources.

According to this view, the EU has tried to use its 'soft power' resources to influence other actors (Nye, 2002, 8–12), whereas the

US is predisposed to the use of 'hard power'. It is indeed the case that some Europeans look with condescension upon US policies and view their own approach as more sophisticated. In the words of Croci (2003, 471), 'Europeans ... tend to regard the USA as a clumsy giant with little *savoir faire*.' The Obama administration has been sensitive to these accusations of US heavy-handedness and has talked explicitly of using 'smart power' as a means to secure its objectives. Smart power represents an attempt to rebuild America's influence in the world through diplomacy and developmental assistance. It reflects a predisposition on the part of Washington to listen to the views of other countries.

These transatlantic differences have been starkly exposed in international crises. Basic differences of grand strategy have been in evidence on such occasions. On the one hand has stood the US as a dominant, hegemonic power that defines its security interests globally and assesses risks conservatively. On the other hand has stood the EU, focused inwardly on integration and self-construction, perceiving itself as upholding different values. These divergences of approach, highlighted within the US-led 'War on Terror' and the 2003 invasion of Iraq, have caused grave damage to the cause of transatlantic unity. They have raised the question as to whether the two sides of the Atlantic are travelling in different directions.

Conclusion

No one would deny that the US possesses a strong power identity. Both before and after the Cold War it has been the foremost power within an international system that it has played the dominant role in shaping. US policymakers have held a clear view of their country's national interests and they have zealously guarded its sovereign capacity to act. America has defined its interests globally and has amassed the capability to project its power on a global stage. Yet at the same time, part of America's claim to be a superpower rests on its leadership position within Europe (Holbrooke, 1995). It has placed a premium upon working with its allies and has been reluctant to lose its position as leader within NATO.

The EU has not possessed a power identity as strong or as clear as that of its transatlantic ally. It has been less united and more hesitant as a security actor. Nevertheless, the EU presents an alternative model to that of the US: a non-coercive power that embraces globalization and is committed to multilateralism. Its power of attraction, due to the legitimacy of its model, is significant. Lindberg (2005, 6) captures this idea well when he notes that American 'exceptionalism is now matched by an emerging sense of "European exceptionalism" '. The interesting question is whether these exceptionalisms can complement one another or whether they will ultimately become mutually exclusive.

Both sides of the Atlantic are aware of the many security challenges that confront them. They also realize that only by working together can they have any realistic prospect of managing and overcoming them. After all, if the US does not work together with the EU then the fundamental question is raised as to whom it can work with.

Chapter 2

States and Institutional Relationships

Introduction

States normally provide for their own security. By doing so they can preserve their sovereignty and maximize their freedom of action. They do not have to place their trust in others to come to their assistance and they are not in fear of being let down in a crisis. But if states are unable to guarantee their own security, because the level of threat exceeds their strength, they may seek to join with others. This may remain an informal arrangement within a coalition or it may be formalized within an alliance (Riker, 1962). The results have the advantage of creating patterns of regularized behaviour and expectations of reciprocity amongst participating states (Haas, 1997). Liberal institutionalists argue that by choosing to invest responsibility for security activity in an institution, states become socialized into patterns of working together. They begin to develop norms and agreed ways of conducting their relationships. The bureaucracy that services the institution may evolve over time to assume a life of its own, and the institution itself may outgrow the role for which it was originally intended.

This was essentially the story of post-war Western Europe. The common threat presented by the Soviet Union was the catalyst for the coming together of a group of European states that had been erstwhile adversaries. They banded together with a superpower: a strange marriage due to the obvious disparities in power amongst the actors. Despite these inequalities in power, the relationship worked and their combined strength served to deter external aggression for over four decades. The NATO organization evolved into a framework both for guaranteeing the security of its members and for overcoming the nationalist rivalries that had caused tensions amongst them. The alliance became only the outward, legal embodiment of a set of deeper political, economic and

37

cultural ties that kept the two sides of the Atlantic in patterns of close cooperation.

Ikenberry (2001) argues that the US played the role of a 'benign hegemon' in relation to its European allies. There was an implicit bargain between the two sides: US power would be constrained within the relationship and cooperation would proceed on the basis of consultation. America allowed itself to be treated as the 'first among equals' and subordinated its strength and the superiority of its power by exercising it within the constitutional order of the Western alliance (ibid., 9). 'The distinctive features of this system – particularly its transparency, the diffusion of power into many hands, and the multiple points of access to policy-making' (Deudney and Ikenberry, 1999, 185), meant that European voices were heard in all aspects of the process. This US practice of mediating power through an institutional framework gave no incentive for European countries to pursue policies aimed at counterbalancing US power (Risse-Kappen, 1995). European states did not feel militarily threatened by their superpower patron because of the political, economic and cultural values that they shared and because of America's geographical distance. They chose to align with the US and served as reliable allies.

However, the end of the Cold War signalled the demise of the Warsaw Pact and the emergence of new security challenges. NATO had been constructed to accommodate American power and its *raison d'être* was the preservation of the security of Europe. It was unclear what role would remain for the organization in deterring residual threats on the continent and addressing conflicts on its periphery. Such conflicts contained significant dangers because they could spill over and escalate, but it was far from certain that the transatlantic relationship would be able to adapt to these demands. Furthermore, new and pressing security challenges were to arise outside of Europe and were likely to absorb American attention. Would the NATO architecture that had been predicated on the assumption of interstate warfare in Europe be appropriate for dealing with these diffuse and complex substate threats?

In the face of new global security threats, what was now at issue was the extent to which the US would be willing to act multilaterally to overcome them. In the Cold War era the US had exercised its power within the constitutional framework of the Western alliance, but now it had the option of expressing its power unilaterally (Stanzel, 1999). Instead of being tied down, as in the story of

Gulliver and the Lilliputians, the US could act alone. Such a course might be attractive if the expectation of US policymakers was that little contribution would be forthcoming from Europe. Ironically, the US was deciding whether to abide by the rules of the very institutions that it had helped to create in the post-war period. It remained to be seen whether America would regard the multilateral system as serving its interests or as a hindrance and a constraint.

Unlike the US, Europe did not have the ability to turn away from international institutions. As their relative standing in the world had declined, European countries had been forced to coordinate their positions in international fora in order to generate the maximum impact. Their own histories had led them to use organizations to contain nationalistic excesses and find ways of working together. They had come to regard institutions as part of the framework for pursuing global governance and they lacked the power to exercise influence through other means. At the same time they had less reason to defer to American leadership and were more likely to advocate policies that did not accord with US thinking.

This chapter looks at the post-1990 choices available to the US over how to work with its allies on security matters. It is argued on the one hand that NATO declined in relative importance, due to the fact that Europe became substantially safer and the new global challenges less susceptible to military solutions. On the other hand, however, it is argued that the EU has not risen to fill the space vacated by NATO. The inability of the EU to realize a muscular foreign and security policy left the US with options as to how best to pursue its relations with Europe. Although the US relationship with the EU has increased in stature, it still lacks the necessary framework to address global challenges effectively.

US bilateral relations with Europe

Bilateral relations between the US and individual European states have been one of the three principal forms of transatlantic interaction. It is relevant to the debate about institutional frameworks because European countries can play decisive roles within security organizations, for good or ill. For example, an individual country can block the capacity of an international organization to work with the US and thereby exercise a power of veto. Amidst the uncertainties of post-Cold War transatlantic security relations, bilateral relations have offered the US and European countries certain types of opportunities. For the US it has provided a way of focusing cooperation on specific issues with trusted countries. In the case of substate challenges, where intimate intelligence needs to be shared, this has been particularly appropriate. It has provided the US with the means to shape opinion within security organizations, to achieve its objectives, and even to exercise influence within organizations, such as the EU, where it is not a member. In some instances it has enabled policymakers in Washington to sidestep the complexities of consensus building by concerting its actions with a small group of countries who share its perspectives. For example, the US created the 'Contact Group' to act on the problem of Bosnia outside of NATO and the EU.

For European countries, the attraction of bilateral relations with the US are readily apparent. Obtaining US support can provide states with the means to realize foreign policy goals at minimal cost. It can serve as a source of prestige, both amongst allies and domestically, to be seen to have the ear of the American president. This is evidenced by the unseemly scramble to be the first European leader invited to the White House after a presidential inauguration, or, even better, to the president's private retreat. The US has sometimes been guilty of abusing its position of strength by playing off European countries against each other. This 'divide and rule' approach has served its interests when there has been opposition to US policies. In President George W. Bush's first term, there was a deliberate policy of disaggregating Europe. Countries with leaders sympathetic to US policies, such as Spain and Italy, were deliberately courted whilst other countries were shunned. The result of these policies was to widen the rifts amongst European states and prevent any possibility of a common European position emerging.

Forsberg and Herd (2006, 2) have identified five possible configurations of European identity in which a country may play a leading part. Three of these configurations reflect the enormous changes that have occurred on the continent since 1990. 'New' Europe – the enlarged members of NATO and the EU – represent for the US a novel source of influence as countries such as Poland have been strongly pro-American in orientation (see Chapter 5). 'Non-aligned' Europe is another, comprising formerly neutral states such as Sweden, Ireland and Finland. Although the nature of neutrality has changed on the continent since the end of East–West confrontation, it still has some resonance, as demonstrated when Austria refused NATO aircraft use of its airspace during the war in Kosovo.

'Periphery' Europe represents those states that are neither members of NATO or the EU, and symbolizes the way in which the political geography of the continent has changed. But two of the configurations, 'Atlantic' Europe and 'core' Europe, represent long held tensions in transatlantic relations between those states committed to perpetuating a close relationship with the US and those countries eager to develop closer European integration.

Countries that are part of 'Atlantic' Europe have changed over the years and have included the UK, the Netherlands, Portugal and Denmark. These saw the US as the continent's most important security actor. They appreciated the role that America has played in gathering states together around its position. Such a country as the Netherlands was firmly pro-European in orientation but was sceptical of any alternative to American leadership, believing that the many and competing interests of continental states would undermine attempts to forge a common defence framework.

The foremost Atlanticist state has been the UK, whose 'Special Relationship' with Washington has made it both the subject of envy and criticism. The US has valued the contribution that Britain has made as a channel and interlocutor for American policies, ideas and trade into the continent. It applauded, for example, the UK's part in obstructing a defence role for the EU during the 1990s and its solidarity with NATO. The US never went so far as to encourage the UK to oppose the process of building political and economic union in Europe, but rather wanted the UK to be exerting a moderating influence in order to ensure that American interests were not marginalized.

Britain has cherished the special status and influence it has derived from being both close to Washington and a leading actor within NATO. The UK's scepticism towards EU integration was not just about placating Washington, it was genuinely felt. It has doubted the ability of European states to act in the absence of US leadership. Its privileged relationship with a superpower has granted it access to nuclear technology, at a fraction of the cost of developing it alone, and intensive intelligence sharing. It has also been accorded special status in the purchase of defence equipment, such as the Joint Strike Fighter programme, and in admittance to the US domestic arms market by British companies such as British Aerospace.

Nevertheless, the UK's instinct to align itself closely with the US has been seen in European capitals as evidence that it will choose

Washington over Brussels. Some critics contend that such special relationships with the US have served to undercut the EU's capacity to speak to America with a united voice (Witney and Shapiro, 2009, 6). British diplomats have always contended that the choice between Europe and America is a false one, that Britain must straddle both sides of the Atlantic if it is to realize its interests. Yet even a leader like Prime Minister Tony Blair, who said that he wanted to place Britain at the 'heart of Europe', came to find that his loyalty to America detracted from his credibility in Europe. He was prepared to speak frankly to US policymakers in private – even engaging in a major argument with President Clinton over unwillingness to put ground troops into Kosovo – but Blair was always supportive in public. Those same priorities were less in evidence under the leadership of Prime Minister Gordon Brown who was aware that Blair had been damaged by his identification with unpopular American policies. Brown was determined to appear less tied to the Bush administration (Dumbrell, 2009, 67). Prime Minister David Cameron has signalled his intention to weigh British interests carefully and to eschew an automatic positioning of the UK alongside the US.

The US has welcomed the UK's willingness to help address global security challenges and to commit forces to operations. In the first Gulf War, in the creation of safe havens for the Kurds, in bombing operations over Iraqi non-compliance with UN Security Council Resolutions, and in the 2003 war against Iraq, the UK participated in military operations. This role was often substantial, second only to the US; in the two wars against Iraq the UK fielded a fully equipped armoured division. Such crises offered opportunities to re-cement the Special Relationship in its core area of security. The UK rationale was that it would share US tasks even in difficult circumstances, so that Washington would not be left to carry these alone. It believed that unless US burdens were shared appropriately, America's commitment to leadership of the West and the well-being of its allies was likely to wane.

Countries including Belgium, Luxembourg and, in the past, Spain and Italy have deserved to be counted as 'core' Europeans. Germany and France have been regarded as providing the momentum for this group, based upon their close bilateral relationship. Germany has been careful to pursue its political, economic and security interests within the framework of the EU and NATO, in order to reassure its neighbours and placate the fears of Russia. Its attraction to

Washington has been magnified by the central role it has played within the EU. For Germany, there was a switch in the relative importance of the EU and NATO once the threat from the Warsaw Pact dissolved. Whilst German leaders have continued to emphasize the importance of the Atlantic Alliance and made efforts to avoid alienating the US, the importance of transatlantic relations has declined. The US is no longer the mainstay of Germany's security and the EU has become an even more important vehicle for the realization of its interests.

Germany was the principal object of post-Cold War US bilateral policy. President George H. Bush saw a united Germany as America's favoured European interlocutor (Stares, 1992), due to its size and economic power and the expectation that it would increasingly assert its own national interests. The country's special status in the eyes of Washington diminished, however, when it became clear in the first Gulf War that Germany still operated under a constrained culture regarding the extra-territorial use of force (Bartlett, 1992, 171). This reflected a post-war tradition within the German polity in which 'the use of force is no longer regarded as a justifiable tool of foreign and security policy' (Longhurst, 2004, 46). It was not until the Kosovo campaign in 1999 that the German military undertook their first combat missions, and this was only possible after considerable soul searching within the Bundestag. Data from opinion polls confirms that the German public take a fundamentally different view from their allies about the role that their country should play in European security. For example, when asked whether Europe should acquire greater military power in order to be able to act independently of the US, only 53 per cent of Germans agreed compared with 71 per cent of French respondents (Transatlantic Trends, 2004). The continuing sensitivity of the issue was underlined at the end of May 2010 when President Horst Köhler resigned after comments he made were construed as meaning that Germany had to resemble other countries in its preparedness to use force (Boyes, 2010).

Contending approaches towards the issue of multilateralism has also caused tensions in US–German relations. Germany has been a staunch advocate of obtaining UN approval for overseas interventions. In 1994 the Federal Constitutional Court ruled that German forces could only engage in operations outside of the NATO area if they had been approved by the UN Security Council and voted upon in the Bundestag (Hyde-Price, 2000, 147). In the lead up to war in

Iraq in 2003, German Foreign Minister Joschka Fischer made clear that he did not find the US rationale for the use of force convincing and argued that the UN weapons inspectors should be given more time to complete their work. When it became clear that the US was determined to remove Saddam Hussein's regime by force, Chancellor Gerhard Schroeder signalled that Germany would oppose American policy even if a second UN Security Council Resolution was forthcoming. The resulting tension between Washington and Berlin was palpable and President George W. Bush refused even to speak to the Chancellor on the telephone. Schroeder's successor, Chancellor Angela Merkel, has sought to repair US–German relations after the nadir that was reached over Iraq and has worked hard to play the part of America's close ally in Europe.

France made no secret of the fact that during the Cold War it saw the US as a hegemonic power engaged in a largely ritualistic antagonism with the Soviet Union. French leaders argued for a 'third way' between the two superpowers. The objective was not to isolate the US but to rebalance the relationship in such a way as to avoid deferring to American interests. The Fouchet Plan of 1961 called for a European 'Union of States', with a foreign and security policy separate from NATO. France progressed to the Elysée Treaty of 1963 and sought to detach the Federal Republic of Germany from America's security embrace (Haglund, 1991, 85). Bonn declined, making clear that it regarded its relationship with Washington as the key to its post-war rehabilitation and the cornerstone of its security. After that crucial period, the Franco-German relationship acted as the motor for closer European economic and political integration, but defence was left to NATO.

The post-Cold War period was seen in Paris as a potential opening of the door to a multipolar world in which Europe could assert its interests independently of US domination. Its leaders went so far as to envisage the EU as a potential counterweight to America. In contrast, the US regarded its unipolar dominance as a benign phenomenon that helped to further peace and freedom in the world. US National Security Advisor Condoleezza Rice (2003, 3) talked of multipolarity as 'a necessary evil that sustained the absence of war but did not promote the triumph of peace'. Paris was hostile to NATO remaining the centrepiece of the European security system: it was content to leave the Alliance as the repository for a collective defence guarantee, but it desired a European framework to address new security challenges.

Where French leaders were less transparent was over the leadership role they envisaged for their own country as Europe became more responsible for its defence. Their allies were suspicious and hostile to these plans because the *'grandeur'* of France appeared central to the vision that was being promoted. One commentator talked of a fundamental tension in French policy: 'on the one hand was the quest for independence: on the other the desire (based partly on a recognition of the inability of France to achieve such independence) to create European defence structures' (Menon, 2000, 138).

The slow development of EU defence structures and the weakness it demonstrated in the Balkans in the early 1990s altered the perceptions of French policymakers and convinced them of the need for more influence within the Alliance. Criticizing NATO from the sidelines was no substitute for having a voice in the military policies that were being decided upon. France decided to draw closer to NATO in an effort to procure influence commensurate with its power and to benefit from NATO's common standards and operating procedures (Schake *et al.*, 1999, 35). Part of France's price for such a volte-face in policy was to be given NATO's Southern Command (AFSOUTH) in Naples, that was held by the US. This would have been a significant loss for the US as it was from AFSOUTH that the US oversaw operations in the Mediterranean as well as the Balkans. President Clinton was unwilling to go that far. In the words of Rynning (1999, 117), 'letters exchanged between Presidents Chirac and Clinton leaked to the public ... and effectively ensured that both were trapped by the symbolism of the issue'. The deal fell through and France did not rejoin NATO's military structure until many years later.

With the 2003 war against Iraq, France positioned itself in open opposition to US objectives. Like the US, ironically, France has possessed its own sense of exceptionalism (Giegerich, 2006, 78) and saw this as the moment when it could realize its goal of developing Europe as a counterweight to America. Yet the unreality of this vision was quickly apparent in the temporary triumvirate that emerged, led by Chirac, Schroeder and Putin. It was apparent that only opposition to Washington's policies in Iraq tied these three leaders together and their relationship fell apart. US National Security Adviser Condoleezza Rice argued after the conflict that American policy should be to 'punish France' for its behaviour (Albright, 2008). This quickly dissipated once the new government of Nicolas Sarkozy came to power with his pro-Atlantic orientation and his desire to repair relations with Washington.

The mixed and sometimes contradictory objectives of the UK, Germany and France have had three implications for transatlantic relations. First, it has prevented the development of a coherent EU foreign and security policy. On major issues the three leading powers on the continent have tended to adopt different priorities. Smaller countries have been drawn into temporary coalitions with these states and constellations of countries have changed over time according to the issues. In the face of dissension amongst the foremost powers, the EU has experienced gridlock, with the result that its influence has been limited.

Second, there has been no single European voice to which the US has been forced to listen. The EU has been unable to present a united front, particularly during times of crisis. This has enabled Washington to marginalize its allies and pursue a policy of selectivity. It has been able to choose with whom to engage according to their congruence with America's own position. Sometimes the US has worked with the EU as a whole, while at other times it has cooperated with individual countries that have shared its approach.

The third aspect is that differences in strategic direction have not divided neatly between the US and EU members. There are often major differences between the policy positions of EU states. In the absence of a well developed European strategic culture, states sometimes side with the US. As Tetrais (2008, 19) points out, where European countries possess special responsibilities, they frequently share American perceptions. For example, on nuclear matters, as on the role of the UN Security Council, Paris and London play a special role alongside Washington. On matters relating to terrorism, those countries that have suffered attacks over many years have tended to side with the hard-line stance of the US (ibid., 20). This renders it more difficult for the EU to present a united front across the Atlantic.

The failure of the EU to fill the NATO vacuum

A second option for America in working with Europe has been to concentrate its energies on NATO. The Alliance was a tried and tested instrument for ensuring US security leadership and offered a sense of continuity in an uncertain period. The US was the dominant power within the Alliance with the ability to mobilize its allies around its policies. It retained sizeable forces in Europe, its commanders enjoyed the leading positions within NATO's military structure and it was in America's interest to preserve the Alliance as its principal security linkage with Europe.

Neither the US nor the Europeans were clear about the post-Cold War role that they wanted the Alliance to play. The American government appeared to be ambivalent about NATO's future importance and was busily engaged in reducing the size of the forces it deployed in Western Europe. NATO had always focused narrowly on military issues – the Article V collective defence of its members' territories – and it was uncertain what place this would have in the future security agenda. The relationship between the EU and NATO was also in doubt. The Treaty on European Union declared that the CFSP would include 'the eventual framing of a common defence policy which might in time lead to a common defence' (European Council, 1992, Article J4.1). There was understandable nervousness in Washington that the EU could take over the leading part in the defence of the continent and thereby undermine all of the investment that the US had made in the Alliance up to that point.

The early to mid-1990s witnessed a deep-seated debate about the future of the continent's security 'architecture'. To a large extent, carving out a role for the EU would depend on the extent to which the US wanted NATO to remain the leading organization in European security. There was optimistic talk in the early part of the 1990s that an interlocking architecture could be fashioned, and Assistant Secretary of State Richard Holbrooke asserted (1995, 5) that the EU and NATO would be 'mutually supportive'. France mooted its return to NATO structures. Asmus (2005, 97) has postulated that such a move could have 're-harmonized the Atlantic and Europeanist projects'. But in reality the two organizations failed to develop a closer relationship and competition and rivalry characterized their interaction. Within a context of changing roles and responsibilities, as well as an evolving threat environment, the two organizations found collaboration difficult and tended to revert to mutual suspicion.

At the 1994 Brussels Summit, US determination to preserve the centrality of NATO was made apparent (North Atlantic Council, 1994). The US seized the initiative and welcomed the building of an ESDI within the Alliance. This was regarded as a way to give European states a bigger say in Alliance policy whilst at the same time preserving the centrality of NATO. The US also took the lead in starting the organizational enlargement of NATO by launching the 'Partnership for Peace' policy with those states eager to accede. These US initiatives were made easier by the lack of European cohesion that had been evident in the conflicts in the Balkans.

Whilst the US adapted NATO to deal with residual European security problems, it experienced greater difficulty in configuring the Alliance to address new challenges. These have included nuclear proliferation and, particularly since 9/11, the threat from transnational terrorism. Senator Richard Lugar (2002) warned that NATO would face irrelevance unless it addressed the issues of WMD and terrorism. Similarly, Clarke and McCaffrey (2004) argued that NATO should embrace the counter-terrorism role by appointing a dedicated assistant secretary general for this issue. At the NATO Summit in Prague in November 2002, the Alliance took on a counter-terrorism mission and began to assemble a NATO Response Force (NRF) to give it a capacity for swift intervention. This force was declared operational at the Riga summit in November 2006, but, subsequently, NATO member states have been seen to have different views on how best to address terrorism, with the result that the NRF has seen little use. It has come to be viewed as too large for most sorts of rapid deployment missions, yet too small for a major intervention. The size of the NRF has been scaled down from 20,000 troops to 13,500. It has only been employed for limited humanitarian operations, such as the 2005 earthquake in Kashmir (Webber, 2009, 54), and discussed as a possible facilitator for action by the African Union (*Economist*, 2006b, 23).

The US has been in the forefront of efforts to create a new Allied Command Transformation, with the aim of changing the Alliance from the collective defence of the territories of member states to an overseas expeditionary posture. These efforts have met with varying levels of commitment, however, from other NATO states. Without the existential threat from the former Soviet Union, it has been hard to generate a sense of shared interests amongst NATO members. The attempt to sketch out a global agenda of issues has been treated by some states with relative indifference. There has been a questioning of NATO's suitability for these sorts of roles: trying to turn NATO into a counter-terrorism actor was described by one commentator as a 'misguided choice' (Stelzenmüller, 2008, 9). Overall, NATO has struggled to prove its relevance to new security challenges because of its relative inflexibility. The strategic purpose of the Atlantic Alliance has become unclear (Andrews, 2005, 1) as it is one of several operational frameworks to respond to new types of threats (Cottey, 2007, 71). The decision to develop a new Strategic Concept in 2010 has been a recognition of NATO's need to reinvent itself to ensure its continuing relevance amidst an evolving environment (NATO 2010, 5).

US dissatisfaction with NATO's process of transformation led Washington to downgrade its importance. Despite the apparent success of the 2002 Prague Summit in acknowledging a role for the Alliance in global interventions, the Bush administration signalled that it no longer regarded the organization as fulfilling a central role. It did not request NATO assistance in the military operations that were initiated after 9/11, and Defense Secretary Donald Rumsfeld pointedly called for ad hoc coalitions instead, thereby undermining the collective nature of the Alliance. In its desire to reconfigure the Alliance to address global security concerns, the US called into question its utility. This demotion in its significance was commented upon by Chancellor Gerhard Schroeder when, at the 2005 Wehrkunde conference in Munich, it was argued that NATO was no longer the main forum for transatlantic relations (Schroeder, 2005). The low-key return of France to NATO's Integrated Military Structure in 2009 has underlined the reduced stature of the Alliance. An event that would have been of major significance in the 1990s has caused little more than a ripple due to the reduced importance of the Alliance.

In light of NATO's diminished importance, it could be expected that the EU would become more of a partner of the Alliance in military operations and fill some of the space it had vacated. With the creation of the ESDP in 1999, the Union had formed a military instrument that would enable it to act more assuredly in defence (see Chapter 3). The ESDP has provided more of a European contribution to security and helped to crystallize their interests. The EU and NATO have worked together in the Balkans and cooperated at an operational level. Regular meetings now take place between the EU High Representative and the NATO Secretary General as well as between the North Atlantic Council and the EU's Political-Security Committee. An EU–NATO Declaration on the ESDP was drawn up in December 2002 that outlined the modalities in their relationship and went as far as to declare that a strategic partnership existed between them.

Yet beneath the surface the EU has been unable both to compensate for the reduced stature of the Alliance and to become a more active partner of the US. The EU has failed to define an agreed set of security interests amongst its members and has continued to defer to NATO and US leadership. In spite of the drawing together of NATO and the EU in functional terms, they have remained far apart strategically. Rivalry between the organizations has mirrored tensions within the broader US–EU relationship. The American Ambassador to NATO, Alexander Vershbow (2001), complained as early as 2001 about the lack of institutional contact between the EU and the Alliance. This lack of cooperation has persisted. The former NATO Secretary General, Jaap de Hoop de Scheffer (2007), commented that 'when one looks at how diverse and complex the challenges to our security have become today, it is astounding how narrow the bandwidth of cooperation between NATO and the EU has remained'. Insufficient effort has been invested into getting the two organizations to work together on the military and non-military aspects of crises. Although there is less ideological opposition to cooperation, the political will has not been forthcoming to transform the relationship. In 2008 US Ambassador Nuland (2008b, 4) called for 'a stronger EU, we need a stronger NATO and ... we need a stronger, more seamless relationship between them'.

The EU still lacks the sort of military capabilities and the political will that would enable it to act on the global stage in place of the Alliance. This is exemplified in the case of Afghanistan where NATO's International Security Assistance Force mission represented its first operation outside of Europe. NATO suffered from a bifurcated command structure and an unclear set of political and military objectives (Gallis, 2006, 6). There were differences between the Europeans and Americans over poppy eradication and the support that was to be given to the Karzai government in Kabul. Whilst countries such as Germany, Spain and Italy signed up to the reconstruction effort carried out by Provincial Reconstruction Teams, the US continued to conduct Operation Enduring Freedom, hunting al-Qaeda and the Taliban and executing cross-border raids into Pakistan. Some European states expressed misgivings that they risked being draw into an American counter-insurgency campaign over which they had no control. As a result, highly restrictive caveats were placed on the deployments of some European forces, preventing them from engaging in combat missions. This led US Defense Secretary Robert Gates to talk of a 'two tier' commitment by Western countries to Afghanistan, between those prepared to send their troops to die and those without the necessary political will (*Economist*, 2008a, 31).

The EU has played only a minor role in Afghanistan, remaining in the shadow of NATO. It is a large aid donor to the country, has assisted in countering the drug problem and, in June 2007, its EUPOL mission took over from Germany the task of training the Afghan National Police. But it has provided only a modest contingent of training officers – less than 300 out of the 400 that were intended, and much less than the 5,000 called for by Washington (Dempsey, 2008, 2). In February 2009 President Obama committed a further 17,000 troops to the Afghanistan theatre, consistent with the recommendations of an earlier report (Afghanistan Study Group Report, 2008, 13), and in the following year another 30,000 troops were pledged (Reid and Whittell, 2009, 6). At the same time as increasing its troop levels, the US has reduced the expectations about the goals of nation-building. Yet President Obama's call for additional European forces in Afghanistan led to commitments of only 10,000 troops. There was barely disguised disappointment in Washington at the modest and grudging responses it received from its European allies.

Afghanistan has encapsulated many of the tensions that lie at the heart of European relations with the US: the outside-of-Europe mission, the debate about appropriate roles for NATO and the EU, the use of force amidst a complex political environment, and the attempt at nation-building. It has exemplified many of the limitations of EU members including the diversity of their interests and their reluctance to resource the Union's involvement adequately. Witney and Shapiro (2009) argue that the EU has failed to focus on the issue of whether the conflict in Afghanistan is a vital European interest or not. The Union has approached it as an issue in transatlantic relations and has sought to provide only a level of effort that will assuage US demands. Many European countries do not believe in the cause in Afghanistan and are sceptical that a worthwhile outcome can be salvaged. For example, 55 per cent of west Europeans and 69 per cent of central and east Europeans would favour the withdrawal of their forces from the theatre (Transatlantic Trends, 2009). There has been little European attempt to engage with questions as to what strategy should be adopted and whether the goals in Afghanistan are appropriate. Witney and Shapiro regard this as indicative of a European mindset that fails to embrace global challenges and continues to abdicate leadership to the US.

US–EU institutional relations

The third option for the US has been to engage more systematically with the EU. The attraction of the Union to Washington is that it provides a point of contact with all the major European states simultaneously and one that has transformed its breadth of competences since 1990. This made it a much more attractive prospective partner and opened up the possibility of cooperation with the US across a spectrum of security issues.

The main test for the EU and the US has been to rectify the inadequate institutional relationship that has existed between them. Their past pattern of interaction was narrowly preoccupied with economic matters, reflecting the traditional competences of the Union. The evolution of new shared security interests necessitated an innovative institutional forum. A senior figure in the administration of George H. Bush, Robert Zoellick (1990), called for this early on so that an 'alliance of values' could prevent US and European paths diverging. Zoellick feared the emergence of a fortress Europe mentality that would treat the US increasingly as an outsider. The first steps for building a new dialogue between the US and the EC/EU began in November 1989 when Secretary of State James Baker gave a speech entitled 'A New Atlanticism' (Baker, 1989). He called for 'a significantly strengthened set of institutional and consultative links' on foreign policy matters of mutual concern. This was to be structured around the US and European Political Cooperation working groups. It resulted in the signing of the 1990 Transatlantic Declaration that mapped out a revised agenda of security priorities between the two sides. It inaugurated meetings between the President of the European Council and the US President, as well as the EC foreign ministers and the US Secretary of State. It also began a series of consultations with the US under the auspices of the country holding the EU Presidency (Steffenson, 2005, 33).

In 1995, President Clinton and Prime Minister Felipe González of Spain inaugurated a New Transatlantic Agenda (NTA). It reflected the influence of the US Ambassador to the EU, Stuart Eizenstat, who was keen to reinforce transatlantic links and to establish multiple dialogues between business actors, parliamentarians and civil society. The major contribution of the NTA was that it focused the US–EU relationship on 'new global challenges', including international crime, terrorism and the spread of WMD (Gardner, 1996).

This was flattering for the EU as it signalled that the US was prepared to treat the Union as a global actor. It contributed to a growing institutionalization in US–EU relations at a variety of levels: intergovernmental, transgovernmental and transnational (Pollack, 2005, 901). These took the form of a series of structured dialogues in biannual summits (reduced to an annual basis after 2000; *Economist*, 2009b, 41); biannual meetings of EU Foreign Ministers and the US Secretary of State; working groups to prepare the agendas for summits; and a Senior Level Group to oversee the implementation of policy decisions.

Ivo Daalder and James Goldgeier (2001, 77) describe US policy during the 1990s as 'putting Europe first', and they argue that it was part of a concerted effort to encourage the EU to assume global responsibilities alongside the US. As part of that effort, in June 1999, the Clinton administration met with the German Presidency of the EU and agreed the Bonn Declaration that committed both sides to strengthening the US–EU partnership. Steps were taken by the EU that were designed to enhance its potential to partner the US.

There can be no doubting that there were ambitious ideas behind the NTA. The results, however, have been disappointing (Peterson and Steffenson, 2009, 27). As Pollack noted (2005, 916), although policy integration between the US and EU is deep, institutional relationships have remained shallow. The Europeans have been predisposed to rely upon the US to address global security concerns and have been reluctant to invest in their own capabilities (Asmus, 2005, 100). The NTA itself has been criticized for drawing up an unreflective lists of issues and failing to prioritize. There has been constant pressure for eye-catching initiatives that have not always been followed through. A major study on the NTA, initiated by the European Commission, concluded that it was overloaded with issues and falling short of its potential. The study recommended that the NTA should be revamped and relaunched with a more strategic focus (Peterson, 2005, 5–6).

The US has found the EU to be a constrained actor in foreign and security policy. It has struggled to construct a strategic vision and remains only as powerful as its member states allow it to be. Foreign policy is 'an example of multilevel governance, including a range of mutually dependent actors across different policy levels, with multiple powers and interests, complementary functions and overlapping competences' (Keukeleire and MacNaughton, 2008, 32). This predisposition towards separate national policies led Zbigniew

Brzezinski (2007), a former US National Security Adviser, to argue that the EU is still basically impotent as a global actor, especially during international crises. A group of former EU leaders agreed and described its foreign policy as 'invisible and ineffectual' (Prodi and Verhofstadt, 2010, 22).

Prior to the passing of the Lisbon Treaty in 2007, policy issues ranged across all three pillars (Lebl, 2007): economic competences rested in pillar one; foreign and security policy in pillar two; and internal security in the third pillar. The instruments for dealing with these issues were interwoven into all three pillars (Stetter, 2007) and progress depended on coordination between a host of committees and agencies (Council of the European Union, 2005a). The Treaty of Lisbon has removed the pillar structure. For their part, the European Council and the European Commission have enjoyed control over different facets of the Union. The Council has controlled foreign and security issues whilst the Commission has enjoyed the leading role in conflict prevention and development assistance. This has led to tensions. For instance, whilst the European Council had stewardship over relations with third countries, if sanctions were decided upon then these came under the trade competences of the Commission. Similarly, issues of intervention lay within the purview of the Council, but post-conflict nation-building was the responsibility of the Commission.

US officials have frequently expressed frustration about working with the EU. They are confounded by the Union's complexity and the time delays that it imposes. Although the Treaty of Lisbon was supposed to simplify the EU, it has failed to do so. Washington has expressed dissatisfaction at the practice of the Union in the way it arrives at common positions, before negotiating with third parties. This has led to an inbuilt reluctance to unpick a position that had been achieved by negotiation amongst the EU members. Hence, analysts have argued that the US needs to influence EU policymaking at an early stage if it is to prevent obstacles appearing later on (Lebl, 2007, 1).

In turn, the EU has found the US a difficult actor with whom to deal. To attach credence to a single foreign and security policy emanating out of the US ignores a policymaking process that is the hostage of competing power centres. A variety of powerful bureaucratic actors, such as the State Department and Pentagon, shape US policy through a bargaining process. There is the influence of a range of interest groups to add to the menu. The two Houses of

Congress also exert a substantial power over foreign policy, beyond the simple control over the budget (Everts, 2001, 8).

The EU's Constitutional Treaty, signed in Rome in October 2004, sought to enhance the decision-making efficiency of the Union and its ability to act. In 2005, referenda in France and the Netherlands rejected the Treaty. This exposed the constraints on the EU. Enlargement fatigue in European countries allied to a perceived disconnect between the political elite and mass support was judged to be behind this unexpected obstacle. The subsequent Lisbon Treaty was submitted as an amending treaty but a referendum in the Republic of Ireland rejected it. The EU was plunged into a period of paralysis as attempts were made to take the reform process forward. A further vote in Ireland, and the final signature of the Czech Republic, eventually allowed the Lisbon Treaty to be implemented in December 2009.

The Lisbon Treaty attempts to improve the Union's foreign policy machinery. It abolishes its pillar system and gives the EU a single legal personality. The post of President of the European Council has been created and replaces the six-month rotating presidencies in foreign affairs. The rotating presidency was blamed for short-term thinking and agenda-setting within the Union. The position of High Representative for Foreign Affairs and Security Policy was also instigated, a role combining the former office of High Representative within the European Council with the Commission's External Relations Commissioner. Javier Solana, a former Spanish Foreign Minister and NATO Secretary General, had done much to carve out a role as the first High Representative for the CFSP. He had presided over a Policy Planning and Early Warning Unit and the establishment of a Situation Centre in Brussels. Solana succeeded in becoming the voice of the EU in matters of foreign policy but had suffered from being perceived as the servant of the national foreign policy ministers within the Council.

These new positions of EU President and High Representative afford an opportunity to raise the profile of the EU in the world. The High Representative will chair meetings of national foreign ministers, possess a considerable external relations budget and will oversee a potentially powerful External Action Service – a diplomatic corps drawn from Council, Commission and seconded staff from national foreign ministries. However, the actual appointments of a President and a High Representative have fallen short of expectations on two counts. In the first place, the external identity of the

Union is left opaque, due the profusion of figures serving as its representatives. As well as the new appointees, these include the EU President and the President of the European Commission. Second, the people appointed to the new positions left commentators disappointed. Herman Van Rompuy is a former prime minister of Belgium and Catherine (Baroness) Ashton is a former EU trade commissioner with little foreign policy experience. National governments seemed to decide that, in the area of foreign and security policy, they did not want EU-level officials to overshadow them (*Economist*, 2010f, 46). They indulged in the usual horse-trading that left only lowest common denominator appointments. In the words of Richard Haass from the Council on Foreign Relations, 'from the perspective of many Americans, rather than building up someone of the stature of Javier Solana, it looks as though Europe has retreated' (quoted in Charter *et al.*, 2010, 1).

The perception that there exists an inadequate institutional linkage across the Atlantic prompted debate about a dedicated US–EU global forum that could replace the NTA. Much has indeed changed in transatlantic security relations, and the actors have sought to muddle through by adapting organizations to new tasks. Yet a report conducted under the auspices of the US Council on Foreign Relations recommended caution over such an approach. It argued that if the main countries in the Atlantic relationship do not agree on policy, then institutions can do little to alleviate the problem (Kissinger and Summers, 2004, 20). Institutions can assist in mediating between transatlantic interests but only if there is the political will on both sides to engage actively. Creating new institutions is an inherently risky business. It seems more likely that the US and Europe will have to reform existing institutions to ensure that they act more effectively.

Multilateralism and the UN

As Steven Everts (2001) notes, there has been growing transatlantic divergence on the issue of global governance. The two sides have differed not only over broad approaches but over specific issues as well. The US and the EU believe that legally constituted international bodies regularize patterns of interaction, contribute towards achieving objectives and help to underpin international order. Institutions accord legitimacy to actions and, in an increasingly globalized world, this is acknowledged to be an important commodity. There is a difference of degree, however, between the US and the Union. In the face of deadlock in some international institutions and the declining importance of alliances, the US has acted unilaterally. This American ambivalence towards multilateralism should not be exaggerated as the country remains committed to the majority of international institutions. It played a leading role during the Cold War in creating and sustaining many organizations. Nonetheless, the end of the Cold War loosened some of the bonds. Its unique strength provided the US with the ability to act through the assertion of its national power. Multilateralism is a preferred approach for American policy, gathering allies to its side. But while Europeans see the construction of a multilateral security order as an end in itself, 'for Americans, multilateralism is strictly a means to an end' (Drezner, 2008, 194). It was precisely because the US had restrained itself within multilateral frameworks during the Cold War that its partial disengagement from these structures in the post-1990 period caused such consternation amongst its allies.

The EU, with its own culture of seeking negotiation and compromise, has called for a 'renewal of the multilateral order' (European Council, 2008, 2). In the face of cracks in the international order, it has sought to shore up institutions as diverse as the International Criminal Court, the International Monetary Fund and the G8. This has partly reflected the lack of alternatives available to the EU but it has also demonstrated a predisposition to act multilaterally. The US has been particularly incensed that some EU countries have berated them for acting unilaterally whilst using the argument of multilateralism as a pretext for inaction. In 2003 the US regarded countries such as France and Germany as using high principled arguments about multilateralism to constrain and delegitimize America's capacity to act. These contending approaches to the legitimacy of international action have been at the heart of transatlantic tensions (Kagan, 2004, 66–7).

The US has some justification when arguing that the multilateral system is weak and flawed. States have often been reluctant to act in the face of flagrant abuses of human rights unless their own national interests are involved. It is also the case that the UN Security Council can be paralysed by the refusal of a single member to approve an intervention under Article 7, even when the case is overwhelming. The system is far from perfect, yet it is the only system that exists for approving multilateral action. Presidential Directive 25, in 1994, declared US policy to be 'assertive multilateralism', signifying that the US was not prepared to remain passive when international institutions failed to act. The US has long seen itself as the key player within the international system, the 'indispensable nation'. It has perceived itself as performing the role of sheriff within a world order that has no overarching form of security management (Haass, 1996). Former Secretary of State Madeleine Albright (1998) summed this up in the phrase that America should 'behave multilaterally when we can but unilaterally when we must'.

This thinking was evident during the 1990s and was then amplified by the administration of George W. Bush, which came into office with the view that several international treaties were flawed and deserved to be repudiated. These included the 1972 Anti-Ballistic Missile Treaty that was regarded as preventing the US from deploying a missile defence system; the 1997 Kyoto Protocol on climate change that was regarded as inhibiting economic growth; and the International Criminal Court on the grounds that it might indict American personnel. The 1996 Comprehensive Test Ban Treaty was not submitted for ratification (Mahncke *et al.*, 2004, 145). The Bush administration was amenable to cooperating with those governments that shared its priorities, but it was not prepared to be bound by agreements that did not serve its interests. Bosch and Ham (2007, 5) describe its approach as 'a policy of multilateralism "by invitation", asking others to ... follow its leadership, and trust its judgement'.

American distrust of multilateral organizations was focussed particularly on the UN, where scepticism stretched back to a time when the Security Council was paralysed by East–West division. The UN was seen as politicized and its bureaucracy bloated. America had reacted to this situation by withholding its peacekeeping dues throughout the 1980s. In the post-Cold War period, UN failures in situations such as Rwanda and Bosnia, when NATO commanders had to place requests for the use of force through UN offices in New York, fuelled a sense of American disillusionment. As a result, a UN Security Council Resolution was not regarded as a prerequisite for action.

The 9/11 attacks hardened US attitudes because the country considered itself to be at war. America was no longer willing to support the status quo and actually became a power seeking to overthrow hostile regimes. The White House was determined to exercise the country's military strength regardless of the views of international organizations. Multilateralism became linked in US government discourse with weakness, with externally imposed limits on its power and a process of endless negotiation (Ikenberry, 2004, 8–9). This view was shared amongst the wider American public: in 2009, only 51 per cent of Americans polled believed that their country should cooperate fully with the UN (Pew Survey, 2009).

In contrast, the EU has treated the UN as the only viable instrument of global governance and has wanted the Security Council to be the decision-making framework for international crises. The Union regards the UN Charter as the building block of global order and contends that 'everything the EU has done in the field of security has been linked to UN objectives' (European Council, 2008, 2; 2003b). EU states have contributed soldiers to UN operations and they have continued to pay into the peace-keeping budget when the US held back (Sangiovanni, 2003, 200). Instead of berating the UN for its failures in crises such as Rwanda, European governments have sought to bolster its capacity to act. The EU conducted the mission to the Democratic Republic of Congo in June 2003 at the request of the UN Secretary General and put resources at the disposal of the African Union in the case of Sudan. This differs with the US which has refused to place its forces under UN command and has been wary of any constraints imposed upon its own freedom of action.

In adopting this stance, the EU has enjoyed a good deal of support from commentators as well as from its own public. James Dobbins, a former senior official in the US government, argued that the UN is actually a frequently underrated actor in crisis management. He opined that 'the UN should remain the West's nation builder of first resort ... It is cheaper, more experienced, and, via its greater legitimacy, more generally acceptable in most circumstances' (Dobbins, 2005, 238). The UN alone has the ability to draw upon resources and financial contributions from the whole of the international community. It has at its disposal a range of agencies specialized in the reconstruction of national infrastructures and it can deploy forces at a fraction of the cost of Western countries (Dobbins, 2008, 33). A poll found that 70 per cent of European respondents opposed the use of the armed forces of their own countries without the prior approval of the UN (Espinosa, 2005, 48). This contrasted markedly with the opinions of US citizens: only 46 per cent of them opposed the use of American armed forces in similar circumstances.

In the case of the war against Iraq in 2003, President George W. Bush had to be convinced of the utility of seeking UN approval by his Secretary of State, Colin Powell, and by his ally, Prime Minister Tony Blair. The British leader considered it vital that the US be seen to exhaust all the channels of diplomacy before resorting to force. When President Bush did eventually decide to seek Security Council approval he made it clear that it was a fundamental test of the UN's own resolve to enforce its resolutions on Iraq. 'Will the United Nations serve the purpose of its founding, or will it be irrelevant?' he asked (quoted in Coulon, 2003, 540). President Bush had reluctantly chosen the UN route under pressure from the UK, but made it clear that he would act even if Security Council authorization was not forthcoming (Meyer, 2006a, 249).

After the Iraq War was over, the EU made an effort to draw closer to the US position and heal some of the divisions that had been exposed. Although the European Security Strategy affirmed its commitment to the United Nations, it argued that 'effective multilateralism' needed to be the watchword for future policy. This was an implicit recognition that international institutions could not always guarantee international peace and security. In certain cases, force may be necessary. The ESS accepted the need for a better EU military capability in the event that coercion would be called upon.

President Barack Obama has worked to change the perceptions of US foreign policy from that of the previous administration. He has emphasized the importance of a rule-based international order and reaffirmed the role of international organizations such as NATO and the UN. In an address to the UN, the President declared 'a new era of American engagement with the world, in word and deed' (Obama, 2009a). During his election, Obama made a high profile visit to Europe, and as President he made three trips across the Atlantic within his first year to attend meetings of the EU and NATO. He appears to be sincere in efforts to find new collective ways of resolving security needs. Yet there are limits to the power of even a popular US President as some of the stumbling blocks between the US and EU are due to the actions of Congress rather than the Executive.

There remains, nevertheless, a challenge in the approach of the Obama team that carries over a theme from the George W. Bush era. The challenge is to organizations to demonstrate their value in the face of the new security threats that exist. The US government does not believe in international organizations for their own sake but rather as vehicles for getting things done. Organizations need to prove themselves relevant to the contemporary environment if they are to enjoy the long-term support of the US.

Conclusion

As a result of its power and status within the international system, the US interfaces with Europe in a variety of ways: with NATO members, with the EU and with individual member states. The post-Cold War period has been one in which the US has pursued a new equilibrium with these various expressions of Europe. President Clinton's time in office witnessed the reassertion of NATO, though this was primarily to deal with residual continental security issues. The George W. Bush presidency marked a distinct refocussing of America's attention upon global security challenges, characterized by a turning away from multilateral frameworks. The US worked bilaterally with a few key European countries and made no attempt to persuade the majority of states, either in NATO or the UN, to follow its lead. This resulted in what Kupchan (2005, 248) describes as 'the sense of common purpose and identity, that has served as the foundation for Atlantic unity ... slipping away, risking the gradual return of balance-of-power logic'. Europe can argue justifiably that it was the US that changed during the Bush era, rather than Europe. America disengaged itself from the institutional constraints on its power that had for so long rendered its hegemonic position acceptable. In doing so, the US did much to weaken the transatlantic relationship as well as its own standing in the wider world.

Whilst acknowledging the damage that was done to US–European relations between 2000 to 2008, it has to be noted that an opportunity was afforded to the EU. The diminution of NATO provided a strategic space in which the importance of the EU could be emphasized. The Alliance was no longer the default position for US interaction with Europe. The EU's strengths in diplomacy, aid policy, law enforcement and judicial matters were relevant to dealing with states that threatened the prevailing international order and with transnational terrorism. Yet the EU was unable to capitalize upon this opportunity. Its relationship with the US, as well as with the Alliance, remains underdeveloped.

This underdevelopment in the US–EU relationship reflects some structural weaknesses that have not been rectified. The EU's own weaknesses include a largely intergovernmental approach to foreign and security policy and an unwillingness amongst the member states to allow the Union to represent them. This continues to be exhibited in the limits placed upon majority voting on CFSP and in the stature of the individuals, resulting from the Lisbon Treaty, that have been appointed to lead the Union. It remains to be seen whether the steps taken within the Lisbon Treaty can help the EU to become a more effective foreign policy actor in the future.

Where the US must share some of the blame is in the poor institutional framework that underpins US–EU relations. There is a need for more effective mechanisms for consultation and decision-making between the two sides (Steinberg, 2003, 137). The US is only too aware of the inadequacies of the Union in crisis situations. In American eyes, the EU has been too preoccupied with building institutions and procedures and insufficiently focused on outcomes. There is substance to this but it also misunderstands how the EU works – it is not a state, hence it can only act if it has the procedures to bring its members together. It illustrates once again that the US and the EU are different sorts of actors who neither know nor understand each other well.

Chapter 3

From the European Security and Defence Identity to the Common Security and Defence Policy

Introduction

The demands of the post-Cold War security environment have imposed strains on US–European relations as well as exposed differences in strategic culture and operational doctrine. On the one hand, this has stemmed from the differences in size and capability: the US has devoted around 3.8 per cent of its gross domestic product to defence compared to a European average of around 1.9 per cent (*Economist*, 2006b, 23). This has made it difficult for other countries to work alongside the US. It has made the US reluctant to rely upon the less capable military power of its allies in coalition operations. On the other hand, it has stemmed from the strategic culture that has flowed from American ascendancy. The 'Powell doctrine' (formulated by Colin Powell when he was Chairman of the Joint Chiefs of Staff) stipulated that America must conduct expeditionary operations only with overwhelming force: that it must have a clear objective and enjoy widespread public support: that it must be in a position to impose a solution and then it must extricate itself before it becomes bogged down. This culture has proved problematic in the face of complex, hybrid emergencies into which the US has been drawn. Such conflicts have not been susceptible to resolution by the short-term application of military power.

The US entered the 1990s as a European power with military bases on the continent. Yet it has been focussed increasingly upon global security challenges and the type of military posture required to manage them. Although it intervened in European conflicts in the 1990s, the Pentagon viewed the principal threats as arising from other parts of the world. It devoted considerable effort to force projection capabilities and the creation of smaller and more agile military forces. Washington found that most European states did not share its preoccupation with global operations and were unwilling to expend the necessary resources to overhaul their armed forces. This left Europe, in the eyes of Ivo Daalder (2003, 150), performing a 'supporting role' in US security policy, rather than acting from a position of equality.

These differences in transatlantic capability and strategic outlook occurred at a time when European countries were struggling with the question of whether to build a defence identity within NATO or whether to embody it within the EU. Europe contained a range of strategic cultures and there were differences amongst states about the centrality of NATO and the desirability of a European-based alternative. In the case of the EU, the transition from a 'civilian power' to one with aspirations for a common security and defence policy (CSDP) added an important new dimension. The milieu goals of the EU – including preserving the safety of the Union's neighbourhood and preventing conflict amongst neighbours – arose alongside national goals of territorial security (Kirchner and Sperling, 2007, 221). This raised a fundamental debate about the sort of military actor that the Union might become and how it might relate to other security organizations.

In this chapter I will argue that since 1990 the US has misjudged its response to European efforts to build a defence capacity within the EU. The US has treated such efforts as a direct threat to NATO as well as to American leadership. In fact, the real risk of European efforts has been that they will be insubstantial and lacking in significance. The suspicion and hostility that has been evident from Washington has increased these risks and made it more likely that the EU will not succeed. It has also made it more difficult for American policymakers to appreciate the contributions that the Union can make to security operations both within and outside of Europe.

The ESDI

During the Maastricht negotiations of December 1991, countries such as France, Belgium and Spain were eager to give the EU responsibilities over the use of force. Other states such as the UK, Denmark and Portugal were sceptical about a European defence identity. The 'Atlanticist' states were reluctant to see the tried and tested framework of NATO put at risk for a European political project that was unproven. The compromise that was reached was to use a hitherto moribund, intergovernmental organization – the WEU – as the bridge between both the putative defence role of the EU and the established framework of NATO (Rees, 1998, 51). The Declaration on the WEU that was attached to the Treaty on European Union stated that 'the WEU will be developed as the defence component of the European Union and as the means to strengthen the European pillar of the Atlantic Alliance' (Declaration on WEU, 1992, para. 4).

Those countries eager to construct a European defence entity proceeded to create a 'EuroCorps' of 50,000 troops that was put at the disposal of the WEU. In 1992 they sketched out the 'Petersberg' tasks – namely peacekeeping, humanitarian operations and military crisis management – as the missions that the WEU might undertake (Petersberg Declaration, 1992). But the WEU was always inhibited by the fact that both the UK and the US opposed its development. The UK's membership of the WEU enabled it to veto all developments of which it disapproved, including its deployment in crises such as the Balkans. The WEU was accorded no operational structures, no military command and planning capabilities, and the US insisted that the EuroCorps also be made available to NATO. The US expressed two of its own reservations from the sidelines. One was the worry that the WEU represented a defence structure separate from NATO that would lead to estrangement between the US and its allies. The Clinton administration's Deputy Secretary of State, Strobe Talbott (1999), warned against an ESDI that could emerge out of NATO but eventually grow to compete with the Alliance. The experience of the UN arms embargo in the Adriatic in the early 1990s, policed by both NATO and WEU forces simultaneously, exemplified the danger of duplication. The other worry was that a WEU-led operation could get into difficulty. The risk was that this might necessitate the involvement of US forces to rescue them, thereby dragging Washington into a conflict from which it might prefer to remain aloof.

The offer by President Clinton to build an ESDI within NATO provided a limited way forward for enhancing the operational potential of the WEU. As part of the concept of Combined Joint Task Forces (CJTF), the US offered to make NATO military assets and decision-making structures available for WEU-led operations (North Atlantic Council, 1994). This came to be known as the Berlin Plus arrangement and it appeared to assuage some of the European debate about 'autonomy' from US control. It was possible

to conceive of a mission in which the US would not want to participate but would not oppose action by its allies. In such a scenario, the
WEU would detach the necessary command and control capacities
from the Alliance, under the headship of the Deputy Supreme Allied
Commander (D-SACEUR), as well as any necessary assets (Hunter,
2001, 16). Whilst NATO and the US would not ostensibly be
involved in the operation, they would facilitate the action of the
WEU.

Howorth and Keeler argued (2003, ch. 1), however, that the
Berlin Plus arrangements exposed the limits of American willingness
to relinquish leadership in European security. Whilst appearing to
endorse European ambitions to possess 'separable but not separate'
capabilities, the concept emasculated European pretensions to independence. The US gained a power of veto over whether a European
operation could go ahead, and it preserved its own right of first
refusal to act. It was hard to envisage a military task in which
America would release assets to its allies but stand back from
involvement. It was also hard to see how the sorts of assets that the
Europeans might need could be released to them in a crisis without
prior training and exercises.

The CJTF concept solved a political problem within the
EU–WEU–NATO relationship by giving European states, on paper,
access to enhanced military capabilities that were compatible with
the Alliance. As many European countries were reluctant to increase
their defence spending anyway, it was a face-saving formula. But in
practical terms the arrangement was largely hollow and it was never
put to the test. For countries that took defence seriously, it represented a temporary fix that would need to be revisited in the future.
France was dissatisfied with what they regarded as continuing
European dependence on the US (Menon, 2000, 129). The UK was
satisfied that the primacy of NATO had been safeguarded but was
under no illusions that a workable expression of European defence
aspirations had been achieved. This was not to come until the end of
the 1990s when the UK allowed a defence dimension to be invested
within the EU itself.

Balkan conflicts and transatlantic strategic divergence

The conflicts in Bosnia and later Kosovo proved to be a stringent
test of the capacity of the transatlantic relationship to adapt to the
new post-Cold War environment. At first, those states impatient to

assert a European defence identity regarded the conflict in the former Yugoslavia as an opportunity to prove themselves. Yet it quickly became clear that the fighting could not be ended by European promises of economic assistance and that the EC/EU's 'civilian power' was insufficient. Having raised expectations, the EC/EU was found to be unable to deliver. Resolution of the Bosnian crisis was contingent on US leadership, because within Europe there was neither the means nor the determination to enforce its will. The EC/EU was bounced into the recognition of Bosnia by the German government with the result that the three ethnic groups of Bosnian Serbs, Bosnian Croats and Bosnian Muslims became embroiled in a vicious conflict of ethnic cleansing. The conflict sucked in European military forces, who, under a United Nations Protection Force mandate, sought to distribute humanitarian aid whilst the warring parties conducted their conflict. European armed forces found themselves attempting to act impartially amidst an intrastate war.

The attitude of the US to the independent role played by the Europeans was instructive. The war inflicted major strains upon the relationship as the transatlantic allies pursued contending approaches to the war and disagreed over how to bring the bloodshed to an end. The US was reluctant to become deeply engaged in a conflict in which they had little interest. At the same time, the American government was highly critical of the unwillingness of the Europeans to take sides in the conflict and impose a peace. The US declared the Bosnian Serbs to be the aggressors and secretly began to arm the Croats ready for a counter-offensive. Washington advocated a policy of 'lift and strike' – lifting the UN arms embargo against the Bosnian Muslims and striking the Bosnian Serbs with airpower. When the Vance–Owen Plan was put forward in 1993, the US government castigated it and denied it support (Owen, 1995). Nevertheless, the peace agreement that was eventually imposed on the warring parties by the US, over two years later, closely resembled the Vance–Owen Plan.

It was not until the period 1994–95 that the Clinton administration intervened to resolve the conflict in Bosnia. Washington came to fear that disunity amongst NATO members over the war in the Balkans was damaging the Alliance and with it the fifty years of American investment in its security relationship with Europe. America assembled the 'Contact Group', comprising the US, the UK, France, Germany, Russia and the UN, to put more pressure on the Bosnian Serb leadership. When this proved insufficient, the US took the lead in the NATO bombing campaign, 'Operation Deliberate Force'. This bombing campaign, in conjunction with a Croat offensive stemming from the Krajina region, proved decisive in making the Bosnian Serb leadership in Pale sue for peace. The US imposed the Dayton Peace Accords in 1995 and a NATO Implementation Force (IFOR) was sent to enforce the agreement.

The campaign in Kosovo, in 1999, drew upon the lessons that had been learned in the conflict in Bosnia. NATO, under American leadership, was determined not to procrastinate, as it had done in the case of Bosnia. The majority of Alliance members seemed to believe that force was the only language that President Milosevic of Serbia understood. After the failure of peace talks at Rambouillet in France, a NATO military activation was ordered and a sustained bombing campaign of Serbia and its military and paramilitary forces in Kosovo followed. This was quickly extended to include strategic targets in Serbia itself (*International Affairs*, 2009). The conflict lasted for seventy-seven days and the Alliance found itself under pressure, urgently desiring the Milosevic regime in Belgrade to back down. There was a real fear that the bombing campaign would have to be superseded by a ground invasion. Fortunately, Finnish and Russian diplomacy led Belgrade to announce the withdrawal of its forces from Kosovo and the acceptance of NATO's terms. At face value, the military action appeared to be a triumph because it forced Milosevic to back down and to allow a Kosovo Force (KFOR) into the province to police the agreement. But it had been a near run thing and it had exposed evidence of strategic divergence in the transatlantic relationship (Mandelbaum, 1999).

In addition to tensions between the US and Europe over their geostrategic interests, Kosovo illustrated the widening military gulf between the two sides (Daalder and O'Hanlon, 2001). The Kosovo War was fought by airpower: the Europeans argued for the sending of ground forces into the province but the Clinton administration was not prepared to suffer casualties in a land offensive. The US and Europe disagreed over the choice of targets in the aerial campaign with American planners eager to enlarge the number of targets significantly. The vast majority of air sorties were carried out by American combat aircraft because European countries lacked the technological sophistication to deliver precision-guided munitions and to fly combat missions at night. Russian demands to send forces to Pristina airport led to a sharp disagreement between the American SACEUR, General Wesley Clark, and the British commander on the ground, General Sir Mike Jackson (Jackson, 2007, 257). The conflict in Kosovo demonstrated the reluctance of the Pentagon to be constrained in its application of force by allies that added little to US war-fighting capacity (W. Clark, 2001).

More fundamentally, the conflicts highlighted that the US had little interest in the Balkans. For the Europeans it was of vital concern because of its proximity and because it was linked to a host of additional problems such as refugee movements and the spillover of drugs, crime and people trafficking. European nations provided the bulk of the peacekeeping forces in both the Bosnian Stabilisation Force (SFOR that replaced IFOR) and KFOR. They also took the lead role in reconstructing the war-torn societies, providing the overwhelming share of the financial resources and appointing the political viceroys. The Europeans drew two lessons from the conflict. The first was that their military capabilities were limited even for operations based within their own region, let alone for extra-European roles. The second was that the US could not always be relied upon to share their strategic assessments of conflicts.

In contrast to the long-term commitment of European peacekeepers and resources, it became apparent that the US rejected long-term nation-building efforts. Both the Clinton and the Bush administrations sought to draw down the US military presence and hand it over to European allies. These ideas were floated by Condoleezza Rice, the National Security Adviser, in October 2000, as the Bush administration was preparing to take office (Riddell, 2003). They resulted in a flurry of European concern that a withdrawal could reignite the conflict. Once in the White House, President Bush decided to keep a US presence in the Balkans but at much reduced levels. An uneasy status quo was established between the transatlantic allies. In 2004, the EU took over the peacekeeping role in Bosnia, thereby enabling the last of the US forces to be released for other operations. America was eager to devote its attention to risks elsewhere and wanted its remaining troops in Europe to be treated as forward deployed units for extra-European emergencies.

In pursuit of its global power projection capabilities, America was anxious to invest in technologies that could enable it to fight and win decisively. This strategic thinking derived from the financial investment it had made in the so-called 'Revolution in Military Affairs' (RMA): the application of information technology to warfare. This focussed on creating network-centric capabilities, that integrated information acquisition and distribution systems amongst land, sea and air forces, and married them to precision-guided weapons. The RMA led the US military to seek to skip a generation of equipment. The US was determined to preserve its strategic dominance, and the experience of the 9/11 attacks reinforced its desire to be able to strike at enemies at long distances from its homeland (United States National Security Strategy, 2002).

America encouraged NATO to adopt these technologies into its own inventory by scrapping the former Atlantic Command (SACLANT) and creating a new Allied Command 'Transformation'. This attempt to reconfigure the Alliance for expeditionary warfare was always going to be difficult to achieve because such a small percentage of European forces were capable of undertaking such a task. Only the UK and France had invested in force projection capabilities, due to their historical commitment to a global defence posture. Even a country like the UK had balked at the cost of developing network-centric armed forces and had been satisfied with network-enabled capabilities (Interview, 2006). Countries such as Germany, by contrast, orientated their forces for the defence of national territory by retaining conscription. Nevertheless, the experience of the 1990s led the EU members to agree upon a new framework for expressing their defence ambitions. The result was the ESDP, which moved the focus of the debate about a European defence identity from within NATO to the EU.

The ESDP

The UK and France seized the initiative in developing the concept of an EU security and defence policy at a bilateral meeting at St Malo in 1998. It was designed as an intergovernmental, rather than a truly common, policy. In 1999 the Helsinki European Council adopted the 'Headline Goal' of 60,000 troops to be deployable within sixty days and capable of being sustained for a period of up to one year (European Council, 1999a). To facilitate this, a Political Security Committee (or COPS) was created, supported by a Military Committee (EUMC) composed of representatives of the national Chiefs of Staff and served by a Military Staff (EUMS) in Brussels.

The ESDP was recognition of a need for the EU to be able to exercise military power: that its diplomacy and economic muscle would sometimes need to be underpinned by force. 'Europe may insist that force is used within the framework of law, but they also understand that sometimes force must be used to uphold law. So we want to add some muscle to our civil power' (Solana, 2003, 2). This was not an attempt to compete with US military strength (Moravcsik, 2003, 83) nor an attempt to establish a European army (Salmon and Shepherd, 2003). Rather, it was an initiative to give the Union a capacity to undertake crisis management, towards the lower end of the 1992 Petersberg tasks, and to be able to act globally. The Kosovo War had convinced EU governments of the need to be able to act separately from the US. It had both an external and an internal justification: it was a lever for European powers to express their influence vis-à-vis NATO and an avenue for advancing the goal of European integration.

The response that it provoked from the US was predictably hostile. Something resembling schizophrenia has characterized US attitudes to European defence initiatives historically. Whilst the US has called for greater burden-sharing from its allies, it has reacted to their efforts with a mixture of suspicion and alarm. This was driven partly by scepticism from within the Pentagon, as to whether anything of substance would come out of the ESDP. It was suspected that the policy would be largely 'window dressing', focusing on institutional form rather than practical substance (Interview, 1999). Partly, the US was fearful that its own interests would suffer. There was the risk that greater autonomy by allies would leave Washington's voice less influential. Also, greater European cohesion could become evident in industrial policy, resulting in fewer American arms being exported to the continent.

With a European tendency to splinter over defence matters, American policymakers found it hard to believe that a new era of European solidarity would be forthcoming. The US Ambassador to NATO, Alexander Vershbow (2000, 3), gave voice to this view when he questioned whether force goals would be 'achieved using smoke and mirrors, or through a real commitment of the resources needed'. Such scepticism appeared to be vindicated when the EU, despite declaring the Headline Goal to be operational in May 2003, subsequently disowned the target of a 60,000 strong force. It was abandoned in favour of the more achievable target of creating thirteen (later eighteen) 'battle groups' of 1,500 men each (*Agence Presse*, 2004a, 7). The need to be able to deploy combat capability more flexibly, within a shorter period of time, was the driving force behind this thinking, with the expectation that larger formations would reinforce the initial interventionary force (Lindstrom, 2007). This was a much more modest goal and it was driven principally by political expediency. No clear strategic rationale has been forth-coming about the role envisaged for the battle groups.

There were also fears in Washington that the ESDP could lead to greater European autonomy. Defence efforts conducted through the framework of the EU potentially sidelined the US and detracted from NATO. President Clinton's Secretary of State, Madeleine Albright (1998), warned of the dangers of 'discrimination, duplica-tion and de-coupling'. She cautioned that European members of NATO, not present in the EU, could feel ostracized by the initiative and might obstruct the realization of the Berlin Plus arrangements. This was indeed to be the case, as in 2000 Turkey vetoed EU access to NATO assets unless it was accorded a full role in the decision-making process. Howorth (2007, 140) notes that Turkey's exclu-sion contrasted sharply with the position of four neutral states, Ireland, Austria, Sweden and Finland, that were fully involved in ESDP decisions. Secretary Albright was disturbed by the prospect of a European caucus that served to undermine transatlantic solidarity. The Bush administration echoed many of these same concerns. It treated EU unity as potentially threatening American interests and expected Europeans to act as supporters of US policies rather than as independent actors.

Unease about the primacy of NATO and an unnecessary duplica-tion of its military capabilities were also components of US concerns. In the light of Europe's disappointing contribution to collective defence, the US was worried that the ESDP would replicate what NATO already provided. Speaking at the annual Munich security conference, Secretary of Defense Donald Rumsfeld noted that 'actions that could reduce NATO's effectiveness by confusing dupli-cation ... would not be positive' (quoted in *Economist*, 2001, 28). Contrarily, France argued that some duplication of NATO was necessary if the EU was to be furnished with the capacity to act inde-pendently. Schake agreed, contending that 'constructive duplication' would be desirable if the EU was to possess the ability to act without America. There were certain capabilities that the EU would need to possess, and she identified, amongst others, reconnaissance capaci-ties, strike capabilities and military research as necessary areas for overlap (Schake, 2003, 119). For example, the ability to transport a European force to a conflict zone, in the absence of US involvement, would require strategic lift aircraft as well as air-to-air refuelling. Similarly, the European Galileo project aims to provide a global positioning system that duplicates the existing American system.

The answer to the questions about duplication and autonomy depends upon whose vision of the ESDP is being discussed. From the outset, there were different visions of the ESDP between the UK and the French governments. The British government, consistent with its traditional pragmatism towards European defence, saw the ESDP as subordinate to NATO. Prime Minister Tony Blair envisaged a 'NATO First' policy in which the EU would only be considered as a last resort. The UK consistently opposed collapsing the WEU into the EU but relented at the end of the 1990s when they realized that Europe's ability to act as a military partner of the US was diminishing. The ESDP was treated as a means to galvanize European allies into doing more for the common defence without risking the alienation of the US. Tony Blair went to considerable lengths to reassure the US that Britain was not selling out, but using a new mechanism to leverage more effort from its European allies. The Chief of the Defence Staff, Sir Charles Guthrie, said in 2001 that 'a stronger European military capability will be good for NATO ... Europe needs to deliver or NATO will be irrevocably damaged' (quoted in Evans, 2001, 2).

According to Dominique Moisi (1999, 124–5), 'if any meaning remains to the word "Gaullist" today, it is France's enduring ability and propensity to say no to the United States'. President Jacques Chirac talked openly of the need for a multipolar world and envisaged an autonomous EU military capacity as one of its vital ingredients. France wanted an ESDP that was fully capable of independent action and that could draw upon military capabilities separate from NATO. It resisted attempts by the US to subsume the ESDP within the embrace of the Alliance and pursued a division of labour between the two organizations. Howorth (2003) refers to it as a deliberate policy of 'constructive ambiguity' that enabled both the UK and France to work together on the ESDP while holding opposing views as to its long-term objective. The Nice European Council in December 2000 exposed this clash of visions between Chirac and Blair. This centred on the issue of 'enhanced cooperation' that would allow states more capable of taking military action to forge ahead and operate under a system of qualified majority voting. The issue of enhanced cooperation was settled some time later but only by allowing both ends of the defence spectrum to restate their own interpretations of its meaning (*Agence Presse*, 2003b, 5). In practice it has never been used and unanimity has continued to be the requirement for conducting foreign and security policy.

The issue of a military planning facility and operational head-quarters was the key test of these contending visions. On 29 April 2003, a summit between France, Germany, Belgium and Luxembourg proposed the creation of a planning facility for the ESDP at Teuveren (Meetings of the Heads of State, 2003). This seemed to confirm the worst fears of the US government because the plan envisaged creating an autonomous European command centre that duplicated the role of the Supreme Headquarters Allied Powers Europe (Sangiovanni, 2003, 193). The UK, sceptical of Europe's ability to undertake independent military operations, was instrumental in watering down the proposals. A compromise was secured in which NATO was accorded the right of first refusal to run a military operation, followed by a European 'lead nation' providing a national headquarters. Only an operations centre was added to the EU Military Staff in January 2007, thereby rendering the EU an independent actor of last resort. The cell would only be strengthened and transformed into a full-scale planning centre if all the alternatives had been rejected, and even then it would only exist on an ad hoc basis until the specific task had been completed. Counterbalancing the establishment of the planning cell, an important EU–NATO liaison was authorized to enable military staff from each organization to be embedded in the other (*Agence Presse*, 2003a, 5).

American hostility and suspicion was mistaken: it treated the ESDP as a threat rather than an opportunity (Moens, 2003). American opposition gradually waned as it became apparent that Europe's capacity to act autonomously was modest and there remained a considerable degree of dependence on US support. This was acknowledged by the US Ambassador to NATO, Victoria Nuland (2008a, 3), when she said that 'an ESDP with only soft power is not enough'. Implicit in this statement was an assumption that the ESDP had not yet delivered significant hard power capabilities. The Ambassador accepted the need for Europeans to be able to act independently from the US but betrayed Washington's view that this capacity had not yet been realized. It remains true that a decade after the launch of the ESDP concept, only small-scale military operations can be undertaken in relatively benign environments. The conduct of high intensity military operations at any distance from Europe still depends upon the involvement of the US. The reality of the situation was one of the factors that led France to decide to rejoin the NATO integrated military structure in 2009. The Sarkozy government argues that the EU and NATO should be seen as complementary in their defence efforts and that the Union may operate in areas such as Africa, where the Alliance would have no interest.

To answer why European capabilities remain modest comes down to two points. First, the motivation amongst some European countries has focused more on identity and institution building than on building capabilities. This has reflected an absence of political will amongst certain governments as well as a reluctance to sacrifice national perspectives in order to cement a stronger capacity for collective action. In the absence of a leading European state more powerful than the rest, there is a tendency to disagree in a crisis and the time taken to reach a consensus severely undermines the ability of the Union to act effectively. Although building up expertise in military matters is a gradual process, the EU has found it difficult to accommodate the variety of strategic cultures amongst its member states. This helps to account for why the EU looks for UN authorization before it considers engagement: because this is something around which its members can coalesce. In the case of the Lebanon operation, for example, this was carried out under the authority of the UN rather than the ESDP.

The second point is that there have been structural weaknesses in EU defence spending. One problem is the disparity in overall spending between countries, as only a few countries devote significant resources to defence. In 2003 the European Commission estimated that the EU's military capability was only around 10 per cent of that of the US, illustrating the enormous gap between the two sides (Marsh, 2006, 93). This looks likely to be squeezed further as a result of financial constraints in Europe after the 2008–09 economic downturn. It is unlikely that any European state will see substantial increases in defence spending in the next three years. Another problem lies in the duplication of spending amongst Union members. Over half of spending goes on personnel costs (Neuss, 2009, 118) and each country fields separate land, sea and air forces. Lastly, European countries have tended to finance operations out of their military budgets, rather than voting for additional resources. This has meant that operations detract from the maintenance and modernization programmes for their armed forces (Dobbins, 2008, 35).

There has been no shortage of analysis of the weaknesses of European systems. The EU Capabilities Conference in November 2001 pinpointed the main shortfalls and led to the European Capabilities Action Plan in May 2003. This established a new

Headline Goal for 2010 and sought to align EU targets with those of NATO's Prague Capabilities Commitment of 2002. The principal shortfalls were identified as air-to-air refuelling, nuclear-biological-chemical capabilities, theatre missile defence, strategic airlift, precision-guided munitions, command and control, and unmanned aerial vehicles. These deficiencies are particularly important in relation to projecting military power into distant theatres amidst high intensity conflict. But all these technologies are expensive. For the foreseeable future, even Europe-only military operations would be dependent on the provision of US assistance, such as satellite intelligence systems. This assessment was echoed by Steinberg (2003, 129) who advocated the 'crucial necessity for Europe to develop at least some "high-end" military capabilities to allow European forces to operate effectively with the United States'.

This sharper focus on European defence requirements has been complemented by trends in defence industries. There has been a process of restructuring and merging firms across the continent in order to establish larger corporations capable of competing in an environment that is dominated by the major US manufacturers (Jones, 2007, 137). The European Aeronautic, Defence and Space company – comprising French, German and Spanish firms – British Aerospace (BAE) and Thales (French) have emerged as transnational champions in Europe in the face of American global giants such as Boeing and Lockheed Martin. France and Germany have argued for Europe-wide firms, whilst BAE Systems alone has been successful in penetrating the US domestic arms market. In 1998, France, Germany, Italy and the UK decided to orchestrate their procurement policies through the Organisation Conjointe de Coopération en Matière d'Armement. In July 2004 this was overtaken by the European Defence Agency that was created with a mandate to promote cooperation in procurement amongst the member states. It was designed to help rectify some of the shortfalls in European capabilities (Cornish and Edwards, 2005, 805), although some European countries saw it as a mechanism to oppose US domination of the international arms market.

But rationalization of the European defence industrial base has not resolved some of the fundamental tensions. First, a European defence marketplace is still a long way away (defence goods have been exempted from European single market rules). EU countries have preferred to spend their budgets on national industrial champions rather than European consortia, especially when 'buying

European' has risked compromising operational requirements (Menon, 200, 141). France, for example, chose to build its own air superiority fighter, Rafale, rather than join the Eurofighter consortium. Second, there are a multitude of similar weapons platforms – tanks, armoured personnel carriers, fighter aircraft – being pursued simultaneously by European countries. The production of each item results in high unit costs and therefore small numbers purchased. This usually results in unfavourable comparisons with the cost of purchasing US equipment 'off-the-shelf'. Third, research and development spending is spread thinly, leading to slow development times and delays in bringing equipment into service. US companies are often reluctant to share technology with their European counterparts because they fear them as potential commercial rivals and because European firms are rarely in a position to contribute to American programmes.

In sum, the EU's aggregate defence spending buys limited capabilities and little force projection capacity. The broad range of potential tasks in a contemporary conflict and the reluctance of individual EU countries to specialize in certain capabilities means that a little bit of everything is procured. Because the Europeans have not regarded global security issues as relevant to them they have not acquired the appropriate military capabilities to undertake them. For example, the A400M aircraft, many years behind schedule, has been subject to the vagaries of national purchasing decisions even though it is destined to provide the backbone of Europe's long-range transport capacity. Much will depend in the future on the willingness of EU countries to spend their resources more strategically and alter their procurement policies in order to obtain more for their money (Witney, 2008, 37).

Operations under the ESDP/CSDP

Since the creation of the ESDP, there have been over twenty military and civilian crisis management operations, varying from interventions in developing crises to interventions after conflicts have subsided. What all these interventions have shared in common is that they have been relatively small in scale: only the Bosnia operation has amounted to a large deployment of 7,000 personnel. Because of the diversity of views amongst European nations it has been unlikely that the EU would seek to carry out a high risk, intensive operation. Brimmer (2007, 31) argues that 'NATO is for hard security in relatively hostile environments, EU forces are for stabilisation operations in more permissive settings'. It has been the US assumption that EU members would lack the necessary confidence as well as the requisite military capabilities to conduct large-scale military operations autonomously. A more condescending US assessment was forthcoming from Robert Kagan in 2003. He contended that European weakness had consigned them to 'washing the dishes' after the US had employed military power decisively in a conflict situation (Kagan, 2003, 23). Critics have alleged that the Union has been more concerned with operations serving the cause of European integration than their practical value.

In the cases of Operation Concordia in Macedonia and Operation Althea in Bosnia, the EU took over as the executor of a peacekeeping mandate. It was envisaged originally that crises would lead to choices being made between the deployment of either the EU or NATO; but these operations saw the EU following on from a NATO force. In these situations, the Union borrowed assets under the Berlin Plus arrangements. This reinforced the linkage between the EU and NATO and reassured the US that the EU was acting in a subordinate role to that of the Alliance. The Union carried out these tasks on the understanding that if there was a deterioration in the situation and a resumption of conflict then NATO forces would return and assist. This was a recognition that the EU needed to have contingency plans for worst case scenarios (Menon, 2004, 636).

The EU has undertaken independent operations at long range overseas, notably in Africa. These tasks have focused upon a limited objective and have been conducted under the aegis of a European 'framework nation', performing the planning and coordination functions. In the case of Operation Artemis, in the Democratic Republic of Congo (DRC) in June 2003, France assumed the role of framework nation. The mission resulted from a request by the UN for the Union to facilitate the return of refugees displaced by the civil war. The operation drew criticism from the US for the perceived symbolism of the EU conducting a mission thousands of miles from Europe (Giegerich, 2006, 62). A follow-on mission in the DRC was later authorized to supervise the holding of elections.

Another operation in Africa, between 2005 and 2007, involved the EU sending equipment and funding to support the African Union mission in Darfur, but it held back from actual intervention. A small force, under French leadership, was situated in the neighbouring state of Chad to protect refugees. There was considerable debate about the possibility of the EU intervening to provide peacekeepers in Sudan and, according to Menon (2009, 15), this could have been an ideal opportunity to undertake a task that would have served the humanitarian and ethical goals of the Union. There was unease amongst some EU countries that they could be sucked into a quagmire in Sudan from which it would be difficult to extricate themselves. There were also suspicions that countries such as France could be using the EU as a cover for national ambitions that drew upon colonial links with Africa.

Yet focusing narrowly upon the size and geographical spread of EU operations underestimates their significance. The Union has engaged in a diverse range of complex peace support operations that have necessitated the use of many different policy instruments, especially police units to combat crime (Giegerich and Wallace, 2004, 164). For example, the EU mission in Bosnia–Herzegovina began with a police mission (European Union Police Mission) and the Proxima mission in Macedonia involved police officers assisting the government there against organized criminals and drug traffickers (Jones, 2007, 203). This was followed by a border assistance mission to the Palestinian territories in 2005 and a policing support mission in 2006. The Themis mission to Georgia was focused on judicial reform and the overhaul of the country's prisons, whilst the EUJUST Lex mission in Iraq was aimed at the training of judges and officers in the prison service (Hanggi and Tanner, 2005, 36). In 2008, a rule of law mission was authorized to Kosovo, the largest civilian crisis management mission so far. According to Hagman (2002), 'the EU's comparative advantage lies not in high-intensity warfare, but in conflict prevention through the coordinated use of diplomatic and economic measures, and crisis management with civilian and military means'.

From the time of the Feira European Council (European Council, 2000) EU governments appreciated that complex interventions designed to prevent the breakout of large-scale conflict require a hybrid range of capabilities (*Agence Presse*, 2007b). This was a logical progression of the civilian power model, using reconstruction, aid, technical assistance, judicial and administrative instruments for a number of different purposes. These included incentivizing communities to eschew violence; policing ceasefires and keeping warring factions apart; rebuilding war-torn areas; and promoting a range of governance mechanisms – rather than just winning a military victory. As well as military security, post-conflict reconstruction necessitates the resumption of a range of public services. Several non-military agencies had been identified to enhance capabilities in crisis management. For example, 'rule of law' operations have been provided with a pool of police officers from the European Gendarmerie Force based in Vicenza, deployable within thirty days. In addition, lawyers, judges and administrators have been designated as available for service overseas. A Committee for Civilian Aspects of Crisis Management was created in 2000 and capability conferences convened to provide the necessary range of resources (Howorth, 2007, 125, 129).

This is not to suggest that complex operations only require non-lethal security capabilities. Post-conflict territories can be deeply unpredictable and usually require military forces to impose and monitor a peace before reconstruction projects can take place. A peacekeeping mission can rapidly deteriorate and hard power military means may need to be brought to bear. Nonetheless, the EU has been in the forefront of thinking about the spectrum of tasks that may be important: 'from the first glimmerings of a problem through the use of force and the "phase IV" post-conflict operations, including nation-building' (Hunter, 2005, 60). It has excelled in such circumstances because it has actively sought to prioritize them. In doing so, the EU has appreciated that a range of agencies, competences and skills need to be integrated together in complex operations. Based upon experiences in Bosnia, Kosovo, Afghanistan and the DRC, the Union has expertise in administering aid, in overseeing elections, in policing and administering societies, and in coordinating non-governmental organizations. It has been able to draw upon the experiences from amongst its member states to furnish these capacities.

The Union's efforts in phase IV capabilities are not above reproach. Critics have pointed to the fact that the EU has failed to reach its targets under the Civilian Headline Goals and it has struggled to find the personnel with the requisite expertise to execute its missions. Korski and Gowan (2009, 24) go as far as to accuse the EU of conducting missions that have been 'strategically irrelevant' and contend that only countries like Denmark, Germany, the Netherlands, Sweden and the UK have taken the requirements of these operations seriously. They argue that the EU has been wedded to a model of intervention that was based on experiences in Bosnia in 2003 and has not adapted to the more demanding types of tasks represented by missions in Somalia and Afghanistan.

The US has come to recognize the value of EU civilian crisis management capacities in which it has not itself invested hitherto. Post-Cold War experiences of conflicts have demonstrated the value and relevance of the skills that the EU has amassed. The Bush administration came into office with a dismissive attitude towards peace-building. Condoleezza Rice made the infamous remark that 'we don't need to have the 82nd Airborne escorting kids to kindergarten' (quoted in Ashdown, 2007, 13). This derived from the Powell Doctrine that envisaged rapid and overwhelming US interventions followed by timely withdrawal. But since that time, US ambitions increased and the administration of George W. Bush attempted to topple dictators and bring democracy to parts of the Middle East. This involved prolonged interventions in which countries had to be rebuilt after a conflict, operations which exposed America's inexperience in post-conflict occupation and stabilization. The new forms of interventions have necessitated the US becoming engaged in long-term and costly commitments. In the cases of Iraq and Afghanistan, relatively straightforward military victories were followed by prolonged and bloody insurgencies. Referring to American policy, Daniel Hamilton (2003, 547) noted that 'the imbalance between our robust ability to wage war and win war and our feeble facility to secure the peace afterwards threatens to undermine our security goals'.

The US has realized that only by rebuilding post-conflict societies can it avoid them slipping back into instability and violence (Rice, 2008). It has turned to the EU for assistance and for a sharing of the burden because NATO has no pre-existing capacity in this field. The NATO New Strategic Concept acknowledges that the organization is not necessarily the appropriate actor for global operations (NATO, 2010, 9). Having access to EU civilian capabilities offers significant 'added value' to Washington – the US Ambassador to NATO went so far as to suggest that a new EU headquarters could be designated to plan such operations (*Economist*, 2008b, 33). The Americans have been building their own capacity, including a dedicated section entitled the Office of the Coordinator for Reconstruction and Stabilization within the US Department of State (Interview, 2008c). Dobbins (2005, 40) argued that this area of policy might provide a foundation for building closer collaboration between the US and the EU: 'where better for a US–EU security dialogue to start than on issues like security sector reform, police training, the deployment of gendarmerie, the building of civil society?'. This is an important rebalancing of the 'Kaganesque' criticism that the EU has become unable to contribute to conflict situations.

Moravcsik (2003, 75) argued for a new transatlantic bargain, based on an American recognition of the value of the Union's efforts. He argued for a division of effort between the US and Europeans: the former to focus on war-fighting whilst the latter concentrates on conflict prevention and on post-conflict reconstruction. This is based on the rationale that Europe should make the most of its comparative advantage and exploit its complementary role alongside America. It was apparent from conflicts such as Iraq that the US has little need of European assistance in conducting high intensity conflict but it does need assistance when it comes to prolonged post-conflict reconstruction and policing. Moravcsik's argument is a version of a long-standing debate about role specialization within the transatlantic security relationship. On one level it is attractive because it makes a virtue out of an apparent necessity (Nicolaidis, 2005, 93).

Yet such a division of labour carries with it major risks. It assumes that in future scenarios the US will be content both to conduct the war-fighting and suffer the majority of the casualties. It presumes that European governments will trust the Americans to lead in all situations and that their interests will always be coterminous. Lastly, it presupposes that Europe will be prepared to pick up the bill for long-term reconstruction efforts. Such assumptions are highly suspect. In the cases of Bosnia and Kosovo, transatlantic strategic assessments diverged and led to considerable friction. In the case of Iraq, there was a fundamental breakdown in trust between countries such as France, Germany and the US. Consequently, US Ambassador Alexander Vershbow (2001, 4) contended it would be unwise for a division of labour to emerge 'where Europeans were equipped for light peacekeeping missions, with the US left holding the bag on high intensity warfare'. What is needed is a more cooperative relationship that involves both sides sharing the tasks. Only in this way will the US and the EU find the common ground on which to act together and resolve the long-term challenges of each situation.

The Obama administration has approached the ESDP/CSDP more positively than its two predecessors and it has helped to soothe some of the tensions with its European allies. A senior official affirmed that 'it is the policy of this administration to support a strengthened European defense capacity' (Gordon, 2009, 5). Obama acted quickly to consign transatlantic tensions over Iraq to the past and acknowledged the need for the help of European allies in future interventions. However, the outlook remains uncertain. Obama inherited the war in Afghanistan and has made a successful outcome there a central plank in his presidency. This means continued frictions with European allies about their contributions to a major military operation – albeit under the aegis of NATO – and to a national reconstruction effort (*Economist*, 2009a, 71).

Conclusion

The ESDP/CSDP has moved the EU away from its unique civilian power status and generated a modest coercive instrument. Its development of hard power capabilities and its conduct of a range of operations have led some to question the 'militarisation' of its security policy (Barbe and Kienzle, 2007, 519). The EU has undertaken a variety of complex tasks. The purposes for which they have been used – humanitarian and crisis management operations – has enabled the Union to argue that it has remained true to its values. Despite acquiring military instruments, the EU has attempted to preserve its status as an ethical actor. Its critics would argue that its operations have been determined more by the lowest common denominator it can agree upon than by what is right.

The significance of the Union's defence efforts can be interpreted in different ways. Despite different visions about the nature of the ESDP, the policy has made significant strides within a relatively short space of time. This is important within a post-Cold War strategic context in which the US has proved itself reluctant to deploy forces in Europe's neighbourhood. In the cases of Bosnia and Kosovo, the US avoided ground force interventions and, once stabilizing forces had been judged to have achieved their objectives, was eager to withdraw. The EU has gradually assumed more responsibility for the security of the continent, providing peacekeepers to oversee political agreements and funding the bulk of the reconstruction efforts. It has also created a military capacity that can act in various parts of the world and has undertaken its first operations. It has sent military and policing missions to the DRC, supported the African Union in relation to Sudan and most recently conducted anti-piracy duties, as part of Operation Atalanta (2008), around the Horn of Africa. Through the ESS it has moved to formulate common views amongst its members about the use of force and it has put its military resources at the disposal of the UN.

The US feared that European defence efforts were putting the transatlantic relationship at risk, whilst adding little in terms of additional capability. Under both the Clinton and George W. Bush administrations, an alarmist attitude was adopted towards the issue. This hostility and suspicion stemmed from a lack of clarity about what the US wanted from its European allies. There has been a tendency to see the EU as a complicator of US strategy rather than an ally with its own unique set of views. France was open about the fact that it saw the ESDP as a way of developing the EU into a global actor and contributing to the formation of a multipolar world that would detract from US hegemony (Giegerich, 2006, 116). But this was far from a danger to America and it was not a view widely shared amongst EU members. Meanwhile, the Bush administration demonstrated its disdain for the importance of Europe and inflicted its own damage upon the transatlantic relationship.

In reality, the EU has been unable to develop significant new military capabilities and it has not drawn closer, let alone rivalled, those of the US. Analysts who expressed these concerns – over damaging US–EU tensions related to questions of autonomy (Menon, 2003) – have not seen their fears realized. European defence efforts have not grown to the point where the US can feel itself being squeezed out of Europe. In the words of Robert Cooper, 'if Europe wants to influence the US they must bring something to the table – and that means military capability' (Cooper, 2003, 167; Lundestad, 2003, 288). They need to be able to offer functions that complement the roles of American forces.

In the new strategic environment the US must judge the ESDP/CSDP by the contribution it makes to European security and to global concerns. It needs to welcome all efforts to contribute to the Western security burden, because there are such an extensive range of tasks to fulfil (Interview, 2008b). The EU's capacity to contribute to hybrid politico-military emergencies should be embraced wholeheartedly in Washington, and at the same time the US should reassure its allies that they will not be treated as the civilian arm of NATO.

Chapter 4

The Enlargement of the European Union

Introduction

Organizational enlargement should be seen as an issue at the heart of the security debate in US–EU security relations since the end of the Cold War. It has represented an attempt to overcome the military security divide in Europe and return the continent to normal, rather than 'securitized', politics. It has therefore raised a question mark about the 'overlay' of superpower interests and the future role of the US in European security. Mindful that decisions taken by the EU would impact on its interests, American policymakers were concerned at the risk of being excluded from decisions about an enlarging Europe. The influence that the US could wield derived also from the decisive role that it could play in the enlargement of NATO.

The process of enlargement has focused attention on the special 'civilian power' contribution that the EU can make within international relations. Rather than confronting central and east European countries (CEECs) or attempting to coerce them, the Union has sought to absorb them. It has drawn them into a cooperative relationship through its power of attraction and offered them the prospect of accession. It has required new members to emulate its policies and values and has provided them with incentives and assistance to achieve these targets. Once it has deemed the aspirants to be ready, the Union has granted them membership.

In this chapter I will argue that EU enlargement has been one of the success stories of the transatlantic security relationship. Although it has received comparatively little attention, the EU and the US have cooperated together to overcome the historical division of the continent. American policymakers have expressed concerns about the impact of EU enlargement on NATO but they have nevertheless embraced and encouraged the Union in its mission of building a Europe whole and free and centred around values shared by both sides.

Differing transatlantic conceptions of enlargement

There was much about the issue of enlargement that united the US and the EU. Both shared a common vision for the continent that included increasing the number of democratic governments and market economies. The Clinton administration put 'democratic enlargement' as one of the centrepieces of its policy agenda. In Brussels, as in Washington, there was a shared belief not only that democracy was the best form of government but that it reduced the likelihood of future conflicts and would promote reconciliation amongst former adversaries. There was an appreciation that physical security would need to be complemented by economic security and a sense of common identity. National Security Adviser Anthony Lake described US policy as 'strengthen[ing] the community of market democracies' and 'foster[ing] and consolidating new democracies and market economies' (quoted in Ikenberry, 2001, 235). Both the US and the EU regarded the process of enlargement as a way to guide central and eastern European countries in a desirable direction. It would help them to conform to a variety of prescribed targets including free economic interaction; peaceful relations between neighbours; democratic control over the armed forces; adherence to human rights; and respect for minority rights. These were objectives that reflected some of the core values of the West.

But enlargement has also meant different things to the EU and the US, reflecting their divergent natures. The enlargement process has been an example of the Union's mission to civilize its continent by exporting peace, its own identity and values to other states. Through membership, the EU has sought to extend its influence and economic opportunities but it has also offered accession states the opportunity to enter into a security community by which military insecurity can be transcended. The Union has recognized that former adversaries have wanted to 'return to Europe' and to the mainstream of political and economic life from which they were detached by the former Soviet Union (Ridder *et al.*, 2008). Enlargement has sought to alter the nature of the interaction between the states involved, moving from the realm of external to that of internal relations. By drawing states into a system of multilevel governance, the EU has 'domesticated' dealings between the actors.

The EU enlargement process was made more complex by the fact that it was simultaneously enlarging both its functions and its membership (Croft *et al.*, 1999). The Union was contending with internal questions about the range of its competences and was taking on responsibility for a large number of additional dossiers, such as Justice and Home Affairs. These policy areas have evolved dynamically and this has ensured that the size of the Union's body of legislation, its *acquis communautaire*, has grown rapidly. It has stimulated an important discussion about the relationship between enlargement of membership and the process of closer political and economic integration: the so-called 'widening versus deepening' debate. Some members were concerned that a larger Union would require closer integration if it was to avoid paralysis in decision-making. At critical times in the enlargement process the EU was to be found balancing the issue of expansion against considerations of closer integration.

The US attitude towards enlargement has been more detached. This has been understandable because the US has not been seeking to absorb countries into a close relationship in the same way as the Union. There are two main interpretations of US policy towards enlargement: a sympathetic and a manipulative one. The sympathetic interpretation sees the enlargement process as a continuation of America's post-war policy of institution building in Europe. The US extended its defence guarantees to new NATO members and limited its own hegemonic power by acting through Alliance channels. America regarded the EU as providing a normative and economic home for CEECs and it provided the leadership within NATO to ensure that these countries were given the necessary defence guarantees. America treated NATO as the necessary backcloth against which the enlargement of the EU was facilitated (Toje, 2008).

This sympathetic reading of America's stance towards enlargement contrasts with the manipulative interpretation. The latter view contends that the US pushed for the enlargement of NATO at the same time as the EU process in order to balance the influence of the latter. According to this view, expansion of the Alliance became a vehicle for preserving America's hegemonic status within Europe. Drawing countries into the Alliance reinforced US leadership and gathered around it states that saw themselves as indebted to Washington. Ensuring NATO enlargement came first can be understood as a US strategy to ensure its own position and undermine that of the more cautious enlargement of the EU.

A source of complication in the early 1990s was the overlap between NATO and the EU. This was embodied in the WEU, which sat equidistant between the EU and NATO. Without an integrated military structure and with only minimal military obligations, the WEU was an attractive organization to aspirant states because it contained binding defence guarantees and was organically linked to both the Union and the Alliance. In fact, its Article V defence guarantee was operationalized by NATO (Rees, 1998, 99). The WEU developed a category of 'Associate Partnership' for ten of the CEECs and a 'Forum for Consultation' by which states could involve themselves in a security dialogue with west European countries. Some aspirant states regarded the WEU as a stepping stone to NATO membership and the US was fearful lest NATO guarantees were extended to aspirant states by a backdoor arrangement. This unease was heightened by the fact that the WEU had included the three Baltic states as partners; something which became one of the most prickly issues between the West and Russia.

Part of the complexity of enlarging the EU derived from the competing perspectives and bargaining processes amongst its leading members. Germany was a particularly influential state. Its own division had placed it on NATO's frontline during the Cold War and it felt a historical guilt towards many of the countries to its east, especially Poland. It was acutely sensitive to tensions within its neighbourhood and it looked upon EU enlargement as a means of exporting stability. Germany's 'Ostpolitik' with its eastern neighbours since the 1970s had enabled it to build close relations with the CEECs. It emerged in the early 1990s with a 'vision' for enlargement led by politicians such as the Defence Minister Volker Rühe (Hyde-Price, 2000, 149–53). Germany was a passionate advocate of enlargement although it did not regard this as an alternative to closer European integration. It desired a united and borderless Europe and was prepared to provide a substantial proportion of the resources to pay for this process.

The UK shared Germany's support for EU enlargement, arguing that the post-war division of the continent had to be overcome. Yet the UK saw in enlargement a mechanism to restrain the momentum of European integration. It was apparent that new countries entering the EU with vastly different backgrounds would make decision-making more complex. They would bring with them a range of new perspectives and might, once they were members, seek to opt out from parts of the Union *acquis*. CEECs could also be expected to join with the UK in being lukewarm towards political union. Having just thrown off the yoke of communist oppression they were likely to be sceptical about relinquishing sovereignty.

France was the most cautious about enlargement amongst the big three states. It advocated reforms of the EU prior to expansion, in order to guarantee that it would work efficiently with a larger membership. Whilst it was willing to champion the cause of particular countries, such as Romania, France was suspicious of Anglo-Saxon motivations towards enlargement. This extended beyond the EU to NATO as well. France argued that NATO should concentrate on its core task of the collective defence of the continent; it did not want to see the Alliance reinvigorated by taking on new members and new tasks. Paris expressed misgivings that expansion could have the effect of weakening the Union and making it an unwieldy actor. Whether this was a fair analysis is open to question. In the words of Forsberg and Herd (2006, 70), 'the key obstacles associated with EU decision-making are not generated by the small EU member states but by the inability of the larger states to elaborate and agree upon a common position'.

There were fears from the French government that the CEECs could become 'Trojan horses' for the US within the EU. This was illustrated during the lead up to the war against Iraq in January 2003 when an open letter from a group of countries, including CEECs on the threshold of joining the EU, came out in support of the American position (*Financial Times*, 2003). Just a month later the 'Vilnius Ten' – comprising Albania, Bulgaria, Croatia, the Baltic states, Macedonia, Slovakia, Slovenia and Romania – declared their support for US policy towards Iraq. This was a slap in the face to France and Germany because it diverged from their anti-American stance. This behaviour drew a sharp rebuke from President Chirac who accused them of missing a good opportunity to keep silent – just the sort of arrogant attitude that had led the CEECs to side with the US.

Countries such as Poland and the Czech Republic demonstrated their continued support for the US by sending proportionately large number of troops to assist the US-led mission in Afghanistan. They also endorsed American policy on deploying missile defences in Europe as they were eager to see a hard-line adopted against Russia. Romania and Bulgaria signed ten-year agreements with the US in 2005 and 2006, respectively, to host US forces on their soil. Most of these forces would come from troop redeployments from Germany once US forces were drawn down in Iraq. This appeared to confirm the jibe made by US Defense Secretary Donald Rumsfeld that 'new' as opposed to 'old Europe' supported the orientation in American policy. The process of enlargement seemed to be pushing the centre of gravity in Europe to the east where there was no shortage of states that disagreed with Franco-German priorities and were sympathetic to US global security concerns (Treverton, 2006, 45).

On a superficial level, this thesis of east European countries being inherently Atlanticist in orientation looks plausible. Many of these countries that emerged from Soviet domination regarded America as the saviour of the West and a beacon of democratic values. The Baltic states, for example, saw American defence guarantees, operationalized through the Alliance, as the only way of offsetting Russian preponderance (Smith and Timmins, 2000, 61). The US would be vital for these countries, not only in its political commitment to their security, but also in supplying them with the weapons and technology to overhaul their outdated armed forces. In the words of Ekengren and Engelbrekt (2006, 8), 'an obvious sign that most CEE governments are more concerned about classic military, territorially based, threats is the unambiguous preference for NATO as a security instrument on European soil'.

Yet the CEECs have recognized that they must perform a balancing act between America and the EU. They have considered the EU as the source of their long-term economic prosperity and have not wanted to put this at risk. Governments in central Europe were under no illusions that the US could replace the Union as their principal economic relationship. The CEECs have also found themselves sympathetic to EU positions, such as on climate change, where European and US policy prescriptions have diverged (Nye, 2006, 31–2). Their only concern, in relation to the EU, was that they could be forced to choose between well-proven defence guarantees operationalized through NATO in favour of alternative defence arrangements through the uncertain ESDP framework.

CEECs have also been sufficiently realistic to accept that US interest in the security of Europe is waning. They have appreciated that Washington may enter into deals with Russia that neglects their interests and that too much dependence on the US is risky (*Economist*, 2009g, 47). An illustration of this was the Obama administration's call for a 're-setting' of its relations with Moscow. It appeared to many of the CEECs that George W. Bush's tough approach towards Russia was being replaced by an attempt to draw close to the Kremlin. This thinking was reflected in levels of approval expressed towards the Obama administration in 2009. Whilst Obama received an 86 per cent approval rate amongst west Europeans, he received only 60 per cent approval in central and eastern Europe (Transatlantic Trends, 2009).

EU enlargement to central and eastern Europe

It was originally foreseen that EU and NATO enlargement processes would be coordinated and mutually complementary. This was based on the assumption that the EU and the Alliance were composed of many of the same states and that their pro-Western interests were compatible and supportive. There would be an agreed strategy for the two organizations and their accession processes would proceed in tandem. There was much to commend this presumption, as similar issues faced both organizations and the priorities laid down by one would affect the other. There were common criteria that qualified countries for membership: namely the 1993 European Council Copenhagen criteria of democratic government, market economies, the rule of law and democratic control over armed forces.

The Clinton administration encouraged the EU to take the lead in relations with the east. The US advocated economic assistance to the CEECs in the hope of underpinning the market reforms that were taking place. Washington recognized the value of locking in post-communist countries, preferably by early accession into the EU. There was a fear that governments in the east could quickly become disillusioned if left in a political and economic vacuum after the implosion of the Soviet-run system. There was a tendency on the part of America to treat the Union as a subordinate organization to the Alliance and see the prospect of EU accession as a possible 'compensation' for failure to join NATO (Wallace, 1997).

However, in spite of these similarities, the enlargement policies of NATO and the EU were pursued largely independently. Their enlargement processes were conducted in parallel, but there was a lack of coordination between them. According to Sperling (1999, 13), the 'progressive disengagement of the (NATO and EU) enlargement processes reflected an unwillingness to leave NATO enlargement hostage to the enlargement of the EU'. EU enlargement thus took place within a context structured by NATO yet in the absence of a detailed master plan. In an important sense NATO enlargement provided the foundation on which EU enlargement could occur. The Alliance was the source of defence guarantees and assurances against Russia that enabled the CEECs to proceed to integrate economically with western Europe.

Prior to 1994, there was a great deal of uncertainty surrounding the issue of NATO enlargement due to doubts about the role of the US in Europe. The announcement of the Partnership for Peace policy at the NATO Brussels summit in 1994 marked a turning point in which the US seized the initiative in what became a 'NATO First' enlargement policy (North Atlantic Council, 1994). President Clinton and National Security Adviser, Anthony Lake, saw in enlargement a vehicle for reasserting an American leadership role on the continent (Goldgeier, 1999, 20). The US has always enjoyed a unique ability to shape the agenda within NATO; there is no state in a comparable position within the EU. The US set about driving forward the policy of admitting new members as a means for assuring the future of the organization. At the NATO Madrid Summit in 1997, the offer of membership was extended to Poland, Hungary and the Czech Republic, and these countries duly entered the Alliance at the Washington Summit in 1999.

Whereas the NATO enlargement criteria were largely political in nature, prospective members of the EU had to bring themselves into conformity with a huge body of legislation and regulation that comprised the *acquis communautaire*. Whilst there was a lack of clarity in some aspects of the *acquis*, aspirant states were left in no doubt that membership would require them to make deep-seated political and economic change (Grabbe, 2006, 33). Through the Agenda 2000 document, aspirants were acquainted with the reforms that they needed to undertake and the wide range of portfolios with which they would be expected to comply (European Commission, 1997).

It was decided that all states would begin from a common starting point and that there would be no preselection of an elite group of countries that could accede in a first wave. This would prevent accusations of a new policy of exclusion. The EU provided advice on the necessary legislative framework, technical assistance, as well as the secondment of officials and twinning arrangements. The European Commission closely monitored the progress of each country through an annual scoreboard. This process of making accession conditional upon the implementation of a reform programme was at the heart of EU policy (Grabbe, 2006, 14). The Union imposed its evolving policies on the CEECs and expected them to implement the whole package without any significant input. It was a stark example of the Union's belief in the universality of its own model.

The reforms demanded by the EU were deep and far reaching and caused considerable dislocation for the states involved. The Union wanted to ensure that the political and economic structures of new members were compatible with those of existing members and would not prove to be a major drain on its finances. The principal security concern of the west Europeans was over the potential influx of organized crime groups from the CEECs and measures were agreed in May 1998 to create a Pre-Accession Pact on Organised Crime (Council of Ministers, 1998). This involved cooperation with the European Police Office (Europol), the compilation of anti-money laundering measures and the drafting of legislation against criminal organizations and corrupt practices. As the accession process drew closer, additional worries were expressed about the effectiveness of new states in serving as the common external border of the Union. These aspects led the EU to focus its energies on internal security matters and highlighted a gulf between EU and US security preoccupations.

In order to facilitate accession the Union offered considerable financial assistance. Robert Cooper (2002), a central figure under Javier Solana, described this approach as 'speaking softly and carrying a big carrot'. The EU assisted countries by channelling funds through the PHARE programme (*Pologne et Hongrie assistance à la reconstruction économique*) and followed this with the signing of Europe Agreements that mapped out the political and economic links that would be pursued with the CEECs. The Union was under no illusion that once states were granted entry, its ability to exercise influence over them would wane (Monar, 2003). States could be expected to promise much in order to qualify for accession but the delivery, once the spotlight had been removed, would run out of steam. An illustration of this was the slowing of economic and judicial reform in Romania and Bulgaria after they gained admittance in January 2007 (*Economist*, 2008d, 14).

The burdens placed on existing EU members were considerable. Not only was the homogeneity and decision-making capacity of the 'Fifteen' to be placed under strain but significant financial costs would be incurred. The price of supporting the transition of the CEECs, with their relatively poor levels of economic development, was borne within the EU budget. The member states also faced longer term costs, such as diminution in Common Agricultural Policy (CAP) support and structural funds spending, as resources were spread more thinly. Fears over losses in CAP and structural funds helped to account for resistance towards enlargement on the part of long term budget beneficiaries such as Ireland, Greece and Portugal.

The US government has been critical of EU enlargement policy on the grounds that it has been too slow and has taken too long to project stability to the east. It was not until May 2004 that the EU allowed ten new members to join: Poland, Hungary, the Czech Republic, Slovakia, Slovenia, Latvia, Estonia, Lithuania, Malta and Cyprus. This was five years after NATO had opened its doors, and was followed in 2007 with the accession of Bulgaria and Romania. The US saw it as vital to reassure CEECs that their interests were being taken into account and that they were not being allowed to languish in the vacuum left behind after the collapse of the Soviet Union (Serfaty, 1997). The concern expressed in Washington was that reformers in governments in the east that did not deliver the much heralded 'return to Europe' would be at risk of being replaced by more nationalistic hardliners.

The western Balkans and Turkey

The EU has been in the forefront of reaching out to states in the western Balkans. The area has come to be seen as the next in line as part of the enlargement process, following the accession of CEECs. The US has been pushed into the background but it has played an important part in advancing the agenda of democratic governance and helping with economic assistance. It is also worth remembering that it was US military intervention in both Bosnia and Kosovo that facilitated the Union's enlargement process (Patten and Lamy, 2003, 8). The Balkans proved to be the most conflict-prone region in the Union's neighbourhood during the 1990s and without US intervention it is difficult to imagine that it would now be drawing close to the EU.

The US acknowledges the positive role that the Union has played in building institutions and embedding democratic norms in post-conflict societies. It has valued the way in which the EU has led the reconstruction and reconciliation efforts in Bosnia–Herzegovina and the leadership role it has played in Kosovo. The US has exhibited frustration, nevertheless, with the hesitancy and prevarication of the Union. The EU launched its Stability and Association Process in May 1999 that opened the prospect of membership, but since then the US has felt that the region has been in limbo. America has been desirous of stabilizing the Balkans as quickly as possible due to its endemic problems of low economic development, organized crime and corruption. The EU feels that the US underestimates the complexity and implications of its enlargement process and has argued that the speed of accession is dictated by the Balkan states concerned (European Council, 2003a, 15). Accession has offered a way to end the turbulent history of this region but the EU insists that its own credibility is on the line in ensuring the security and stability of the region (European Council, 2003b).

The fact that the Union has placed stringent preconditions on countries such as Serbia – for example, to surrender indicted war criminals like General Ratko Mladic – before gaining accession, illustrates contrasting priorities with the US. Whilst it has recognized that countries like Croatia, Bosnia–Herzegovina, Macedonia and even Kosovo need to be offered membership if stability is to be assured, the EU has been wary of sacrificing the rigours of its own process (*Agence Presse*, 1999, 3; *Economist*, 2008b, 16). In order for conditionality to have a disciplining effect on accession states, it has been necessary for the Union to suspend the process in the face of non-compliance (European Commission, 2006). It has appreciated that premature enlargement could lead the EU to import problems as well as limit the leverage it can exert over accession states.

Enlargement has proceeded alongside the deepening of the Union's competences and this has raised the stakes and made it all the more important that the EU admit only those states that have adopted the *acquis communautaire*. This has opened the EU to accusations that it has been focusing upon its own interests in the enlargement process. For example, Community Assistance for Reconstruction, Development and Stability funding in the Balkans has gradually switched from spending on promoting democracy to Justice and Home Affairs issues in which the EU has a selfish interest. Similarly, the EU has tied trade and aid agreements to a country's compliance with EU strictures on the readmission of illegal immigrants and counter-terrorism cooperation – positive inducements as well as threats of punishment. Such practices are judged by some to be incompatible with the Union's sense of itself as an ethical power (Smith, 2005, 71). Lavenex (2004) has described the European Union's actions as a form of 'external governance',

imposing its will upon neighbouring countries. The US has been critical that states have been left in the EU's waiting room and have
slipped backwards in their reform processes. Bosnia has been a
particular cause for concern and it was warned by Vice President Joe
Biden in May 2010 that it had lost its way (*Economist*, 2010c, 67).

In relation to Turkey, the US has diverged with the EU over the
prospect of the country's accession. America regards Turkey as a
bridge between the Muslim world and the West, as well as a state
inhabiting a vital geostrategic position in relation to the Middle
East. The US enjoys a close relationship with Turkey, especially
with its military, through NATO, and it has been muted in its criticisms of Ankara's policy towards the Kurdish Workers Party
(PKK). Although Turkey denied Washington access to Iraq during
the military campaign of 2003, Turkish military forces have
demonstrated their utility by serving within Afghanistan and twice
taking command of the International Security Assistance Force.
Washington has bemoaned the way in which Ankara has been kept
waiting by the EU and pointed to the unwelcome side effects that
can result from keeping the country in an indeterminate position.
For example, Ankara made it clear after the launch of the ESDP
that 'acceptance of an automatic EU access to NATO assets and
capabilities is out of the question' (*Agence Presse*, 2000, 3). Turkey
did not relent on its refusal to accept the Berlin Plus arrangements
until 2003, only after it had been lobbied strenuously by
Washington and London (Kidd, 2009). The US has warned the
Union that its procrastination could spark an anti-European backlash in Turkey.

America's attempts to lobby for Turkish accession have been
perceived by the EU as an unwarranted intrusion into its internal
affairs (*Economist*, 2009c, 16). Washington must tread a careful
path between interacting with and trying to influence the EU, as
compared with being seen as meddling in its internal affairs. The
Union has responded that the US fails to understand the complexities of granting membership to Turkey. It is relatively poor, largely
agricultural and would represent a major voting block within the
Union. Turkey also has a bad domestic record on human rights
towards its Kurdish minority and a history of military intervention
in politics. In spite of its early application to the EC, it was not until
1999 that the country was accorded candidate status, by which time
a group of other states had leap-frogged its position. Actual accession negotiations were only started in 2005 and in December of the

following year eight out of the thirty-five EU accession chapters were suspended over Turkey's relations with Cyprus.

There have been considerable divergences amongst EU members towards the question of Turkey's entry. Germany and France have openly opposed its membership and President Sarkozy has insisted on a referendum being conducted in France prior to accession. Berlin and Paris have proposed a special type of partnership for Turkey instead of membership. In contrast, the UK has always championed the country's right to become a member, arguing that it would send a powerful political signal that the EU did not represent a closed Christian club. In July 2010, the new Conservative Prime Minister, David Cameron, visited Turkey and reaffirmed support for its accession. Nevertheless, this equivocal stance by the Union as a whole could undermine Turkey's determination to put the necessary reforms in place to render itself eligible to join (*Economist*, 2009f, 48). US Defense Secretary Robert Gates warned in June 2010 that the EU was at risk of making the historical mistake of 'losing' Turkey (*Economist*, 2010e, 51).

The Mediterranean and the European Neighbourhood Policy

Geographical proximity and historical linkages have enabled the EU to assume a position of leadership in relation to countries in north Africa, the Middle East, eastern Europe and central Asia. The US has been eager to encourage the EU's outreach towards regions where American policy has little contemporary influence. In the past, the southern Mediterranean region was neglected because it was treated as no more than the southern underbelly of NATO, but the US has welcomed the Union's development of ties to north Africa. This area has increased in geopolitical significance due to its role in the War on Terror. Eastern Europe and central Asia were previously regarded as off-limits to Western influence because they were part of the Soviet sphere. The lessening of Russian control over the region since the Cold War has offered opportunities for the penetration of both American and European influence. The US has encouraged EU involvement where its own or NATO intervention would be seen as overly provocative.

As far as the EU's southern neighbours were concerned, they were regarded as the source of a variety of complex problems such as transnational organized crime and drug trafficking. These problems impacted upon the EU because they leaked into the territories of its member states. The response was initially to create a 'fortress Europe' that kept these problems at bay through the maintenance of a hard geopolitical boundary (Smith, 1996). Over time the EU has come to realize that it would have to help to shape its external neighbourhood, rather than withdraw behind the walls of a twenty-first-century fortress. It recognized that it would have to engage more actively with these countries and try to address some of their problems at source.

The first sustained effort by the EU to reach out to the Mediterranean and Middle East regions was through the 1995 Barcelona Process. Security was a key aspect of this project with an emphasis on preventing the spread of nuclear, chemical and biological weapons. This drew enthusiastic support from the US that was worried about the region's volatility leading to a race to acquire WMDs. Libya, Syria and Iraq were major sources of concern. But EU influence tended to diminish in proportion to distance from its territory. The Barcelona Process failed to achieve the impact that had been intended, despite efforts after 2000 to reinvigorate it with additional measures. President Sarkozy of France launched an intergovernmental initiative, the Union for the Mediterranean, in 2007, but this received such lukewarm support from other European states that it was decided to fold it into the Barcelona Process as a way of further developing it.

The European Neighbourhood Policy (ENP) was launched in May 2004 as an instrument for the EU to overhaul and upgrade its relations with countries in north Africa and the Middle East (Cameron and Balfour, 2006, 14). The aim of ENP has been to project stability, prevent conflict and export European values. It has been fuelled by states such as Cyprus and Malta acceding in 2004 and reinforcing an orientation among southern members of the EU towards the Mediterranean. The EU has tried to modify the behaviour of neighbouring countries by offering them a broad range of incentives embodied within a policy based around the concept of joint ownership. These have included trade and cooperation agreements, technical assistance with border control and measures to speed up the supply of visas for entry into Europe (Barbe and Johansson-Nogues, 2008, 86). The EU has provided help with governance and has seconded officials to advise with the drafting of legislation. The Union has tried to address some of the root causes of these difficulties such as poverty, unemployment and very high birth rates. It has also concerted strategy towards its neighbours and tried to develop linkages within regions. In sum, the Commission was eager to share the EU's values with ENP countries and draw them 'into an increasingly close relationship, going beyond cooperation to involve a significant measure of economic and political integration' (European Commission, 2004, 5).

A central feature of the action plans that the EU has negotiated with each ENP country has been internal security cooperation. This has reflected the EU's traditional concerns about north African countries, that they are a major source of security problems that impact on the territories of the member states. The EU has been particularly concerned about illegal migration and drug trafficking and this has been the focus of its efforts through agencies such as Europol and Frontex. ENP states were expected to work with the EU on controlling migration and asylum, and negotiate readmission agreements to return those found to have unsuccessfully claimed asylum (Boswell, 2003). The US was less interested in this issue because it did not impact directly upon its interests. In addition, the threat of terrorism was accorded a high priority. Some of the extremist groups emanated from north Africa and it was feared that individuals could slip into Europe to carry out terrorist attacks. The US shared European concerns in relation to terrorism and added to it the threat from nuclear proliferation in the region.

But ENP countries have been sceptical of the value of these EU initiatives. Many of the eastern European countries regard the influence of the EU, other than through its economic power, as limited. Ukraine, for example, has been unimpressed with what ENP has to offer and has considered itself worthy of a more substantial relationship with the Union (*Agence Presse*, 2007a, 4). The same has been the case for Armenia and Georgia, whilst countries like Belarus have largely ignored the Union. North African states have little in common with each other and have tended to view the EU as pursuing its own vested interests (Khasson *et al.*, 2008). The difficulty for the ENP has been that it was targeted at states with no prospect of accession and this has robbed the EU of its principal means of influence. The ENP has been about avoiding enlargement whilst at the same trying to draw states into a cooperative relationship. In practice, the incentives have been inadequate for the task.

The inclusion in ENP of states in eastern Europe has reflected the EU's growing global stature and its inability to ignore important geopolitical neighbours (Asmus, 2006, 24; Daalder *et al.*, 2006).

The US has been closely interested in EU activities, because of its own desire to obtain new sources of energy from a region with such important oil rich states as Azerbaijan. In the Caucasus the EU sought to assist in some 'frozen conflicts', such as in Nagorno-Karabakh and Moldova, drawing upon its expertise in conflict prevention and crisis management. The Moldovan example has involved the threat from criminal gangs exploiting the trade in illicit goods and has drawn in the Russian military who serve as an intermediary force between the Moldovan state and its Transnistrian (also known as Trans-Dniestr) separatists (Barbe and Kienzle, 2007, 523). The EU has provided considerable financial assistance as well as a border monitoring mission (EUBAM) along the Ukrainian–Moldovan border.

Russia and enlargement

The US was the principal interlocutor with Russia, due to the respective sizes of the two countries and the breadth of their common security interests. This resulted in a 'Yalta' complex amongst European governments, based on a fear that a deal could be done between Washington and Moscow over their heads. The US has wanted cooperation from Russia in relation to extra-European issues: for instance, access to air bases in central Asia as part of its War on Terror, or Russian pressure to be exerted on Iran over nuclear non-proliferation. There will always be global security issues that lead the US to seek cooperative relations with Russia. Europe has feared that its interests in relation to Moscow have been neglected in favour of US national interests.

A counter-balancing fear has existed on the part of the Europeans. This has been over the extent to which their relations with Moscow could be jeopardized by the ups and downs of the US bilateral relationship with Russia. This was evidenced in the fallout from the American abrogation of the 1972 ABM Treaty, the crises over the 2003 War against Iraq and in Moscow's threats to target new nuclear missiles on Europe due to central European participation in US missile defence (Meyer, 2009). Although EU states were on the margins of the decisions that were taken in Washington, they suffered from the worsening in US–Russian relations through no fault of their own. In addition there are interests that the EU shares with Russia, separate from that of the US, that can be put at risk by a downturn in relations. Tensions with Russia also have the capacity to divide EU governments amongst themselves. For instance, countries such as Germany and Italy have become highly dependent on Russian natural gas supplies – in 2004, Russia supplied 43 per cent of Europe's gas and 42 per cent of its oil (Niblett, 2005, 49). These dangers were realized in January 2009 when a dispute between Russia and Ukraine led to the disruption of gas supplies to several European countries. The US has warned its European allies about the risk of becoming overly dependent on Russian energy supplies and wonders aloud why they do not take this issue more seriously.

Russia has remained a sullen actor in its relationship with the US and Europe. It has focused its opposition on NATO rather than EU enlargement, seeing the former as directed against itself and arguing that it had been offered assurances at the end of the Cold War that the Alliance would not enlarge. Russia's disapproval has varied in intensity but has been particularly vociferous when NATO has considered membership applications from states that were formerly part of the Soviet Union or when membership impacts on the enclave of Kaliningrad. The Alliance came to accept that Russia had to be accorded a special status and created the NATO–Russia Permanent Joint Council. It drew the line, however, at allowing the Kremlin to act as a spoiler; in the words of Secretary of State Madeleine Albright, 'Russia will have a voice, but not a veto' (quoted in Solomon, 1998, 116). Russia has tended to remain quiet in the face of EU enlargement, regarding it as a development without strategic implications for its security.

The relationship with Russia is one of the eighteen 'strategic partnerships' that the EU has negotiated. It involves twice yearly meetings between representatives of the two sides at the highest level (European Council, 2003b). But the partnership has failed to bear fruit and the EU has been unable to exert its power of attraction due to Russia's size and sense of status. The EU and Russia designated four common spaces, of which two were focused explicitly upon security – internal and external (as well as economics and research and education). This was an attempt to target their interactions around issues of concern to the EU, such as organized crime, drug trafficking and terrorism. This concentration on security matters was reminiscent of the US–Russia relationship but it quickly became apparent that the Kremlin was unwilling to treat these matters as a priority.

Three important obstacles have stood in the way of the EU–Russia relationship. First, Russia tends to see security in realist terms, emphasizing hard power and material capabilities. Its slide towards authoritarianism under President (later Prime Minister) Vladimir Putin has rendered its relationship with the EU increasingly uncomfortable (Prodi and Verhofstadt, 2010). It has long craved a return to its past status as a superpower and the restoration of its sphere of interest. Such an approach is in direct contravention with the civilian power ethos and multilateralist vision of the EU. The August 2008 Georgia crisis, when Russia recognized the territories of Abkhazia and South Ossetia, starkly exposed these contending world views. Second, although Russia has not regarded the EU as threatening nor its enlargement a cause for concern, it has not taken the EU's role as a security actor seriously. It has been dismissive of the importance of the ESDP and has resisted any EU peacekeeping forces replacing Russian troops in areas like Moldova. The Kremlin has also tended to view the Union's Justice and Home Affairs (later renamed Justice, Liberty and Security) agenda as self-serving and of little relevance to Russian interests. Third, Russia feels that the EU as a whole does not accord them a sufficiently special status. There is a measure of truth in this perception because Russia is only a relatively peripheral economic actor in the eyes of Brussels. Many countries regard Russia as important only in the sense that it is a supplier of energy (Baghat, 2006) and even in that category it is judged to be erratic and prone to nationalistic excess.

The future of EU enlargement

The US has called for Western organizations to shift their attention to a global rather than a regional focus, on the grounds that the principal security challenges are arising from outside of Europe. In NATO, Washington has argued for the creation of 'Global Partnerships' within which countries from around the world enjoy close relationships with the Alliance, short of actual membership (Rice, 2003). Countries that have been identified for this status include Australia, New Zealand, Japan and South Korea, who have all been associated with NATO missions (Daalder and Goldgeier, 2006). This has exemplified US priorities towards NATO, seeking to make it an organization fit for interventions anywhere in the world. By contrast, the US has felt that the EU has become too parochial, too absorbed with its own 'ring of friends' in relation to enlargement.

There has been evidence of tension between contrasting EU and US visions of enlargement. At NATO's Bucharest Summit in 2008 the Bush administration pushed for Georgia and Ukraine to be admitted to the Alliance's Membership Action Plan (MAP), an important stage in the accession process. This was a signal not only that Washington regarded the anchoring of Ukraine within the West as vital (Asmus, 2003, 23–4) but that it wanted to extend NATO influence into central Asia. The US has regarded such countries as pioneers in spreading democratic values and it has valued Georgia's geostrategic location and access to oil reserves. It was also symbolic of America's perception that the security of Europe was no longer about the western half of the continent. The eyes of Washington policymakers had switched to the frontier states in the east and the consolidation of Western values in these countries.

For its part, the EU fretted about the damage that could be done to Russian relations with the West. The championing of Georgia and Ukraine by the US came at a time when the EU was considering the terms of an association agreement with Ukraine and was preparing to engage in a rule of law mission in Georgia. The US was sending the message to the EU that it needed to go further and faster in responding to an increasingly global security agenda. In the event, President Bush faced opposition from countries such as France and Germany and was unable to secure European support for NATO MAPs with either state (Evans, 2008, 40).

Differences of view between the EU and the US over Georgia and Ukraine were overtaken by events in August 2008 when the conflict broke out between Russia and Georgia over the disputed regions of South Ossetia and Abkhazia. Russia had become alarmed by growing US military assistance to Georgia and the country's desire to accede to NATO. The Union's more measured approach towards enlargement appeared prescient in the light of the risks that NATO might have been drawn into the conflict between Georgia and Russia. President Sarkozy of France, holding the EU Presidency, was able to broker a ceasefire between the warring parties and at the end of September an EU civilian monitoring mission consisting of 200 personnel was despatched to oversee the agreement. The Georgia crisis illustrated two factors for the EU. First, the Union had the ability to act in parts of the world where an American role would have been too sensitive (Neuss, 2009, 118). Second, it showed that Russia remained capable of resorting to force and that close cooperation with America is important for the security of EU members.

Attitudes towards the further enlargement of the Union remain mixed. A strong sense of 'enlargement fatigue' has crept into the EU discourse as well as mutterings that the 'absorption capacity' of the Union has reached saturation (*Economist*, 2008c, 54). The argument is that the EU needs to concentrate on consolidating those countries who have recently joined or to whom a membership perspective has been extended (*Agence Presse*, 2008, 5). Concerns about enlargement and the loss of jobs to immigrants was widely blamed for the failure to pass the EU Constitutional Treaty. Even countries such as Germany, traditional stalwarts of the enlargement agenda, have expressed an unwillingness to go on providing the resources to fund the process. In 2008, German MEP Elmar Brok, the European Parliament's rapporteur on enlargement matters, called for 'time out' on enlargement and argued that the Union needed to develop options for relations with its neighbours that did not go as far as membership (*Agence Presse*, 2008).

This is tied up with perceptions that the outer borders of 'Europe' have been reached and that further enlargement risks admitting states, such as Turkey, that have a Euro-Asian character. The failure of the EU and NATO to synchronize their respective enlargement projects raises problems for the future. For example, at the NATO Sixtieth Anniversary in April 2009, Croatia and Albania were welcomed into the fold (North Atlantic Council, 2009), but it was unclear how this would be reflected in their applications to join the EU. Even if states are drawn to the US in security terms, the economic attractions of the Union will grow to dominate their perspectives. There remains no common agenda towards enlargement between the two organizations and this presents the opportunity for US and European divergences to be exacerbated.

Conclusion

Those that question the EU's claim to be a security actor need look no farther than its process of enlargement (Barbe and Johansson-Nogues, 2008, 87). EU enlargement has been a successful but relatively low profile issue within the transatlantic security relationship. The US has not accorded the EU sufficient credit for the transformational role it has played in central and eastern Europe and the stabilizing influence it has projected into the Balkans and north Africa. EU enlargement has been a triumph because it has facilitated the export of an entire model of political, economic and social development from west to east. The influence of the Union has been extended to its wider neighbourhood, drawing countries into concentric circles of cooperation, some by offering the prospect of accession and others by offering lesser forms of relationship.

The EU's power of attraction has reformed and changed political and economic systems, it has helped to ensure adherence to democratic structures and human rights, and it has fostered the rule of law. In so doing it has served America's interests by reducing the responsibilities that the US formerly carried and enabled it to focus its attention elsewhere. But enlargement has not been without US–EU tensions. The US criticized as insufficient the reforms made by the Union to its own decision-making structures to cope with twenty-seven members. No secret has been made of the fact that America considers the Union to have enlarged too slowly. The US has argued that the EU focused its efforts on the relatively straight-forward countries such as Poland, Hungary and the Baltic states and has left states in the western Balkans and Ukraine languishing outside. Washington accuses the EU of letting Turkey's pro-Western orientation slip away.

Because the US has been focused on global security issues, it has regarded the Union as overly preoccupied with developments on its own continent. There is some justification for this view as the process of EU enlargement has led it to focus on issues like drug trafficking, illegal immigration and organized crime. This has had the effect of reducing the points of common interest with Washington. American policymakers have perceived the EU to be too self-absorbed: to be turned inwards rather than outwards.

Chapter 5

States of Concern

Introduction

The US saw itself during the Cold War as global actor with a commensurate range of interests. In contrast, it regarded Europe as a regional actor. This thinking was made explicit in Henry Kissinger's (1973) infamous 'Year of Europe' speech but it was implicit in US thinking up to 1990. To an extent it was an acceptance that the unique power enjoyed by America enabled it to exert influence in every corner of the world and that it played a decisive role as the leader of the Western world. Many European states, with the possible exceptions of Britain and France, 'believe that their proper role to be that of stabilising the continent while the United States defends common interests elsewhere' (Binnendijk and Kugler, 2002, 121). Wayne Thompson argued that the regional–global split is more complex than it first appears. The US is often drawn to regional solutions to problems whereas Europeans are attracted by global, multilateral solutions through international governmental organizations (Mahncke *et al.*, 2004, 98).

The US focused much of its security efforts before 1990 on Europe. When, in the latter stages of the Cold War, it attempted to get its allies to look beyond Europe – such as in relation to the security of the Gulf region or the use of force against Libya in response to acts of terrorism – it was largely unsuccessful. European allies responded that NATO was designed for the defence of the north Atlantic area and that problems in the Middle East were 'out of area'. But in the post-Cold War period the US believed that the stability of the European continent had been achieved and it was time to reorientate Western attention. In the words of Richard Haass (2002), Director of Policy and Planning at the US Department of State, 'because of the relative peace and stability Europe enjoys today, there is less that the United States and Europe have to do together in Europe and more that they should do together beyond Europe'. There was a hope that the EU would take on some of the

106

security tasks that the US had been carrying. This had echoes of the 'burden-sharing' debate that had previously characterized transatlantic relations (Sloan, 2005, 84). European governments have been willing to take greater responsibility for the security of their own continent, as demonstrated in the Balkans. They have differed with the US, however, in their belief that the continent is still vulnerable to major security challenges.

Europeans have not failed to appreciate that the centre of gravity in transatlantic relations has shifted as their interests with America have bifurcated. A European strategic culture has evolved slowly in relation to the security of the continent, but in relation to global issues it remains embryonic. As extra-European security challenges have assumed a progressively larger role in American planning, dissatisfaction that these priorities have not been shared in Europe has grown. American investment in military capabilities to project force has not been mirrored on the other side of the Atlantic. This has rendered Europeans less useful potential partners because they do not possess the ability to operate alongside US forces.

What is sometimes overlooked, however, is that European and American attitudes towards other parts of the world have often diverged. The Cold War imposed an artificial sense of unity upon the Atlantic allies that was not reflected in other theatres. The Middle East has been the most dramatic illustration of these differences and proved to be a regular source of irritation in transatlantic relations (Daalder *et al.*, 2006). Although the security issues of the Middle East impact on all sides, the US has looked upon the region as one in which its own diplomacy must lead and it has resented any perceived European meddling (Errera, 2005, 72). Washington has expected support from its European allies and it has been dismissive of their alternative views on the nature of the problems.

EU countries have been critical of what they have regarded as unqualified US support for the state of Israel. This was evident during Israel's 'Operation Cast Lead' in Gaza between December 2008 and January 2009. The EU has been more sympathetic to the plight of the Palestinian people, providing them with financial assistance as well as policing and rule of law missions within the Occupied Territories. In spite of the level of resources that it has committed to the area, the EU has enjoyed relatively little influence in the Arab–Israeli dispute. The Union has been a member of the 'Quartet', along with the US, Russia and the UN, that has taken a diplomatic lead towards the region but it has offered no strategic plan or vision for the resolution of the crisis. The EU has been constrained by the fear of arousing US censure and has been content to act in a subordinate fashion to Washington. Even the dialogue between the EU and Arab governments has been hollowed out for fear of stepping on US toes (Aoun, 2003, 297).

In this chapter I will argue that the issue of 'states of concern' has come to represent one of the sharpest cleavages in transatlantic security relations. Differences of threat perception, and over the appropriate instruments to employ, existed during the 1990s but were exacerbated by the 9/11 attacks. The war against Iraq was the culmination of these differences of approach, rather than their inception. Having demonstrated these differences so brutally in 2003, the period since then has been an attempt to repair relationships and try to rediscover common ground.

Contrasting threat perceptions

It was appreciated in the US in the 1990s that there were a multiplicity of threats to security. In its Quadrennial Defense Review, policy was predicated upon a number of strategic assumptions. The first was that residual dangers were left over from the Cold War, such as nuclear weapons on the territories of post-Soviet republics. The second was the possible eruption of a regional conflict, such as between China and Taiwan or the two halves of the Korean peninsula. The third was asymmetric threats, such as a hostile country sponsoring a terrorist movement. This third category was the hardest to prepare for, yet it arose to be the foremost of security fears.

President Clinton's first National Security Adviser, Anthony Lake, catalogued these threats to US security in an article in *Foreign Affairs* (Lake, 1994). He warned against the risks posed by so-called 'backlash' or 'rogue' states. These were countries that were undemocratic, were ruled by authoritarian cliques and disregarded human rights. Many had been former clients of the Soviet Union, but following the latter's demise were now unattached to any other power and were anxious about their own security interests. Such rogue states were hostile to the West and were potential sources of regional instability. They were also frequently sponsors of terrorist groups and states seeking to obtain WMD (United States National Security Strategy for Combating Terrorism, 2003). For example, Iran was categorized as such a backlash state that posed a military threat to Western oil supplies through the Straits of Hormuz; it was a vocal opponent of the Middle East Peace Process and supported both Hamas and Hezbollah and was suspected of possessing a covert nuclear programme (Katzman, 2008, 32–4).

On one level it is not apparent why a superpower should feel threatened by lesser powers. Such writers as Noam Chomsky (1994) contend that US hostility is driven by the US military–industrial complex needing to find enemies in order to justify new patterns of defence spending. Yet more mundane reasons provide a better source of explanation. Rogue states exhibit hostility towards a Western concept of international order that now enjoys almost universal acceptance. This order was created largely by the US, whose overwhelming power now made it intolerant of threats. The US was determined to oppose countries that behaved as outcasts to its order. In the words of Lake (1994, 46), 'as the sole superpower, the United States has a special responsibility for developing a strategy to neutralize, contain and, through selective pressure, perhaps eventually transform these backlash states into responsible members of the international community'. Another reason is that rogue states frequently pose a danger to American allies in their region. The changed distribution of power since the Cold War meant that such countries could cause disproportionate upset within the international system. For example, North Korea poses a threat to South Korea and to Japan, whilst Iran is a direct threat to Israel. Finally, domestic politics helps to drive the policy of US administrations as Congress frequently demands tough action against America's enemies. The Republican dominated Congress used Iran as a way of pressuring the Clinton administration during the latter half of the 1990s (Pollack, 2006, 14).

EU members have not shared America's preoccupation with these 'states of concern'. (Note: the phrase 'rogue states' was rejected in 1999 in an attempt to reduce disagreement over the issue.) European states have grown accustomed to coexisting with a variety of dangers in their region and they looked upon many of the countries as states in need of assistance. The EU viewed the US policy of isolating these states as simplistic and counter-productive. In the case of Iran, for example, European countries have regarded it as important regional power that indulges in dangerous forms of behaviour. Whereas Washington viewed states of concern as irrational and therefore undeterable, Europe has viewed them as subject to the same cost–benefit calculations as other countries. The EU has regarded America's hostility towards Cuba, for example, with a degree of bewilderment. Despite not possessing WMD, Cuba has been categorized as a state of concern whilst Syria, which does possess such weapons, has not (Litwak, 2002, 56).

The gap between transatlantic approaches to states of concern widened after the traumatic events of 9/11. Prior to that, the US sought to contain threats at the lowest possible cost. As noted by Lake, the priority of the early Clinton administration was to 'transform' such states, whilst seeing them as a source of potential danger. This position hardened over time, particularly as the Republicans in Congress put pressure on the administration. After 9/11, the US became determined to eradicate threats (Everts, 2001, 3). It was a 'sea change in American policy, from a status quo guardianship of stability ... to revolutionary destabilization of the existing order to create a better world' (Pond, 2004, 7).

EU countries questioned the implications and relative importance of the link between terrorist groups and states of concern. They have not denied the existence of linkages between states and terrorist movements, such as the Taliban providing sanctuary to al-Qaeda and Syria's relations with Hezbollah, but EU members have resisted American attempts to conflate confronting states of concern with fighting terrorism. Such thinking led the US to identify an alleged association between Saddam Hussein and al-Qaeda and encouraged the development of an open-ended American strategy that sought the defeat of all forms of terrorism everywhere in the world. European governments have argued for a more limited set of objectives and have been willing to enter into dialogue with states such as Syria, Iran and Libya as part of an attempt to wean them off sponsorship of terrorism.

In contrast, the US came to embrace the prospect of regime change and actively sought to destabilize opponents. Funds were channelled, for example, to Iraqi opposition groups in the latter part of the 1990s in order to try and unseat Saddam Hussein. The George W. Bush administration took this a considerable step further. In a speech to US veterans on 26 August 2002, Vice President Richard Cheney argued that old ways of containing threats were no longer sufficient in a world where WMD were more widely available and where these weapons could be transferred to terrorist actors. He argued that such threats would have to be neutralized before dreadful consequences were visited on the US (Gordon and Shapiro, 2004, 99).

The problem of 'failed' states has tended to be seen in different ways by the US and Europeans. The US has viewed such states as threats mainly because they can act as security vacuums into which hostile elements may become established. Organized criminal gangs, drug and people traffickers, and transnational terrorist organizations can all conduct their activities from weak and failing states or use them as sanctuaries from where to avoid reprisal (United States National Security Strategy, 2002). Such countries are at risk of becoming regional destabilizers, either exporting problems to their neighbours or drawing in intervention from surrounding countries. Somalia exemplifies this problem, both through its internal chaos and the intervention of outside powers. President George H. Bush authorized the sending of American troops to Somalia but it was President Clinton that inherited the problem. This resulted in one of the debacles of his period in office when the deaths of US servicemen in Mogadishu in 1993 led to American withdrawal from the country.

US policy has paid particular attention to failed states since 9/11 because it has witnessed the way in which terrorists have exploited the existence of ungoverned spaces in places such as Yemen. Afghanistan, an archetypal failed state resulting from poor governance and Soviet occupation, provided the sanctuary from which al-Qaeda was able to operate and train jihadists. In spite of nearly a decade of Western armed intervention, Afghanistan is still wracked by the Taliban insurgency, it persists as a host for al-Qaeda operatives and it is the point of origin for most of the global heroin trade. The Obama administration has perpetuated much of the approach of its predecessor but it has recognized more explicitly the ties between the problems of Afghanistan and Pakistan. It has built up its military presence within the former and increased the scale of drone attacks in the latter. It has been determined to prevent its adversaries enjoying safe havens in the tribal regions of neighbouring Waziristan.

Conversely, the EU has tended to focus on the vulnerabilities of failed states. The Union has attempted to identify the root causes of problems in what it views as 'pre-modern' states (Cooper, 2003) – countries that are pre-industrial and remain locked in a cycle of poverty and under-development. These problems range from natural disasters, such as famine, to the fall-out from civil conflicts that lead to lack of governance and a breakdown of law and order. Having identified the source of the difficulties, the EU seeks, consistent with its values, to provide aid and other forms of development assistance (European Council, 2008, 8). These range from help with administration and human rights issues to justice and the provision of security.

The European Security Strategy of December 2003 was designed to bridge some of the divide between the EU and US positions (Biscop, 2005, 18). The EU affirmed the importance of the transatlantic relationship and its shared interest with the US in promoting world order. It accepted the American argument that failed states could act as potential sources of threat. An example of this being realized has been the emergence of piracy off the Horn of Africa, resulting in the involvement of navies from around the world (Pank, 2009, 37). In the face of such challenges, the ESS accepted that it may not be sufficient to wait for those threats to grow until they strike at European countries. It argued for the EU to possess the capacity for 'early and robust action', perhaps even leading to intervention on the territories of failed states (European Council, 2003b). It appreciates that such intervention would need to be speedy and on a large scale and would risk encountering resistance from hostile elements. Whilst dropping its call in an earlier draft for 'pre-emptive engagement', the ESS does call for the capacity for 'preventive engagement' (ibid.). It would need to be conducted in concert with military forces to ensure the necessary cover for humanitarian agencies operating on the ground.

Contrasting transatlantic approaches to states of concern

The EU approach towards states of concern has been to interact with them both politically and economically. The Union's experience of socializing states within its own region, through policies of engagement, has been a powerful influence upon its thinking. Consistent with its values, the EU has sought to act in a cooperative and non-coercive manner, believing that its own example can serve as a model and promote peaceful change. The EU has offered states positive incentives to modify their behaviour, such as trade, direct investment and assistance with governance. It is hoped that these interchanges will bring with them new ideas and influences that will help to open up the target country. Germany pioneered the strategy of 'critical dialogue' and this became the common policy adopted by the whole of the EU (Falke, 2000, 157). It is similar to the policy enacted towards China, and the EU saw no reason why it should not work with countries like Iran and North Korea.

As part of the critical dialogue, the EU stands ready to censure countries for aggressive behaviour, for failures in human rights and for authoritarian policies towards their own populations. But the objective has been to preserve a two-way communication and to break this only in the last resort. In the case of Iran, there were strong protests by the French government to Tehran after assassinations took place on its soil. The EU decided to suspend its dialogue with Iran in 1997, after a German Court's decision in the Mykonos case when there was evidence of Iranian complicity in the assassination of its overseas dissidents (Noi, 2005, 87). Nevertheless, the ambassadorial contacts were resumed in the following year, leading the US government to criticize the weak penalties imposed by the EU.

The EU has been reluctant to threaten or use force for a number of reasons. First, the diversity of contacts enjoyed by its member states. Due to their former colonial pasts and their contemporary trading policies, member states have extensive links with countries that the US has designated as states of concern. For example, notwithstanding allegations of sponsorship of terrorism, Libya, Iraq and Iran have experienced close relations with countries such as Germany, Italy, France and the UK. Investments and oil supplies have all played a part in maintaining ties. A second reason is that EU states have not wanted to become targets for terrorist groups (Byman, 2005, 220). Taking a stand on an issue risks retribution by a terrorist movement sponsored by that state. Third, several members of the EU have limitations over their ability to use coercive means. Germany, for obvious historical reasons, is a country with self-imposed constraints over the use of its armed forces. Other countries, such as Finland, Austria and Ireland, have strong traditions of neutralism that limit the recourse to force.

Another tension between the transatlantic allies has been over European advocacy of strategies aimed at conflict prevention. EU members have identified poverty, deprivation and disease as issues that can lead to despair, radicalization and even to violent extremism. They have sought to offer aid and development assistance to such countries and hoped to promote the cause of moderation as a result. The EU has also targeted respect for human rights and the promotion of democracy as important indicators, believing that they contribute to stability and conflict prevention within and between less developed countries (Smith, 2003, 107). John Peterson (2004, 626) characterizes the different priorities between the EU and the US as one in which the latter 'attack[s] the disease by hitting at its symptoms ... The European approach is more classically preventive and holistic'.

In contrast, the US has advocated a policy of containment and isolation of states of concern, arguing that only pressure will force authoritarian governments to change. In the case of Iran and Iraq, from 1993 the Clinton administration followed a policy of 'dual containment', seeking to hold them both in check. America applied a range of instruments ranging from diplomatic pressure to destabilization and economic sanctions. In the case of Iraq, the US Congress passed the Iraq Liberation Act in 1998 that authorized the use of funds to opposition groups in an attempt to overthrow Saddam Hussein's government. America imposed economic sanctions on Iraq and Iran and leaned on its allies to enforce them. It was even willing to threaten and, on certain occasions, actually employ military force (Tanter, 1999).

Both sides of the Atlantic are critical of the other's approach. The EU is critical of the US because they see these states of concern as important actors in their own right and fear that American policy will drive them into a corner with no room for manoeuvre. The US gets locked into dead-end policies from which it cannot extricate itself without a major loss of face (Everts, 2001, 4). The Union's fear is that the government of the target country will justify its domestic repression and its hostile foreign policy on the grounds that it is threatened by America. President George W. Bush's 'Axis of Evil' speech in 2002, for example, left the Europeans aghast (Bush, 2002b). The linking of Iraq, Iran and North Korea in such an arbitrary way was viewed as baseless. The use of rhetoric of 'good' versus 'evil' made the Europeans very uncomfortable because it provided no room for either dialogue or compromise. The US appeared to be committing itself to a protracted confrontation with all states of concern.

In turn, the US has been critical of EU priorities. It argues if dialogue fails, then the West must be willing to back up its threats with the actual use of force. According to poll data, 47 per cent of Americans favour increased diplomatic pressure on Iran with the option of resorting to force, whilst 53 per cent of Europeans would support increased pressure but would rule out the use of coercion (Transatlantic Trends, 2009). US policymakers have perceived that the lack of military capabilities to project force has left the EU unwilling to act (Kagan, 2003, 32). The US has accused the EU states of depending on them for security yet being unwilling to follow their lead. In the past the US has adopted a hard-line stance towards a state of concern but then watched as its European allies gradually defect from the position. Harsh voices from within the US Congress have accused European countries of appeasement: a language designed to cause maximum offence in European capitals.

Economic sanctions

Sanctions are designed to inflict pain upon a target state, and they have been used as an early step in an escalatory ladder of punishment. They have been employed for a range of purposes, such as halting the development of WMD or to adhere to human rights provisions. The Export Administration Act of 1979 provides the formal mechanism through which the US designates those states with whom it will not trade or provide economic or military assistance. Each year the President has to certify to Congress whether these measures are still in place. There has long been a transatlantic debate over the utility of sanctions, whether they are effective and serve the goals for which they are created. There has always been a range of options concerning sanctions, ranging from universal measures agreed upon and imposed by the UN, to unilateral measures initiated by one state. Sanctions also vary according to their targets, whether they are designed to hurt the general population or whether they are 'smart' in nature, such as travel bans, and aimed only at a specific elite. The issue of extra-territorial sanctions, namely those imposed by one state but exacting penalties on allies not abiding by the measures, have caused the greatest tension in US–EU relations.

In spite of the fact that trade is one of the EU's principal areas of strength, it has resorted to sanctions sparingly. The imposition of sanctions has been treated by the Union as a major punishment and one that it is reluctant to use – as cited in its 2004 Basic Principles on the Use of Restrictive Measures (Sanctions) (Niblett and Mix, 2006, 15). The EU has preferred constructive engagement and dialogue, seeking to change countries from within by drawing them into a cooperative relationship that becomes too costly to break. For example, in relation to Iran, the EU was eager to bolster moderate opinion after the election of President Khatami in 1997, in the hope that religious hardliners could be sidelined.

The US has imposed sanctions unilaterally rather than relying on those mandated multilaterally – for example in the case of Libya after the Lockerbie bombing in 1988. By acting alone the US fails to include the EU in its strategy, yet it has expected its European allies to enforce its measures, including bans on credit and dual-use goods. No effort was made, for example, to consult with the Europeans, through the Transatlantic Dialogue, in the case of new sanctions arrangements during the Clinton administration (Leeuwen, 1999, 18). Even though the US was trying to impose extra-territorial sanctions, it had not discussed these arrangements with its partners. As a result the EU did not feel obligated to follow the US lead. They regarded the US policy as hypocritical because the US was drafting laws that impacted on others yet at the same time it was asserting its own sovereignty and rejecting any outside influence.

The Iran–Libya Sanctions Act (ILSA or D'Amato Act) and the Cuban Liberty and Democratic Solidarity Act (LIBERTAD or Helms–Burton Act) of 1996 exemplify the different approaches of the US and EU. In the case of ILSA, the Clinton administration was targeting Iran but Congress forced the President's hand and the legislation was extended to include Libya. This was because of Libya's role in the destruction of Pan Am flight 103 in December 1988 over Scotland and French UTA flight 772 in September 1989 over Niger. The US oil company Conoco had to suspend its activities after its government announced a ban on all trade and investment with Iran. The US threatened reprisals against any European company that invested more than $40 million in either Iran's or Libya's energy industry. These reprisals could have taken the form of banning the company's products or denying them loans from US financial institutions. In the case of LIBERTAD the target was the regime of Fidel Castro and the US warned that any European companies trading with Cuba would be liable to be sued by Cuban émigrés that had suffered the expropriation of their property.

Washington contended that trade and debt rescheduling helped to ensure the survival of target regimes by preventing them from defaulting (Rudolf, 1999, 79). Since then the US has gone on to develop a range of sanctions including financial measures to inflict considerable pain. In the case of North Korea, the US targeted the Macau-based bank, Banco Delta Asia, and banned it from dealing with US financial institutions because of its linkages to the regime in Pyongyang. Similarly, in relation to Iran, the US has barred certain Iranian banks from dealing with their US counterparts, with the result that a large number of overseas financial institutions have severed contacts with these banks (*Economist*, 2010a, 66). US financial pressures on target countries can be very onerous, including making it difficult to obtain export credits. America often compounds the pressure by imposing travel bans on senior government officials.

Congressional policymakers have been particularly unhappy to watch American companies being forced to disengage from contracts whilst European companies filled the vacuum. The US has argued that its extra-territorial sanctions were matters on which security had to take priority but this reasoning was rejected by its European allies. In the case of Iran, the French company Total secured a $2 billion deal over the development of the South Pars gas field (Katzman, 2006, 3). The Anglo-Dutch company Royal Dutch Shell agreed to help construct a pipeline across northern Iran to transport gas (Noi, 2005, 87). Sections of the American government saw this as evidence of European hypocrisy: that the Europeans wanted their protection yet exploited economic opportunities at America's expense. Particular criticisms were made of Germany for its apparent willingness to put its large investments in Iran ahead of security concerns and for the involvement of German companies in developing an alleged chemical weapons facility in Libya.

It is undeniable that the companies of EU states maximized their commercial advantage when US companies were instructed to withdraw. As a non-coercive power the EU has been more focused on economic advantage and on the benefits from trading with other countries. Europe has enjoyed long ties with many of the countries on whom the US has imposed sanctions. Europe has been Libya's main partner in trade, for example, and the importer of most of its oil (Takeyh, 2001, 72). The EU has been Cuba's foremost trading partner. But the Union was unwilling to support the US lead because it did not accept the argument that the ILSA and LIBERTAD Acts were security matters. Instead, the EU defined them as commercial and legal issues in which the US acted extra-territorially and flouted international law. The EU passed legislation preventing its members from acquiescing with US sanctions policy (Niblett and Mix, 2006, 12) and threatened to take the matter to the WTO. European opposition to the US legislation was strenuous and united, seeing it as a direct affront to their sovereignty (Falke, 2000, 157). The Union was quick to point out that America would be outraged if it was expected to implement legislation from an external authority. President Clinton was empowered by the legislation to suspend implementation for six-month periods and this was renewed until a decision was reached on the issue. In May 1998 the EU came to an agreement with the US by which the extra-territorial measures against European companies were waived.

The stance of the EU towards sanctions has aroused considerable hostility within the US and especially from Congress. Critics in America have accused EU countries of placing trade considerations and commercial gain before security concerns of WMD proliferation and state sponsorship of terrorism (Pollack, 2006, 14). It reinforced a perception that only the US was willing to think strategically about global issues. This same issue reoccurred in a slightly different form in 2005 when the EU proposed lifting its embargo of weapons sales to China that had existed since the time of the 1989 Tiananmen Square massacre (Binnendijk, 2005, 6). The US feared that it could one day find itself in a confrontation with China over Taiwan and was worried that it might face European-made arms. American protests, including a Senate resolution calling on the EU to maintain the embargo, led the Union to back down.

The threat or use of force

Debates over the threat or the use of force and the grounds for initiating interventions have been amongst the most prickly areas in transatlantic relations. This is understandable considering that these issues are some of the most important yet contested topics in international relations (Kissinger and Summers, 2004). Tensions were heightened during the era of President George W. Bush by his administration's disinclination in obtaining UN approval for overseas interventions.

In the 1990s the US was reluctant to use military force for fear of incurring casualties. The experience of US intervention in Somalia in 1993 had illustrated the difficulties of employing force in situations where US vital interests were not at stake. The Clinton administration was prepared to use force but not in the form of major ground-based operations. Instead, the US military employed airpower because it leveraged its technological supremacy and lowered the risk of American casualties. For example, in 1998, Operation Desert Fox led to the bombardment of Iraqi facilities for four days in an effort to degrade its military capabilities and any residual WMD programmes.

EU states were more averse to the use of force than the US. This is not to say that all European countries have shied from the use of force per se. The UK resorted to military means in Sierra Leone in 2000 and France deployed forces to Chad. But the EU as a group of states, riven by differences of opinion towards other countries, has been reluctant to use force. Partly, this has reflected doubts about what force will achieve in the longer term and partly it has reflected an appreciation that they would have to live with the long-term consequences of confrontation. European countries stand in close proximity to many states of concern and they would face the security and economic fallout from military action. After the US attack on Libya in April 1986 (Operation El Dorado Canyon), for instance, Libya retaliated by firing a ballistic missile at the Italian island of Lampedusa.

The EU and US also differ on issues of how to legitimize military action. Consistent with EU adherence to the rule of law, European governments have been hesitant to act without the political cover of a UN Security Council Resolution. The US has tended to take a more robust approach. With countries such as Russia and China in the UN Security Council assuming different political positions on states of concern, a mandate for action has frequently been unobtainable. Washington has tended to justify force on the basis of Article 51, Chapter VII, of the UN Charter which tolerates the use of force in self-defence. The US arrogates to itself the right to interpret threats to its security and act against them, rather than obtaining a mandate from the Security Council. Whilst adopting the rhetoric of multilateralism, the US has acted unilaterally. The National Security Strategy (NSS) declared that 'we will not hesitate to act alone if necessary' (United States National Security Strategy, 2002).

It was the events of 9/11 that had the greatest impact on US willingness to use force. The 9/11 attack was momentous in terms of the American psyche, ending its sense of invulnerability and opening a window, primarily in terms of domestic political support, for the Bush administration to wield force proactively. The Pentagon was placed in the driving seat of the US War on Terror as the administration gauged that the public were prepared to accept casualties. Colin Powell, the former Secretary of State, confirmed the significance of the moment when he heralded it as the onset of the 'post-post-Cold War world'. This is endorsed by Robert Kagan (2008) who makes the point that the al-Qaeda atrocity changed America and led it to return to global leadership, after a period in which it had drawn back from undertaking missions abroad. This change was insufficiently appreciated in Europe and masked a growing division between the two sides of the Atlantic to engage in war.

The NSS of 2002 was explicit about using America's military hegemony to effect change and its inherent right to do so. What was even more significant was that the US argued it had to be prepared to act pre-emptively before the threat to its security came into being (Bush, 2002a). According to the NSS, the only way to address this threat would be by anticipatory self-defence that led the US to act before the threat became imminent (United States National Security Strategy, 2002). This strategic posture was reaffirmed in March 2006 when the NSS was updated.

The attacks of 9/11 brought, temporarily, a new sense of solidarity between Europe and America. The nature of the new enemy reminded the West of its many commonalities, that any one of them could have been attacked by al-Qaeda. NATO invoked Article 5 and European allies took steps to support America. But as US policy unfolded, it drew a growing chorus of criticism from European nations. They charged that the US was shifting its stance from defence to one of prevention, which presumed the availability of perfect intelligence about an adversary's intentions (Freedman, 2003). Bush was effecting a revolution in foreign policy, 'not in its goals, but in how to achieve them' (Daalder and Lindsay, 2003, 2). The US was reserving to itself the right to use force whenever it believed that a threat to its security was in gestation. European critics felt that this was sending out the wrong signal to other countries around the world and establishing a dangerous precedent.

The Bush White House did not care very much about what EU governments thought. In the midst of its War on Terror, the US saw the positions of its allies largely as an irrelevance once its own course of action had been decided. EU governments were judged to be unable to add much weight to US military capabilities and they were effectively sidelined. Even the UK government was regarded as important more as a legitimizer than as a contributor of forces. There was an assumption on the part of the Bush administration that it was the duty of its allies to support American leadership: that they would fall into line once the plan of action was clear. Some European governments did support US foreign policy after 2001 but many did not and the result was the worst ever transatlantic crisis.

The US chose to use ad hoc coalitions as part of its War on Terror. 'Operation Enduring Freedom' in Afghanistan led the US to draw upon some of the contingents of special forces of European countries, and it provided a role for UK armed forces, though it refused large-scale assistance. The US judged, perhaps unsurprisingly in light of numerous complaints about the poor military investment of their allies, that it could achieve its objectives more efficiently through the unilateral application of its power. Unlike in the past when the US would have made a case to its allies to convince all of them of the need to act together, the Bush administration was unprepared to make the effort to win over the Europeans (Haass, 2002). It was heedless of how unpopular its policies had become in the eyes of European public opinion and treated its allies as a tool-box of capabilities to assist a US-centred effort.

The Iraq War and the transatlantic alliance

The war against Iraq in 2003 was to prove the supreme example of differing transatlantic approaches towards states of concern. The crisis has been aptly described as a 'perfect storm' within the West: a confluence of unfortunate events and attitudes (Gordon and Shapiro, 2004, 6). It involved a radical US administration engaged in a crisis with a German Chancellor seeking re-election and an avowedly Gaullist President in the Elysée Palace. It exacerbated long and deep-seated tensions between Europe and the US over the Middle East. In this, President George W. Bush was once again an aggravator, rather than an instigator, of underlying issues that had been brought to the forefront as a result of 9/11.

The absence of an agreed perception of the threat between the two sides was the first factor that contributed to the crisis. The extent to which Saddam Hussein's regime represented a danger to the West and its allies, as well as to regional stability, was highly contested. That Iraq had possessed programmes designed to develop WMD was beyond doubt. It had employed chemical weapons against its own Kurdish population at Halabja in 1988 and the United Nations Commission (UNSCOM) on disarming Iraq had spent several years after the first Gulf War destroying its weapon stockpiles. Its nuclear and chemical weapons had been systematically dismantled. Its biological stockpile had been systematically denied by the Iraqi government but came to light after 1995 when Saddam's son-in-law, Kamal Hussein, surrendered 1.2 million pages of documentation that had been kept secret from UNSCOM (Blix, 2010). After August 1998, Iraq suspended UNSCOM's activities and suffered retaliatory bombing by the US and UK as a consequence. From that time onwards it became impossible to know how much of Iraq's clandestine weapons programmes had been reconstituted and further developed. It was also uncertain what links Iraq might have forged with terrorist groups, although there was scepticism outside the US that any links existed between Iraq and al-Qaeda, because of their antithetical ideologies.

The second factor, the imminence of the danger, was also related to perceptions of threat. The American administration argued that Iraq was such a danger that a pre-emptive conflict was justified to forestall the threat. In November 2002, UN Security Council Resolution (UNSCR) 1441 found Iraq to be in 'material breach of her obligations' under earlier UN resolutions and mandated a new weapons investigation under the UN Monitoring, Verification and Inspection Commission (UNMOVIC). UNSCR 1441 itself was an uneasy compromise designed to try to keep the US and Europe together. It papered over the cracks between the US and French and German positions and allowed both sides to interpret the Resolution in different ways. It aggravated the sense of betrayal in both America and Europe when their policy prescriptions were subsequently rubbished by the other side. In January 2003 UNMOVIC reported that Iraq was not providing a full inventory of its weapons and the Bush administration took this as providing the necessary pretext to use force. It had viewed 1441 as granting Iraq a final opportunity to disarm and when this was not taken there was sufficient authority, based on earlier UN resolutions, to disarm Iraq militarily. In contrast, France and Germany had seen UNSCR 1441 as a commitment to pursue the continued disarmament of Iraq through weapons inspections. They felt, like Hans Blix, the director of the weapons inspections, that more time should be given to UNMOVIC to complete a thorough investigation of Iraq's weapon sites. If force were to be used, France believed that a further UNSCR would be required, a view shared by the other Council members of China and Russia.

The Bush administration made no secret of the fact that they had no confidence in Hans Blix, nor his superior at the International Atomic Energy Agency, Mohammed El Baradei. They judged that these figures were more concerned with averting war than securing the disarmament of Iraq. The intelligence services of most other Western countries agreed with the US assessment that Saddam Hussein was hiding WMD. This faulty assessment illustrates the difficulty of gaining accurate intelligence on such a closed society as

Iraq. But other European governments did not accept the US conclusion that war had to be conducted immediately, that Iraq was such an imminent threat that it could no longer be contained by other means. EU governments were convinced that Washington had already decided to use force and was prepared to disregard the views of its allies. America feared an indeterminate outcome over Iraq with endless weapons inspections and was eager to use force decisively (Meyer, 2009). The Bush administration was keeping to a military-dictated timetable in which the huge forces assembled in the region had to be used quickly before a window of opportunity afforded by seasonal temperatures changed (Pauly and Lansford, 2005, 111).

The third factor was US–European disagreement over the utility of economic sanctions. A sanctions regime had been imposed upon Iraq by UNSCR 687, after the first Gulf War. It was accompanied by a no-fly zone over Iraq's northern and southern regions that had been designed to stop the regime in Baghdad persecuting its Kurdish minority and Shia majority. While the US and UK saw sanctions as a means to contain and weaken Saddam Hussein's government, many European countries had become increasingly vocal in their criticism that these measures were poorly targeted. European governments felt that the maintenance of sanctions was reducing Iraq to the status of a less developed country and causing disproportionate suffering on the population. They pressed for sanctions either to be narrowed considerably or scrapped altogether. As part of an attempt to reduce the suffering of the ordinary people, sanctions had been modified in April 1995 by UNSCR 986. This allowed Iraq to sell $1 billion of oil every ninety days with the money going in to a UN account and being spent on food and medicines.

The debate over sanctions had become a growing source of tension between Europe and Washington. The US was impatient with the porosity of the sanctions regime, aware that goods were being shipped in to Iraq by neighbouring countries. American policymakers suspected that their allies were overly influenced by the debts that Iraq owed to European governments and the opportunities to obtain contracts for rebuilding its oil industry and creaking infrastructure (Gordon and Shapiro, 2004, 77). Meanwhile, the Iraqi National Congress, an opposition movement in exile led by Ahmed Chalabi, was coaxing the US towards removing Saddam's regime from power, arguing that America would be hailed as liberators by the grateful population.

The final factor was the predilection of the US to act alone. The US had grown disillusioned with pursuing a multilateral approach to Iraq as it had watched its allies defect from the sanctions regime. As the US moved towards advocating a change of government, if necessary by the use of force, it found itself increasingly at odds with many of its European allies. By as early as the spring of 2002, US Central Command (CENTCOM), under General Tommy Franks, had been given the authority to plan for a military invasion of Iraq. The US might have been able to win its European allies around to its way of thinking but the Bush administration decided it had little need of their support. In the words of Cottey (2007, 65), 'the US has taken an increasingly utilitarian attitude towards its European allies – assessing their value primarily on the basis of their willingness and ability to support US policies'.

To talk of European opposition to the US war against Iraq is a misnomer: it was as much an intra-European rupture as it was a US–European one. EU unity splintered over the crisis as the contrasting strategic interests of the leading members were thrown into sharp relief. There was a divide between those that broadly supported the policies of the Bush administration and those who were opposed. Amongst the supporters, the UK had stood alongside the US in its approach to Iraq since 1991, upholding sanctions and the no-fly zones, and joining in periodic bombing when Saddam Hussein's regime refused to comply with UN resolutions. Prime Minister Tony Blair remained steadfast in support of US policy, contending that Britain shared America's perceptions of the dangers of Iraqi WMD (Riddell, 2003, 58). Blair believed that only by acting alongside the US could the UK exert influence. Critics have made the point that Tony Blair received little in return from the US for his decision to support the invasion (Meyer, 2006a, 248). The UK was joined by Italy and Spain, whose right-of-centre governments were both ideologically supportive of the US and eager to oppose the traditional dominance of France and Germany in Europe. A host of central European states also supported the American policy, including Poland, the Czech Republic and Hungary.

France, Germany and Belgium were firmly opposed to US policies. France had earlier dropped both sanctions against Iraq and the enforcement of the no-fly zone. In January 2003, it blocked Turkey's request for military assistance from NATO in the event of an attack upon Iraq: a gambit that put NATO itself at risk (Pond, 2005, 46). President Jacques Chirac viewed March 2003 as a moment when US–European interests were starkly opposed and as an opportunity to realize France's cherished dream of a stronger European identity separate from the transatlantic relationship. The French government used the crisis to redouble its calls for a multi-polar world to replace the unipolar dominance of a single super-power.

Germany, under Chancellor Gerhard Schroeder, also refused to be a part of what it saw as US 'adventurism'. Public opinion in Germany was against the use of force and Schroeder rejected the involvement of his country, regardless of whether a second UNSCR was passed (Steinberg, 2003, 113). Germany displayed an anti-Americanism that was unknown in its previous fifty-year history.

This was a qualitatively different moment in transatlantic rela-tions, with key European states trying actively to frustrate US policy. France and Germany even aligned temporarily with Russia in opposition to the war (Lindberg, 2005, 10; Kupchan, 2008, 120). A rancorous transatlantic exchange ensued, with one seasoned commentator describing it as the 'near death' of the transatlantic alliance (Pond, 2004). There were huge rallies in major European cities and an outpouring of anti-American feeling. In return, anti-Europeanism was evident in the US, aimed particu-larly towards France, and which became mixed up with accusa-tions of anti-semitism. When the Aznar government in Spain lost the election a year later and the new Zapatero government removed Spanish troops from Iraq there were even accusations of appeasing terrorism.

Neoconservatives and other ideologues within the US accused several European governments of failing to support the freedom agenda promulgated by the Bush administration. This agenda envis-aged that regime change in Baghdad would be part of a wider plan to transform the Middle East. Iraq would partner Israel as the two leading democracies in the region and US attention would be shifted to several other potential dominoes – such as Iran, Syria and Libya. The response from many EU governments was that the US was misguided in thinking that democracy could be imposed by force. They called for the US to consult over an appropriate strategy towards the region rather than take unilateral steps and expect others to follow. US goals would have been served better by work-ing in partnership with European countries.

America's conduct of the war was brilliantly successful and the Iraqi military was defeated within the space of three weeks. It was a triumph for the sort of transformed US military for which Defense Secretary Donald Rumsfeld had been labouring: a small and technologically sophisticated force that was able to manoeuvre and strike with devastating precision. Only about 150,000 US troops were employed in a combat role and they were supported by 45,000 troops from the UK, 2,000 from Australia and 200 from Poland (Daalder and Lindsay, 2003, 147). The speed and decisive nature of the victory lulled the American military into a false sense of security that the conflict was over. A rapid draw-down of American forces was envisaged for the Autumn of 2003.

Yet the optimistic scenario of the neoconservatives was to be overtaken by the course of events in Iraq. The false sense of confidence was quickly replaced by dismay as a situation of post-conflict chaos unfolded. It was apparent that the US lacked the size of forces to police the country effectively and that planning for the aftermath of the war had been neglected (Interview, 2006). Coalition troop levels were insufficient to cope with a Sunni-led insurgency that began to sweep the country, swelled by an inflow of jihadists determined to kill American soldiers in a Muslim country. The situation was aggravated by the imperial ethos that the US brought to Iraq: the head of the Coalition Provisional Authority, Paul Bremmer, chose to disband the Iraqi military and de-Baathify the civil administration (Chandrasekaran, 2006). The result of this was to reduce some 400,000 armed men to a situation of unemployment and to remove from positions of power all those who had experience of running the country. The failure to find any WMD added to the sense of crisis (*Economist*, 2004, 23–5).

To make matters worse, America's enemies in the region were able to profit from the situation. Syria and Iran were emboldened to exploit the situation for their own purposes. Iran's support for the Shia cleric Moqtada al-Sadr gave it special influence in the politics of Iraq, whilst its technical support to the insurgency, in terms of improvised explosive devices, enabled it to bleed American forces. According to Dunn (2007, 3), 'the creation of a weak and strife-ridden Iraq has meant that, geopolitically, Iran is the clearest beneficiary of the American invasion'.

The US was to face a long and bloody insurgency in Iraq in which its forces incurred heavy casualties. Despite its enormous strength, the US lacked the means to impose its priorities. The UN was driven from the country by a disastrous bomb attack in 2003 that killed its head of mission, leaving America to cope with the situation. Washington attempted to reach out beyond the coalition that it had assembled to the wider international community for help. But the perceived illegitimacy of the campaign made it practically impossible to attract wider support, especially amongst European states, to stem the violence and rebuild Iraq. The situation was only brought under some semblance of control in 2007 with the 'Sunni Awakening' against the influence of foreign jihadists, the curbing of the Shia militias and the decision to 'surge' extra US forces to Iraq to smother the insurgency.

Opponents of America's intervention into Iraq were left to look on from the sidelines with a sense of *Schadenfreude*. Whilst the transatlantic relationship reached a nadir during 2003, it was able to improve once some of the main protagonists left the scene. Chancellor Schroeder and then President Chirac were replaced by more avowedly pro-American leaders, although there was no stomach from either Sarkozy or Merkel for their countries to become involved in the situation in Iraq (Interview, 2008a). The EU launched a 'rule of law' mission in Iraq in July 2005 (EUJUST LEX) to train and assist that country's judicial system, but this was a token contribution. The neoconservative ideologues that had encouraged the Bush administration to pursue its invasion also disappeared quickly from the scene. They argued that their vision for the Middle East had been the correct one but that the execution had been botched by the administration.

President Barack Obama has sought to repair some of the damage wrought to America's standing in the Middle East. Whilst this will not be easy in the shadow of the distrust that was engendered by the Iraq War, it is nevertheless vital considering that this is one of the foremost priority areas for any US administration. Only at a very late stage did President George W. Bush attempt to intercede in the Arab–Israeli conflict by initiating the Annapolis peace conference in November 2007. In contrast, President Obama made his Cairo speech at the very outset of his term of office. In the speech he called for a new beginning between Islam and America and promised a new era of American respect towards Muslims (*Guardian*, 2009, 1). Obama also pledged to make efforts to break the deadlock between Palestinians and Israelis and to reach out to Iran.

President Obama also made clear whilst running for office that he was determined to pull US troops out of Iraq at the earliest opportunity. He judged that their presence was an obstacle to political progress within the country and that the security forces and the political establishment in Iraq were ready to handle the situation themselves. Obama also judged, correctly, that the ghost of Iraq still haunted relations with some European countries and needed to be exorcized. He remained true to his word and in August 2010 US combat operations in Iraq were declared to be at an end. Some 50,000 troops will remain in Iraq performing training and support functions.

Conclusion

States of concern have proved to be one of the sharpest and longest running areas of divergence in US–EU relations. During the Cold War, EC members did not always agree with US global policy but they kept their counsel due to the importance of America in the security of Europe. After 1990, contrasting approaches to states of concern have led to open disagreement as EU states have felt less inhibited about criticizing US policy. For America, the dangers posed by states of concern have grown in significance because its agenda has shifted from Europe to issues such as WMD and international terrorism. During George W. Bush's first presidential term the US was prepared to ignore the protests of many of its allies, turn its back on multilateralism and act according to its own national priorities. Thus, the issue of states of concern came to symbolize the structural shift in US–EU relations.

The two sides have approached states of concern with different threat perceptions and with different capabilities. Whilst they have agreed over the objectives – namely, to prevent new states acquiring WMD and to contain regional instability – they have differed over the most appropriate instruments. The US, regarding itself as the guardian of the international order, has believed that it has taken a principled stance and accorded primacy to security issues. It has accused EU members of sacrificing security to selfish commercial interests. After the 9/11 attacks the US assumed a confrontational stance towards terrorism and those countries that it suspected of supporting various groups.

American unilateralism over Iraq in 2003 brought a crisis of confidence in US leadership as it showed the US to be heedless of European views and also naïve in stumbling into a politico-military quagmire. Europeans were made suspicious of attempts by Washington to lead in foreign policy issues (Allin *et al.*, 2007).

Conversely, the EU was made to look weak and incoherent by the crisis. The Iraq conflict exposed the hollowness of the claim that the Union could act as a counterweight to the US. The challenge for the future of the transatlantic relationship will be to try and build a consensus towards states of concern.

Chapter 6

Nuclear Non-Proliferation and Counter-Proliferation

Introduction

The risk of the proliferation of WMD, particularly nuclear weapons, goes to the heart of the debate concerning international order. The states that possess nuclear weapons have traditionally been those that have defined the contours of the order, whilst at the same time opposing countries that have sought to change or overturn that order. The acquisition of nuclear weapons offers an aspirant state a means of disproportionate influence because it provides them with the most powerful instruments of destruction known to man. Since the end of the Cold War nuclear armed states have found themselves trying to perpetuate a system based on double standards: namely, denying the development of nuclear weapons to aspirant states whilst at the same time refusing to divest themselves of their own weapons.

Not all analysts agree that the proliferation of WMD is an undesirable prospect. Probably the majority of experts regard the horizontal proliferation of weapons to threaten strategic stability. As more states acquire the most awesome weapons, the risk of miscalculation is believed to increase, especially as the newcomers will not know the 'rules of the game' that have been learnt over the years by the nuclear powers. But a group of neo-realists, led by such distinguished names as Kenneth Waltz and John Mearsheimer, argued the converse (Waltz, 1981; Mearsheimer, 1993). They posited that horizontal proliferation contributes to strategic stability by making states inherently risk averse. They argued that the logic of deterrence would counsel caution even amongst those states that have most recently acquired the technology.

The issue of nuclear non-proliferation has been a particularly difficult one within the transatlantic relationship for a number of reasons. First, it exposes the differing status of Western countries:

the US, the UK and France as nuclear powers and the rest of Europe as non-nuclear states. Second, historically, the US was the foremost actor on matters of nuclear non-proliferation but the increasing salience of the issue has made it a subject for wider concern within the West. Third, this is one of the topics over the last two decades on which the US has pressed its allies to share more of the burden.

In this chapter I will argue that efforts to counter nuclear proliferation have been central to the transatlantic global security agenda since 1990. America has grown increasingly disillusioned by the apparent inability of the multilateral regime to prevent proliferation. In contrast, the EU has become increasingly focused upon the problem and has devoted its energies to buttressing the regime. I will use the examples of North Korea and Iran to explore the differing priorities of America and the EU towards these issues.

Threat perceptions

During the period of East–West confrontation, European states were used to living with nuclear vulnerability at the hands of the former Soviet Union. They relied upon the US extended nuclear guarantee to deter aggression and ensure their security. After the collapse of the Soviet Union, they did not see themselves as a likely target and therefore saw no reason to acquire such capabilities. EU states believed that the risk of overwhelming retaliation would deter new proliferants from the risk of using nuclear weapons against the West. This reflected, according to Schake (2000, 112), European negligence of the proliferation threat because Europe is actually more vulnerable than the US to ballistic missile attack from states such as Iran. EU countries have been more concerned with the risk to international order and stability from new states trying to acquire nuclear weapons. A policy towards non-proliferation was slow to emerge because the Union's security competences took time to evolve (Tetrais, 2006b, 38). Non-proliferation became a component of the CFSP but there remained a diversity of views amongst the member states towards the issue.

The prioritizing of non-proliferation by the US after the events of 9/11 has focused EU attention on the matter. The EU perceived the need to respond to America with a document published at the Thessaloniki Summit in December 2003, entitled 'EU Strategy against Proliferation of Weapons of Mass Destruction' (European Council, 2003c). This affirmed its commitment to strengthen the existing non-proliferation regime and encourage other states to sign up to the most stringent inspection mechanisms. In addition, the Union appointed a Personal Representative, Annalisa Gianella, to oversee non-proliferation policy.

Unlike many European states, the US has not been prepared to live with the risk of horizontal proliferation, especially by such states of concern as Iraq and Libya (Heisbourg, 2000b, 132). It has feared for the security of American territory and the potential threat to its troops deployed overseas or on expeditionary operations. It has also been concerned about regional allies, such as South Korea and Israel, that find themselves in parts of the world where proliferation is a real possibility. The US has focused its attention on capability rather than intention, having identified those states that show evidence of investing in weapons programmes. It has then pursued a range of strategies to dissuade countries from pursuing a nuclear weapons programme. In the words of one analyst, 'the United States ... has significantly different threat priorities and perceptions from many other countries, including its allies ... this is particularly so regarding WMD and their proliferation' (Valencia, 2005, 18).

The administration of George W. Bush was not the first to link the threat of nuclear proliferation to terrorist groups as this had been done under President Bill Clinton. In a speech at the UN in 1996, Clinton warned that rogue states, terrorism and WMD presented the foremost threats to international security (Clinton, 1996). However, the searing experience of 9/11 raised this issue to a new level of urgency. A nexus of threats was subsequently given overriding priority in US security planning: what has been described as 'the interweaving of terrorism, weapons of mass destruction, and failed and rogue states from Marrakesh to Bangladesh' (Asmus and Pollack, 2002). In 2004, 75 per cent of Americans polled regarded WMD as a key threat to America's security (Transatlantic Trends, 2004). American thinking on this matter helped to drive both foreign policy planning and internal security measures. US Secretary of Defense William Cohen argued that an attack upon the US homeland with WMD was not a case of 'if' but 'when'.

Many EU states have reacted with scepticism to this American assessment, thereby undermining transatlantic solidarity and a sense of shared risk (Fohrenbach, 2006, 52). According to European thinking, there was a possibility but not a likelihood that a terrorist organization would ever be able to attack an EU country with a nuclear weapon because of the difficulty in acquiring such a device.

The only opportunity for a substate group to gain access to a weapon would be through its provision from a state. It would make little sense for a state to provide a terrorist organization, over which it could exercise no control, with supremely powerful weapons (Muller, 2003). Such a country would fear that those weapons would be used against itself and it would be unable to discount the possibility of massive retaliation if a Western government ever discovered from where the weapons had originated.

A more likely scenario would be a terrorist group detonating a 'dirty bomb'. This would involve the acquisition of radiological material from a facility, such as a hospital or a research laboratory, and wrapping it around conventional explosives. Such a device would cause radioactive contamination and would be likely to generate panic on a wide scale. It would not, however, be anywhere near as destructive as a nuclear bomb. The Union also sees the use of biological and chemical weapons as a greater likelihood than nuclear weapons (European Council, 2003b). After all, these weapons have been developed and used by substate actors, such as the Aum Shinrikyo sect in Japan in 1995.

Nevertheless, the US response to this perceived threat focused on preventing weapons falling into the hands of extremists and the consideration of pre-emptive attacks against state proliferators. This stance marked a divergence with many European states – though not all of them. In the case of Iraq, the US alleged that that country's failure to comply with UN Security Council Resolutions to disarm, justified an American invasion. The administration sought to identify a linkage between the regime of Saddam Hussein and al-Qaeda, thereby raising fears that a terrorist organization could secure access to WMD. In the event, neither the Iraqi weapons programme nor the links to al-Qaeda ever materialized.

A strategy of denial

Multilateral regimes

The US and the EU have played a central role in developing the nuclear non-proliferation regime and upholding its principles. The US was the founder of the Non-Proliferation Treaty (NPT) in 1968 that provided the essential underpinning of the international norm against the spread of nuclear weapons. Two other treaties have been essential to the control of other forms of WMD: the 1972 Biological

Weapons Convention and the Chemical Weapons Convention of 1996.

The NPT was never a straightforward treaty. Rather, it represented an explicit bargain between nuclear weapon states (NWS) and non-nuclear weapon states (NNWS). Articles II and IV of the treaty promised the provision of civil technology to the NNWS in order that they might have access to electricity generated by nuclear power. This was to be made universally available on the condition that NNWS eschewed the pursuit of nuclear weapons. In return, the other side of the bargain was that the NWS committed themselves to Article VI, the pursuit of disarmament. Countries such as India regarded the treaty as inherently discriminatory because it created a two-tier system of nuclear 'haves' and 'have-nots'. The US, the UK and France have been subject to accusations of hypocrisy for not disarming as the treaty stipulated. Countries such as Israel never signed the treaty nor saw themselves as being bound by its provisions. Nevertheless, both the EU and the US worked together to renew the NPT and played a part in securing its indefinite extension in 1995. The principles of the NPT resonate with EU values: namely, a multilaterally negotiated treaty that constrains military competition between countries. The EU has worked consistently to promote universal adherence to the NPT and in the Review Conference in 2000 the EU helped to agree new measures relating to states that already possess nuclear weapons.

A further problem in the field of proliferation was the issue of dual use technologies. Many of the technologies relevant to the building and running of nuclear reactors for the purposes of civil technology could be subverted for military applications. For example, the enrichment of uranium could be used as part of a civil nuclear fuel cycle, but enrichment to higher levels provides fissile material for a nuclear bomb. Although it would be very hard to stop a determined state from conducting a clandestine programme, inspections by the International Atomic Energy Agency (IAEA) were designed to give supplier states the confidence that their technology was not being used for military purposes. The policy of signing 'safeguards' agreements, under Article III of the NPT, has been a mechanism for policing the treaty. Yet there has never been clarity on the penalties that would be imposed for contravening safeguards.

The EU has been active in trying to control the horizontal spread of dual-use technology. For example, in April 2004 EU members on the UN Security Council co-sponsored Resolution 1540 that was designed to develop domestic legislation to prevent the export of nuclear-related materials (Bosch and Ham, 2007). The Resolution was focused against non-state actors and is enforceable under the UN Charter's Chapter VII provision that relate to threats to international peace and security. The '1540 Committee' was created to police the agreement and monitor the level of international compliance.

The EU has endorsed measures taken within the Nuclear Suppliers Group (NSG) to restrict sensitive nuclear items that could be exported to countries or sold on to terrorist groups (Council of the European Union, 2004, 2). Although countries such as France and Germany have been amongst the leading suppliers of nuclear reactor technology, they have been mindful of their obligations to restrict the diffusion of sensitive technologies. To this end they have been active participants within the Australia Group and the Zangger Committee that restrict the sales of reactors to states not under IAEA safeguards. The EU also pushed for ratification of the 1997 Comprehensive Test Ban Treaty (CTBT) that was designed to make it harder for new states to join the nuclear club.

The Union has enacted a range of anti-proliferation measures in its wider international activities. For example, it has inserted clauses against proliferation into its trade agreements and, prior to concluding deals, it has expected countries to sign up to the NPT as well as the 2005 Additional Protocol on safeguards. As part of its enlargement process, the Union required CEECs to become parties to the NSG and the Australia Group (Alvarez-Verdugo, 2006, 428). In these ways the EU has demonstrated its determination to support and strengthen non-proliferation.

EU members have worked alongside the US in establishing the 2003 Proliferation Security Initiative (PSI) that interdicts shipments of suspected weapon cargoes at sea bound to or from states of concern such Iran, Syria and Libya (Valencia, 2005, 26). North Korea has been a particular target of the PSI because of its predilection to export sensitive military technologies overseas in order to gain foreign currency. The value of the PSI was demonstrated in October 2003 when a German registered ship en route to Libya was detained and searched (Allison, 2005, 223). On board were materials that would have assisted the Libyan government in efforts to construct a nuclear weapon. The exposure of this shipment was a significant factor, along with the effect of long-term sanctions, in pushing the government in Tripoli to renounce its proliferation programme. It resulted in sanctions against Libya being lifted and the destruction of the country's residual nuclear equipment under IAEA supervision (Denza, 2005, 295–6).

US disillusionment with multilateralism

There are divergences in US–EU attitudes towards non-proliferation. Whilst the EU remains committed to the principles of multilateralism, the US has appeared increasingly disillusioned by the return on its efforts (Interview, 2008a). Two pieces of evidence support this view of an American loss of faith. In July 2004, the US abandoned the goal of seeking a Fissile Material Cut-off Treaty. This was because they could no longer be confident that a cut-off would be verifiable (Quille, 2006, 52) and reversed a commitment it had made at the 1995 NPT Review Conference. The second piece of evidence was the lukewarm US approach to the 2005 Review Conference of the NPT. There were differences of emphasis towards the Conference amongst European states – reflecting the fact that the UK and France were in a different position because they possessed nuclear weapons – but there remained broad-based support overall for the NPT. In contrast, the US seemed to have arrived at the conclusion that it could no longer rely on the regime. In the words of Walker (2007, 439), it had decided that it would have to 'rely on its own power, give full rein to its innovative genius and not hesitate to exploit its superiority'. As a result of America's approach, the Review Conference failed to produce a concluding document and contained no coercive policies against proliferators.

The grounds for US disillusionment were threefold and substantive in nature. First, was the discovery of the A. Q. Khan network in Pakistan. It was revealed in 2003, that the foremost scientist in the Pakistani nuclear weapons programme, A. Q. Khan, had been selling nuclear materials and sophisticated information, clandestinely, to any country in the world (*Economist*, 2008e, 85). This information was thought to include centrifuge technology for the production of fissile material as well as warhead designs for ballistic missiles. Iran, North Korea and Libya were beneficiaries according to Western intelligence agencies (Bertram, 2008, 12). The implications of the Khan network for non-proliferation were devastating. Not only had a proliferant country become a source of nuclear know-how for some of the most dangerous states in the world, but it was actually a US ally and a leading state in the War on Terror.

The discovery that Pakistan was at the centre of a nuclear smuggling ring, with the possible complicity of elements of the Pakistani state and intelligence services, invoked a sense of crisis in American policymaking circles.

Second, was the explosion of a nuclear device by North Korea in 2006. The government in Pyongyang had conducted a secret enrichment programme that undermined confidence in verifying a country's adherence to IAEA safeguards. North Korea declared its intention to resume processing plutonium in 2002 and it withdrew from the NPT in January of the following year (Sur, 2006, 17). It was the first country ever to leave the non-proliferation regime, but there was little that either the US or the EU could do to stop the move. In the lead up to its first test, the North Koreans threatened to pull out of the six party talks that included South Korea, China, Russia and Japan and which had been convened to try and stop the nuclear ambitions of Pyongyang. North Korea had relented in September and agreed to a joint statement on the denuclearization of the Korean peninsula. The nuclear test exposed once more the duplicity of the government and narrowed further the options available to the West.

Not only did the North Korean test highlight concerns about its possession of weapon technology, it also raised fears about the likelihood that such knowledge would be sold overseas. The government in Pyongyang has proved willing to sell its technology and hardware. It has perfected ballistic missile technology: a three-stage rocket was fired over Japan in August 1998 (Niksch, 2002, 3). A subsequent generation of the missile, the Taepodong-2, was tested at the time of NATO's sixtieth anniversary summit in April 2009 (Bosworth, 2009, 1). The North Koreans have sold rocket technology to other countries such as Syria and Iran. It is not implausible that the government of Kim Jong-Il will sell its nuclear know-how in the same way, further undermining the non-proliferation regime.

Third, it has become clear that Iran is determined to develop all the elements of a nuclear fuel cycle. The regime in Tehran has stated many times that it does not seek a weapons capability. This seems hard to reconcile with the evidence, however. Iran possesses plentiful reserves of both oil and gas and there would not seem to be a strong justification for expending valuable resources on nuclear energy. Furthermore, aspects of its nuclear programme, including links with the A. Q. Khan network, and the extreme secrecy with which it has been carried out, have convinced analysts of Iranian subterfuge. It appears probable that Iran desires, at the least, a capacity to build nuclear weapons, if not the determination to acquire a nuclear stockpile. The EU and the Americans view such an eventuality as unacceptable. They believe that a nuclear armed Iran would trigger a proliferation crisis in the Middle East with countries such as Saudi Arabia, Egypt and Syria likely to follow suit (Specter with Bradish, 2006–07, 14). Israel has also made clear that it could not tolerate a nuclear-armed Iran, in light of the statements by Iranian President Ahmadinejad that he would like to see Israel erased from the map.

These factors convinced the administration of George W. Bush that treaties and multilateral agreements were of little value in the face of sustained efforts to acquire WMD. The US had been horrified at the end of the Cold War to find that Russia had possessed huge stockpiles of biological weapons in spite of its commitments under the Biological Weapons Convention. Now the same sort of events seemed to be taking place in nuclear non-proliferation. Washington came to the conclusion that legal agreements, freely entered into, would not be sufficient to protect US security interests. Instead the US would take whatever measures it deemed appropriate to ensure its security. Hence it refused to proceed to ratify the CTBT and subsequently (2002) announced its withdrawal from the 1972 Anti-Ballistic Missile Treaty (ABM). This is not to say that the US withdrew from all multilateral frameworks for controlling arms – America actually pushed for and obtained agreement on budgetary increase for the IAEA. But the Bush administration signalled that the US would no longer be the active sponsor of the non-proliferation regime.

The EU did not draw the same conclusions from these experiences as the US and interpreted Washington's policies as a further source of damage to the non-proliferation regime (Schmitt, 2005, 8). The Union has been eager to strengthen non-proliferation. They have proposed finding new ways to make nuclear fuel available to countries for peaceful purposes, aware that the demand for nuclear energy to supplant fossil fuels is likely to grow in the future. The challenge has been to reduce the risk of fissile material leaking out for clandestine use (Allin *et al.*, 2007, 56). The EU argued that multilateral approaches to non-proliferation must be preserved and reinforced. Through a negotiation process involving incentives, improved safeguards and the threat of punishments, the EU believes that the policies of recalcitrant states can be modified and they can be drawn into cooperative behaviour. It has sought to build upon its long-standing relations with aspirant countries to convince them of the dangers of seeking access to WMD. Thus the Union has come to regard itself as the upholder of a multilateral approach to non-proliferation, grounded on internationally negotiated treaties.

The 2010 NPT Review Conference was a crucial moment to bolster and reaffirm the cause of multilateral non-proliferation. Of particular importance at the Review Conference was the issue of the Middle East Resolution that had been agreed in 1995 and which called for the creation of a nuclear-free zone in the region. With the perceived failure of the 2005 meeting and the pressures that surrounded the issue of proliferation in Iraq and Iran, it was vital that progress be made on this issue if the NPT was not to be viewed as increasingly irrelevant. A text was agreed that called for the implementation of the goal of a nuclear free Middle East and censured Israel for standing in the way of this objective (*Economist*, 2010d, 74). It also underscored the importance of the IAEA, the need to tighten up export controls and called on the international community to enhance safeguards. Where there was Western disap-pointment was over the failure to name Iran for non-compliance, but it was clear that if this had gone ahead there would have been no Final Document produced by the meeting (Irish Chair, 2010).

The change in US attitudes towards nuclear non-proliferation was evidenced in the country's approach to both Pakistan and India. The US expressed outrage and called for sanctions against Pakistan and India after they conducted a series of nuclear weapon tests in 1998. But the American attitude towards Pakistan changed due to the War on Terror. The Bush administration judged that it needed the full support of the government of General Pervez Musharraf to fight international terrorism (Steinberg, 2003, 114). Pakistan had a vital role to play in the conflict against the Taliban in Afghanistan, in cracking down on domestic jihadists and deploying its armed forces in a costly counter-insurgency campaign in Waziristan. In spite of the fact that Musharraf had come to power in a coup and that his country had tested nuclear weapons against the expressed wishes of the US, Washington was prepared to rehabilitate him and provide him with significant levels of military aid. The needs of nuclear non-proliferation were sacrificed on the altar of America's other strategic interests.

A similar shift of American position was evident towards India. In 2005 Washington decided to improve relations with India and enhance its regional power position vis-à-vis China (Perkovich, 2005, 192). The US chose to alter the rules of the NSG by signing a Civil Nuclear Cooperation agreement with India, that assisted both its military and civil nuclear programmes. It was agreed that the US would accept India's nuclear status and ignore the fact that the country had achieved its position outside the NPT and the inspection regime of the IAEA. India faced no obstacles to the continued production of fissile material and no pressure to accede to a test ban treaty (*Economist*, 2006c, 65). This was condemned in Europe as an example of US proliferation concerns being subordinated to other political and economic priorities. The EU felt that the US was undermining the NPT regime by accepting the legitimacy of the Indian nuclear weapons programme and threatening the survival of the NSG (*Economist*, 2008g, 74).

The administration of Barack Obama has shown determination to restore America's commitment to multilateralism. In his Prague speech in April 2009, the President outlined a vision of a nuclear free world and committed his country to significant cuts in its strategic arsenal. He declared 'America's commitment to seek the peace and security of a world without nuclear weapons' (Finkelstein, 2009, 9) and he returned to the same subject in a speech to the United Nations Security Council in September 2009 (Philip, 2009b, 42). No longer is it just a group of retired defence secretaries and military officers speaking of their vision for a nuclear-free world. These initiatives were supported by a special summit in April 2010 on nuclear disarmament in Washington that witnessed Ukraine pledging to rid itself of highly enriched uranium (*Economist*, 2010b, 13). The administration proceeded to underpin these commitments in a New Strategic Arms Reduction Treaty (START) with Russia in the same month. The two sides have agreed to deep cuts in their offensive nuclear systems with warhead ceilings shrinking to 1,550 for each side (Woolf, 2010).

Dissuading proliferation by sanctions

A variety of instruments exist for the US and the EU to discourage the proliferation of WMD. Offering positive inducements is one option that tends to be overlooked. At the end of the Cold War, the US sought to transform its relationship of military competition with Russia through the Nunn–Lugar Cooperative Threat Reduction Programme (CTRP). Sponsored by senators Sam Nunn and Richard

Lugar, the programme involved America contributing some $10 billion over a ten-year period to help pay for the safe disposal of Soviet-era nuclear weapons and providing gainful employment for nuclear scientists (Nunn and Lellouche, 2005, 8). This was an attempt to address the risk of 'loose nukes' that might leak from the former Soviet arsenal and be sold on the black market.

Washington was critical that its European allies did not contribute to the CTRP, despite the fact that Russia is in Europe's backyard. Some authors have accorded Europe the benefit of the doubt by arguing that a transatlantic division of labour was achieved over Russia in which the EU complemented America's efforts by helping with its power stations and facilities under the Technical Assistance to the Commonwealth of Independent States funding programme (Mahncke *et al.*, 2004, 143). The US remained critical of the EU's contribution until June 2002 when the Union announced its participation in the Global Partnership against the Spread of Weapons of Mass Destruction, orchestrated as part of a Group of Eight initiative (Allison, 2005, 222). This will channel funds to continue the work of decommissioning nuclear arms from the Cold War era.

Russia could be argued to represent a special case in transatlantic non-proliferation policy. In relation to other states of concern, there has been a mix of incentives and threats of economic punishment. Whilst Europe and the US have broadly agreed on the goal of non-proliferation, they have often differed on the optimum means of achieving these objectives. The EU has argued consistently in favour of engaging countries in dialogue in the hope of influencing their policies. The assumption has been that moderate leaders within the target government will be encouraged, hardliners sidelined, and that more cooperative policies will ensue. The US has tended to argue for the isolation and containment of proliferants, responding to errant behaviour with measures such as sanctions.

North Korea has presented a complex set of problems, due not only to its clandestine weapons programme, but to its sale of missile technology. The isolated nature of the government of Kim Jong-Il has made it resistant to external influence. The US has led the efforts to contain Pyongyang's nuclear programme because of its troop presence in South Korea and its interest in the security of the Asia–Pacific region. In the first round of the crisis in 1993, the IAEA requested a 'special inspection' of North Korea's nuclear facilities – which was refused. The US pressed for sanctions through the UN and the North responded by warning that such a measure would be tantamount to a declaration of war (Litwak, 2002, 64). An 'Agreed Framework' was reached with Pyongyang in 1994 that stipulated the dismantlement of its existing nuclear facilities, the freezing of plutonium production and compliance with the IAEA. In return, the US and Japan agreed to provide two nuclear light-water reactors plus heavy fuel oil for the country's sclerotic economy.

The EU contributed ECU75 million to the Korean Peninsula Energy Development Organization (KEDO) and obtained a seat on its board (Philippart and Winand, 2001, 454). Nevertheless, the EU was clearly a junior partner to the US and felt that it had been co-opted merely to help pay for the deal. The US made little effort to include the EU in its thinking, whilst at the same time expecting support from Brussels. The Union made a subsequent attempt to act as an intermediary between North Korea and the US when, following a visit by the Swedish Prime Minister Goran Persson, it established diplomatic relations with Pyongyang in May 2001. The administration of George W. Bush appeared unsettled by this independent EU diplomacy and expressed its misgivings. In reality there was little that the EU could deliver to the North, other than humanitarian assistance, and its independent initiative quickly fizzled out.

The US proceeded to take the lead in negotiating with North Korea and diverged from the limited rapprochement that had been pursued by South Korea. America refused one-to-one negotiations with Pyongyang, despite the exhortations of European allies, fearing that this would accord the North Koreans a special status that was undeserved. Policymakers in Washington preferred to work through a six party framework that brought with it the influential presence of China and Russia. America found the regime unpredictable and duplicitous: in October 2002, Pyongyang confessed to a covert uranium enrichment programme at an installation at Yongbyon. This had been kept secret and was clearly incompatible with the obligations that had been entered into with the US.

The US imposed tighter sanctions on North Korea and ended the delivery of oil supplies. In spite of the pressure that was exerted upon Pyongyang it continued to play a game of cat and mouse with the international community, alternating between promises of compliance and dire threats of aggression. This strategy enabled it to sustain its weapons programme and proceed to test a bomb in 2006 (*Economist*, 2006a, 25–7). In February 2007 there was an agreement in the six party talks that North Korea would give up its weapons programme in return for substantial economic benefits. This deal envisaged a carefully orchestrated series of steps in which sanctions would be lifted and aid restored in return for the dismantling of the North's weapons programme. It was hoped that Chinese and Russian involvement would encourage Pyongyang to follow through on its commitments but the subsequent breakdown of the agreement signalled a return to the uncertain negotiation process.

The limited influence the Europeans were able to exert in relation to North Korea contrasts with the much more substantive part they have played in the case of Iran. Three countries – the UK, France and Germany (the 'E-3') – led the Western efforts towards negotiating with Iran. They were joined by the Union's High Representative, Javier Solana, and this enabled them to craft an EU stance towards Tehran. From 2003 they pressed Iran to abandon uranium enrichment, the *sine qua non* of US policy. They justified this on the grounds that the Russian nuclear reactor being constructed at Bushehr could only run on Russian fuel. The EU has seen Iran as the test case of its policy of constructive engagement, namely to incentivize a country to relinquish its aspiration to acquire WMD.

The EU's efforts were undertaken with the blessing of the US, even though Iran made it clear that it preferred to engage directly with Washington (Interview, 2008a). America was willing to see whether the EU could act as a bridge and deliver the prize of non-proliferation. The E-3 offered Iran a range of inducements in the hope of changing its policy through soft power. The regime was offered EU trade and investment and possible admission to the WTO (Kutchesfahani, 2006). A minor success was achieved when Tehran signed the 1997 Additional Protocol to the NPT, increasing the range of safeguards, as well as the Paris Agreement of November 2004 that committed the country to suspend uranium enrichment (Denza, 2005, 307; Katzman, 2008, 20). There have also been efforts around the idea of sending Iranian nuclear fuel outside the country for enrichment. Russia and France offered to facilitate such an arrangement but were rebuffed. In May 2010 Turkey and Brazil offered Iran a similar sort of deal by which it would send some of its low-enriched uranium abroad and would receive highly enriched fuel rods in return (*Economist*, 2010c, 67). It was hoped that the involvement of an Islamic country like Turkey would offer Iran reassurance as well as provide it with a face-saving formula vis-à-vis the West.

The election of President Ahmadinejad in June 2005 appeared to confirm that hardliners were in control of Iranian policy, and shortly afterwards the Paris Agreement broke down. The EU had been reluctant to find Iran in violation of the NPT as they were aware that this would trigger its referral to the UN Security Council and which could put it on a collision course with the US. But in 2007 the UK, with the support of President Sarkozy of France, recommended that Iran be referred to the Security Council on the grounds that there was little more that the EU could do to mediate in the situation (*Agence Presse*, 2007d). The UK's view was that China and Russia needed to bring pressure to bear upon Tehran and that only the US had the influence to obtain their support. China and Russia have both gained substantially from commercial links with Iran and have supplied military equipment to the regime.

The US had grown steadily more sceptical of the EU's approach to Iran and impatient with the lack of progress. Opposition groups within Iran revealed in 2002 the presence of two undeclared nuclear sites, a heavy-water reactor at Arak and a uranium enrichment facility at Natanz, both of which suggested a long-term plan to conceal the country's efforts. These were in contravention of the NPT and had probably been built with the assistance of knowledge acquired from the A.Q. Khan network in Pakistan (Cronin, 2008, 14). In 2006 Iran resumed its centrifuge enrichment, claiming that this was its sovereign right and denying that it had any intention of progressing to a weapons capability. Washington pressed for the second strand of the approach to be ratcheted up: tighter sanctions leading to referral to the UN Security Council.

Two UN resolutions mandating sanctions were debated in December 2006 and March 2007 (*Economist*, 2008i, 32). The EU floated the idea of the US lifting its sanctions and offering Tehran security guarantees (Wright, 2008, A12) but the US responded that it would only be prepared to talk to Iran once that country had suspended its uranium enrichment programme. The US wanted its allies to join in increasing sanctions and the EU has duly agreed to adopt measures exceeding in severity those mandated by the UN Security Council. In the absence of alternatives, the US needs EU members to exert pressure on Tehran through sanctions that withhold investment in its all-important petrochemical industry.

Upon his election President Barack Obama softened US policy towards the government in Tehran. He made an effort to be conciliatory and emphasized that Iran had to be treated with understanding and respect. But Obama has made clear that the US will not tolerate a nuclear-armed Iran because of the destabilizing effect that this would have on the Middle East. In his speech at Cairo University in June 2009 the President stated that Iran's possession of nuclear weapons could result in a regional arms race (*Guardian*, 2009, 1). The administration has carried forward the efforts of its predecessor to secure Russian and Chinese endorsement of tighter sanctions through the Security Council (*Economist*, 2009h, 28). These efforts were successful and in June 2010 China and Russia joined a Security Council majority of twelve in imposing a fourth round of sanctions on the Tehran regime.

Coercion and defence

The possibility of using coercion has always been an option to prevent nuclear proliferation. In 1993 the US Defence Counter-Proliferation Initiative (CPI) envisaged that a range of measures could be used to address the threat from new states acquiring WMD. These included efforts from destabilizing regimes through to the use of military force to destroy nuclear facilities. The CPI emerged from reflections on the first Gulf War where it was feared that US and coalition troops could have been subject to attack by Iraqi forces with unconventional weapons. After the bombings of US embassies in Africa, the Clinton administration ordered cruise missile strikes against a suspected chemical weapons facility in Sudan. President Clinton also authorized the funding of opposition groups in Iran in the hope of bringing about regime change there (Nasr and Takeyh, 2008, 86).

As part of the CPI, the US considered the use of force against North Korea in 1993, but ultimately discounted the option. It concluded that a military strike against its nuclear facilities would have resulted in devastating retaliation against South Korea and was not certain of success (Litwak, 1999, 214). The acquisition of nuclear weapons by the regime in Pyongyang reduces the likelihood of the use of force still further. It is worth pointing out, nevertheless, that military deterrence remains a part of US policy towards countries engaged in proliferation. After the sinking of a South Korean warship, the *Cheonan*, by a North Korean torpedo in Spring 2010, the US responded by a demonstration of its resolve to defend its ally militarily. The naval exercise Invincible Spirit, involving a US carrier battle group, provided a tangible warning to Kim Jong-Il of America's commitment to the region (Lloyd Parry, 2010, 26–7).

In the first term of the George W. Bush administration, the US was openly sceptical about the value of the non-proliferation regime. The appointment of the hardliner John Bolton, as Undersecretary of State for Non-Proliferation, was symptomatic of the more unilateral attitude towards the issue. Walker (2007, 445) contends that the NSS of 2002 signalled the relegation of containment and deterrence within the US approach and a 'rebalancing ... [towards] offence and defence'. If force was going to be used against proliferants, then it was the US that possessed the capabilities to carry this out. Whether it was large conventional forces for an invasion, or technologically sophisticated aircraft for a pinpoint strike on a nuclear facility, these capacities resided within the US military inventory.

This hardening of US policy prompted the EU to publish its own document, the 'Strategy against proliferation of WMD' (European Council, 2003c; Allin *et al.*, 2007, 53). This marked an attempt to narrow the differences between the US and the EU by agreeing that coercive measures under Chapter VII of the UN Charter could be employed in circumstances where diplomacy had failed (Grant, 2003; Ham, 2004, 6). It was evident that there were different priorities amongst the leading European states: France and the UK tended to share some of the US's concerns, whereas Germany was less willing to envisage the use of force. Nevertheless, there was consensus that the US would need to build the largest possible international constituency to support coercive action. In order to be legitimate, European countries argued that force had to treated as the very last option.

There was much speculation during the second Bush term of office that air strikes would be launched against Iranian nuclear installations. In Brussels, in February 2005, the President warned ominously that 'no option' was off the table (Bush, 2005). One theory was that the US would attack before a crucial tipping point in the Iranian nuclear programme was reached. With its army bogged down in Iraq at the time, air strikes seemed to offer America the potential to slow down Iran's nuclear ambitions. It was possible that the use of military force could destabilize the government in Tehran and lead to its downfall. The US made no secret of the fact that it would welcome a change of government in Iran (Tetrais, 2006a, 33). For their part, the EU were not looking to change the government in Tehran but to entice it back to a path that rejected the acquisition of WMD.

No-one was under any illusions that a recourse to armed conflict would resolve the situation. Many analysts were sceptical that air strikes could damage significantly Iran's dispersed nuclear facilities. Attacks would need to be executed on a large-scale and sustained over a period of time to be confident of degrading Iran's well-concealed and hardened nuclear facilities. Whilst they might disrupt and damage Iran's programme, attacks would be likely to aggravate its determination to achieve nuclear status and confirm its rationale for acquiring such capabilities. Iran's ability to retaliate should also not be under-estimated. It could harm the flow of oil exports through the Straits of Hormuz, it could help to radicalize opinion in the Muslim world against the West and it could encourage groups such as Hezbollah and Hamas to attack Israel.

European engagement with Iran after 2003 was driven partly by a desire to forestall the risk of US military action and partly to remain true to its own values. The EU feared that the use of force would be counter-productive and worried about the repercussions that would ensue. The EU called for the carefully calibrated escalation of pressure, arguing that a resort to armed conflict would spell the end of diplomacy. They insisted that their negotiated approach enabled Russian help to be enlisted to put the maximum pressure on the government in Tehran. Indeed in 2007 Russia called for Iran to submit all its facilities to IAEA safeguards and offered to reprocess its used fuel back in Russia (Arbatov, 2008, 69).

There was also a body of opinion within European countries that an Iranian regime armed with a small number of nuclear weapons would not present an intolerable threat (Bertram, 2008, 22). It was argued that Iran was not a state with a record of risk-taking: that there was no reason to suppose that it could not be deterred from the use of its weapons just like other nuclear armed states. Conversely, it was asserted that the threat and use of military action could have highly damaging consequences. Its threat could push states like Iran into acquiring WMD on the basis that only possession would deter a superpower attack. The use of military force could destabilize the already turbulent Middle East and engender an even deeper sense of grievance and alienation within Iran.

Yet the decisive factor preventing the US recourse to force against Iran, during the period of the Bush administration, came from an unexpected direction. In December 2007 a United States National Intelligence Estimate (NIE) report, based on the collective view of sixteen US intelligence agencies, stated that in 2003 Iran had stopped activities designed to lead to the production of a nuclear weapon (National Intelligence Estimate, 2007). The NIE expressed confidence that before this time Iran was working on a nuclear weapons programme and that it retained the capability to resume that programme at any time. However, it judged that Iran would be unable to produce highly enriched uranium of weapons grade until a period between 2010 and 2015 (Maddox, 2008, 42). This was something of a bombshell in both the US and Europe. It pulled the rug out from under hawks in the administration, such as Vice President Richard Cheney, who were arguing for the need to strike. It risked derailing UN efforts to put further pressure on Tehran because it appeared to confirm what Iranian leaders had been saying. It was a deliberate attempt by the intelligence agencies to emasculate a possible US military intervention and forestall the risk of their being called upon to provide the justification for a military operation. The US joined the negotiations in Geneva in July 2008 and the Bush administration entertained the possibility of 'talks about talks' with the government of Iran.

The issue has not left the international security agenda and there has been an impetus to keep the pressure on Tehran to reverse course. The discovery of a secret enrichment facility on a military site near the city of Qom provided further evidence that Iran is committed to a clandestine weapons programme, as did evidence that it was working on a trigger device for a nuclear weapon (Philip, 2009a, 1, 7). All such work is incompatible with Iran's commitments under the NPT. A further complicating factor has been the attitude of Israel, whose attack on Iraq's Osirak reactor in 1981 provided a historical precedent. Israel conducted a raid on an alleged Syrian nuclear facility in September 2007 and this was deemed to be an important signal of Tel Aviv's seriousness.

National missile defence

The US has been the only Western power with the resources and the political will to employ its own technological efforts to counteract the nuclear threat. Although deterrence by the threat of nuclear retaliation has underpinned Western policy since the 1950s, the US has developed a missile defence capability. It is too simple to ascribe this policy to US disillusionment with multilateral efforts to contain nuclear proliferation, although this has been one motivating factor.

The US has long been attracted by the potential of moving beyond a position of vulnerability to nuclear attack, to one in which it can defend its own territory and that of its allies. This thinking was demonstrated by President Nixon's development of a limited anti-ballistic missile system and President Reagan's authorization of funding for the 1983 Strategic Defense Initiative.

President Bill Clinton inherited a well-advanced programme on National Missile Defense (NMD) from the previous administration. Research was progressing into several variants: tactical missile defence to protect forces engaged in expeditionary missions; theatre missile defence to defend regional allies; and NMD to defend the US homeland. Clinton authorized the testing of various technologies under the 1999 National Missile Defense Act and appropriated $6.6 billion in that year for interceptor missiles and radars (Schake, 2000, 115). In the face of an unproven record, however, Clinton took no decision concerning deployment. He went on to argue that the ABM Treaty should be amended in order to allow for the development of a defence against a limited missile attack, knowing that this would have necessitated a renegotiation of the Treaty with the Russian government (*Economist*, 2000, 23).

During the Clinton period, there had been pressure building domestically to proceed to deployment of missile defences. A bipartisan body, the Commission to Assess the Ballistic Missile Threat to the United States, reported in 1998. Headed by Donald Rumsfeld the Commission foresaw that an aspiring nuclear state could acquire the means to strike the US with a nuclear or biological warhead within as little as five years. George W. Bush ran for election promising to deploy missile defences and when he entered the White House he duly authorized the citing of the first land-based interceptors in Alaska.

The US has always insisted that the sole rationale for NMD is to nullify the potential threat from states of concern acquiring nuclear weapons. North Korea and later Iran were argued to be the primary justifications. Yet EU countries have feared the implications that ballistic missile defences could have on relations with the People's Republic of China and the Russian Federation. Both countries, but especially China because of its small strategic nuclear forces, have regarded missile defences as aimed at them. It is possible to conceive of a scenario in which the US could initiate a pre-emptive attack and then could limit the retaliatory damage to itself through missile defence, thereby negating the deterrent power of its enemies. EU countries were wary of the counter-measures that China and Russia might take in the event of US deployment of NMD (Heisbourg, 2000b).

In addition, the EU was alarmed by the example that the US would set by a policy of unilateral steps to guarantee its own security – particularly when this necessitated abrogating the ABM treaty. Once the US was protected by a shield there were fears that different levels of security would exist between the Atlantic allies and that this might result in greater American unilateralism. Even France and the UK could be forgiven for reflecting on the implications for their own nuclear deterrents (Bowen, 2001). Despite the fact that Europe's geographical location renders it more vulnerable to attack from short-range missiles, there has been little appetite to expend the necessary resources on developing missile defence. Europe has been willing to suffer vulnerability rather than follow the US example. The differences over this issue between the US and the EU were sufficiently severe to cause concern on both sides of a deepening rift. Even the pro-American President Sarkozy was quoted as saying that NMD added little to security whilst complicating relations with other countries (*Economist*, 2008h, 48). The decision was taken in the latter period of the Bush administration to tone down European criticism of NMD because it was becoming publicly too divisive.

In 2005, the US opted to put its missile defence plans within a NATO framework that would enable defence guarantees to be offered to its allies. It chose to situate ten interceptor rockets in Poland and a radar in the Czech Republic. The Russian President Dmitri Medvedev responded to this American decision by threatening retaliation by the citing of Iskander missiles in the enclave of Kaliningrad (*Economist*, 2008f, 32). On 17 September 2009 President Barack Obama reversed course and decided not to situate the systems in the Czech Republic and Poland, choosing instead to develop the sea-based version of the Aegis system (Reid, 2009, 6). The decision was believed to be based on US desires to improve relations with Russia over strategic arms control and to elicit their support towards sanctions on Iran. Although this has reassured some EU governments who were eager to avoid antagonizing Russia, it has infuriated others in central Europe who interpreted the measure as the US backing down in the face of pressure from Moscow.

Conclusion

The non-proliferation agenda has proven to be dynamic over the last two decades, witnessing several states crossing the nuclear threshold and the uncovering of a black market in nuclear materials. These events have confirmed America's fears and justified its belief that proliferation presents one of its foremost security concerns. The US has grown sceptical about the ability of the current non-proliferation regime to constrain the process of nuclear diffusion and it has led it to resort to the exercise of its enormous military power. The US was unwilling to tolerate Iraq as a long-term nuclear threat and in relation to both North Korea and Iran it has entertained the possibility of using force. Yet the assertion of US unilateral policies served to undermine Europe's sense that transatlantic interests were coterminous. America's lack of commitment to the NPT, to a Fissile Material Cut-off Treaty and its abrogation of the ABM treaty showed it to be acting in pursuit of narrow national interests.

Attitudes amongst EU countries towards the issue of nuclear non-proliferation have evolved substantially. In the past, EU governments, not possessing the military capabilities of the US, have relied upon Washington to manage the issue of non-proliferation. EU states were willing to consider economic and political pressure on nuclear proliferants but have not accorded the issue the same priority as the US. The war against Iraq, the changing of US policy on non-proliferation and the emergence of new nuclear powers has caused the EU to devote more of its attention to the matter. There has been a growing sense of a common EU approach to non-proliferation (Tetrais, 2006b, 44–5), exemplified by its Strategy against Proliferation of Weapons of Mass Destruction. With the NPT serving as the only legally agreed framework for prohibiting the spread of nuclear weapons, the EU has been determined to reinforce the regime.

The EU and the US have long agreed upon the ends of nuclear non-proliferation whilst differing over the means. With some justification, the US has treated the EU as a junior partner in the past but the Union's greater involvement leads it to deserve a more equal relationship. The EU played an important role in bringing Libyan President Gaddafi's WMD programmes to an end through consistent pressure. It is also apparent that the complexity of trying to arrest Iran's nuclear programme would justify a more coordinated EU–US approach. Tetrais argues that the 'good cop, bad cop' approach that characterized transatlantic efforts over the last few years has given Tehran the opportunity to try to exploit divisions between the US and the EU (Tetrais, 2006a, 31).

There seems to be an opportunity for the EU and US to narrow their differences now that the administration of Barack Obama has signalled new priorities. Dedicating the US to a nuclear-free future, by multilateral means, has given hope to those who believe that America must show renewed leadership on nuclear matters. This approach is consistent with an emphasis on reasserting and reinforcing the goals of the NPT and tightening up the sale of dual-use materials. US and EU attitudes towards multilateralism in non-proliferation may now be moving towards a common set of assumptions.

Chapter 7

Transatlantic Homeland Security Cooperation

Introduction

Transatlantic cooperation in countering international terrorism has been illustrative of the new agenda of security issues. Although not strictly a new phenomenon, after the experience of 9/11 it became the dominant paradigm in Western security thinking. By its nature, terrorism presents a complex set of security challenges. It has global reach, rendering all states potential targets, and attacks can occur anywhere without warning. Terrorism is perpetrated by non-state actors, yet it may receive covert support from a state sponsor (see Chapter 5). It is a form of violence that is difficult to counter with the traditional instruments of state power, because terrorists melt into the civilian population and leave no target against which to retaliate.

America's strategic culture shaped its particular response to international terrorism after 9/11. Drawing upon a variety of strands in its historical experience – a belief in the right to bear arms; of terrorism as an overseas 'evil' that must be confronted; and of the need to mobilize the country's economic and material strength against its enemies – America reacted with a national security approach and declared itself to be at war (Rees and Aldrich, 2005, 905). The Pentagon was placed in the driving seat of overseas policy as the US mobilized its huge military capacity and justified the pre-emptive use of force against any country deemed to be sponsoring terrorism or providing sanctuary. This was based on the assumption that the acquisition of WMD by terrorist groups presented a catastrophic danger that could materialize in a very short space of time. The US would have insufficient warning time and therefore US policymakers believed that they had to be able to resort to force in advance of a threat materializing.

The US found its overwhelming military power to be a blunt

instrument in the War on Terror. Furthermore, its decision to initiate conflicts in Afghanistan and Iraq served to fuel the concept of a global jihad and provided both a recruiting motive and a proving ground for fighters wanting to take up arms against the West. The European response to 9/11 was different: they did not interpret terrorism as such an acute problem. They chose to treat terrorism primarily as criminality to deny it a sense of political legitimacy. They concentrated on combating the problem through intelligence, law enforcement and judicial mechanisms. The EU's High Representative Javier Solana famously contrasted Europe's position to that of America's by stating that 'Europe is not at war' (Frankel, 2004, A15). The EU avoided the employment of military forces: for example, under the ESDP, no substantial role against terrorism was accorded to the military. Even though the ESS named terrorism as its primary threat, the EU did not envisage a significant military response.

Even though the US has looked to its military establishment to play a leading role in its War on Terror, it would be a caricature of American policy to suggest that this has been its only instrument. Analysts have tended to exaggerate Washington's predisposition to use force and have neglected the extent to which it has drawn upon other instruments of national power (Pillar, 2001, 73). As noted by President George W. Bush soon after the 9/11 attacks, 'we will direct every resource at our command – every means of diplomacy, every tool of intelligence, every instrument of law enforcement, every financial influence … to the disruption and to the defeat of the global terror network' (quoted in Luck, 2004, 88). The US has actually been assiduous in using all means at its disposal as part of a comprehensive counter-terrorism strategy (United States National Security Strategy, 2002). In doing so, it has found it necessary to work with other countries in sharing intelligence, enhancing border controls and extraditing suspects. The external dimensions of internal security have become some of the most important areas of development and the US has fashioned its closest cooperation with its European allies.

This internal – or 'homeland' – security cooperation between the transatlantic allies has not been built entirely from scratch: it has been constructed on foundations that were laid during the 1990s to combat transnational organized crime and drug trafficking (Den Boer, 2003). During that time the administration of President Bill Clinton was energetic in promoting international law enforcement action and using its superpower status to encourage the extradition of fugitives and the stationing of its legal attachés and Drug Enforcement Administration officers in embassies around the world (Nadelmann and Andreas, 2006, 170). The US looked upon the EU as an important potential partner and the two sides worked together against common problems, such as cocaine trafficking from the Caribbean and people trafficking from central and eastern Europe. They also collaborated to establish the UN Convention against Transnational Organized Crime in 2000 (Winer, 2005, 107). The chief impediments to this type of activity in the 1990s was its innovative nature and the fact that it was only since the Maastricht Treaty that the Union had acquired competences in Justice and Home Affairs (JHA).

Nevertheless, homeland security cooperation between the US and the EU benefited from these earlier forays against transnational threats and now extends across the full range of counter-terrorism activities (Interview, 2008a). In this chapter I will argue that the US and the EU have demonstrated the capacity to move from the traditional sphere of foreign policy cooperation to working together on internal security matters such as legal assistance, airline security and the monitoring of financial flows. What has emerged has been a major area of activity that did not exist prior to 9/11. It was continued and insulated from the toxic disagreements that swirled across the Atlantic at the time of the war on Iraq. Whilst it has not prevented numerous tensions developing between the two sides over their approaches to counter-terrorism, it has demonstrated the adaptability of their security relationship, as they have found innovative ways of confronting shared problems. The transatlantic partners have recognized their interdependence and one of the leading figures in the first Bush administration, the Secretary for Homeland Security, Tom Ridge, in his final news conference, expressed regret that he had not sought closer cooperation with the EU sooner (Asmus, 2005, 98).

Contrasting threat perceptions

The two sides of the Atlantic have contrasting threat perceptions about terrorism based on different historical experiences. These involved radical left and anarchist organizations, such as the Red Brigades and Baader Meinhof in Italy and Germany, during the 1970s: secessionist movements, such as the Provisional Irish

Republican Army in the UK or the armed Basque nationalist group Euskadi Ta Askatasuna in Spain; and post-colonial movements, such as the Armed Islamic Group (GIA) that fought against France. The national character of these movements made it hard for European states to cooperate against terrorism. They were unable to agree over a common definition of the problem, and their courts often refused requests from neighbouring countries to extradite individuals charged with terrorism offences. Historical European struggles against terrorist groups resulted in all the same mistakes for which the US, in its contemporary War on Terror, has been criticized. These include its over-reliance upon the use of military force, the creation of special courts to try terrorist suspects and the imposition of internment without trial. EU states argue that experiences taught them the optimum means of countering terrorism and prevented the repeat of earlier errors.

In comparison, the US has not suffered from a significant domestic terrorist movement during its history. Apart from single-issue extremist groups resorting to sporadic violence, such as anti-abortionists or animal rights campaigners, there have been no sustained terrorist campaigns against the US government. Instead, terrorism has been largely an overseas phenomenon, visited upon America's military or diplomatic personnel or its interests abroad (Pillar, 2001, 57). The involvement of the US in global politics, especially in the Middle East, has led it to endure a number of murderous attacks upon its military and citizens: the loss of 241 US marines during the attack in 1983 on their base in Beirut, the destruction of Pan Am flight 103 over Lockerbie, the 1996 Khobar Towers attack in Saudi Arabia, and the 1998 bombings of US embassies in Kenya and Tanzania. It was not until 1993, however, that extremists planted a bomb under the World Trade Center, and a terrorist attack violated the assumed invulnerability of the US homeland.

The 1993 perpetrators of the World Trade Center bombing were believed by the US to be representatives of a form of political violence that was qualitatively different from that which had come before. Analysts like Bruce Hoffman identified a 'new' terrorism that was driven by novel motivations and methods (Hoffman, 1998; Simon and Benjamin, 2000). This phenomenon was religiously motivated and sought to avenge the oppression experienced by Muslims in conflicts such as within the Palestinian Occupied Territories, the Balkans, Kashmir and Chechnya. It was being conducted by jihadists who regarded it as their religious duty to wage a holy war against both secular Arab governments and Western influence. Martyrdom was the goal of these holy warriors. They appeared to be uninterested in violence as a form of political communication and sought instead to inflict the maximum number of casualties upon their enemies. They targeted fellow Muslims and those governments that had deviated from the path of Islam, as well as non-Muslims or 'infidels'. Thanks to training camps that had been set up in countries like Afghanistan and Pakistan, and financial support from wealthy donors in countries such as Saudi Arabia, these jihadists were capable of conducting attacks anywhere in the world.

Al-Qaeda was the foremost example of this new form of terrorism. Founded by Osama bin Laden and Ayman al-Zawahiri, it called for the re-establishment of a Muslim caliphate and preached the destruction of both authoritarian governments in the Arab world and the US that supported them. It railed particularly against the American military presence in Saudi Arabia that was seen to defile the holy sites of Mecca and Medina (Wright, 2006, 210). Al-Qaeda's success lay in its all-embracing ideology that allowed disparate groups around the world to unite under its banner. In an increasingly globalized world, the organization acted as a franchise that could be adapted to the needs of diverse groups. Even when most of the core al-Qaeda leaders have either been killed, arrested or dispersed, lip-service to its objectives is still paid by groups of individuals stretching from Indonesia and the Philippines to Algeria and Morocco (Errera, 2005).

The overriding concern that has driven US threat assessments has been the fear of catastrophic terrorism: that a terrorist group might gain access to a WMD. Without the constraint of trying to retain popular support, it is possible that an organization might find a way to procure a WMD and be prepared to use it. The detonation of even a crude improvised nuclear device would result in unimaginable casualty figures (Clarke and Beers, 2006, ch. 14). Vice President Richard Cheney enunciated the '1% doctrine' which argued that even a minimal risk of a catastrophic attack on the US must be considered unacceptable and would need to be acted against (quoted in Allin *et al.*, 2007, 38).

EU states have tended to dispute the 'newness' of the threat posed by Islamist groups (Copeland, 2001; Rees and Aldrich, 2005, 912). They have argued that this terrorism draws on past religious and economic grievances just like others and, as with all forms of violent protest, there are underlying political objectives. They have pointed to the fact that terrorists are using the same sorts of weapons and that there has not been a catastrophic attack. EU governments regard such an attack as unlikely and see a 'dirty bomb' as more probable (Vries, 2004b). Biological and chemical weapons, such as anthrax or ricin, are also feared, and many European countries have conducted exercises to test their abilities to respond to an attack (Nunn and Lellouche, 2005, 8; Kellman, 2007).

The Union has prioritized the threat it faces at home rather than abroad: it perceives the greatest threat to arise from within its own population (Dittrich, 2006; Shapiro and Byman, 2006, 34). The EU posits that 'diasporic radicalisation' amongst the 13 million Muslims in Europe is its foremost danger (Roy, 2003, 64). The July 2005 attacks in London, as well as foiled plots in Germany and the Netherlands, appear to bear out this thesis. These are particularly difficult threats to counter as they often involve individuals previously unknown to the security services (Errera, 2005, 77–9). They may be second or even third generation immigrants who become alienated and disaffected from their host society as a result of poor education, limited job prospects and an absence of social mobility. Members of the Pakistani community in the UK, Algerians in France, as well as refugees from various war torn countries have all been involved. Such immigrants are fertile ground for radicalization through propaganda on the Internet or preaching by extremist clerics. European governments judge that actions taken by the US in its War on Terror have served to inflame Muslim opinion and contributed to the radicalization process.

The US believed itself to be immune from this domestic radicalization problem. There was a belief that its own Muslim community was too affluent to present such a risk and that America's long experience with integrating immigrants into its 'melting pot' would preclude any danger (Interview, 2008f). Recent experience, however, has led US authorities to reconsider their vulnerability. The shootings by Major Nidal Malik Hassan that killed thirteen soldiers at Fort Hood, Texas, and the attempted car bomb attack in Times Square in New York by Faisal Shahzad have demonstrated how extremist violence can be perpetrated by both American Muslims and by legal immigrants.

EU states believe that the US has exaggerated the threat from terrorism and, as a result, has accorded it an undeserved status. From the perspective of most European governments, terrorism results in small-scale violence that aims to exert a powerful psychological impact. European critics of America argue that it has played into the hands of the jihadists by responding to their actions with force and declaring a state of war. The Europeans have not perceived this to be a useful organizing principle because it has created a sense of an endless conflict, a relentless struggle between religious communities. In the eyes of European governments it has risked confirming this in the minds of those who argue that a clash of civilizations has developed between the West and the Muslim world (Huntington, 1997).

The result of these contrasting US and EU threat perceptions has been a subtly different set of counter-terrorism responses. This has contributed to tensions within the transatlantic security relationship as it has been more difficult to agree on how to combat the problem. In the words of Shapiro and Byman (2006, 34), 'the United States and Europe disagree on ... the precise nature of the terrorist threat, the best methods for managing this threat, and the root causes of terrorism'.

Transatlantic internal security cooperation

The US response to 9/11 was to seek a revolution in its internal security provision. Unlike EU governments that have long tolerated a balance of risk, the US pursued a goal of risk avoidance (Stevenson, 2003, 79). It acknowledged that the protection of its own homeland security had been neglected in favour of addressing threats from overseas (National Commission on Terrorist Attacks, 2004). It undertook to redress this oversight with a speedy and energetic programme of security measures, including the overhauling of its intelligence services and the drafting of new legislation. America crafted an over-arching counter-terrorism strategy (United States National Strategy for Combating Terrorism, 2003) and embedded within it a plan for protecting the US mainland (United States National Strategy for Homeland Security, 2002).

The core idea behind the US approach was to engage the potential terrorist threat as far from its shores as possible and rely upon a series of layered defences. In the words of Bobbitt (2008a, 10), amidst a war on terror 'the aim is not the conquest of territory ... but the protection of civilians'. Law enforcement, intelligence, immigration and customs officers based overseas were its first line of defence, preventing dangerous individuals and goods embarking for America. Coastal protection, airline and border security were the next line of defence, preventing entry onto US soil. A third line of defence resided in domestic police and intelligence agencies as well as the private sector. A last line of defence would be the 'first responders' – fire, medical and federal authorities – that would arrive on the scene after a terrorist attack. The cornerstone of these efforts was the creation in November 2002 of a new agency responsible for internal security, the Department of Homeland Security (DHS). The DHS subsumed a variety of smaller agencies that had hitherto dealt with border security, immigration and coastal defence.

The EU response to 9/11 has been more multifaceted, reflecting both a lower threat perception and the more complex, multilevel relationship between the Union and its member states. Most of the operational counter-terrorism capabilities remain with national governments and they have been reluctant to cede sovereign powers to the EU. Thus practical cooperation in transatlantic counter-terrorism is conducted mainly bilaterally (Lebl, 2007, 5) and the US works particularly closely with countries such as the UK, France and Germany (Rees, 2009, 112). Whilst the EU's own legitimacy is enhanced by providing internal security for its citizens, it has needed to show where it can add value before being accorded a greater role. The heads of the member states placed the main responsibility for counter-terrorism efforts in the Union's Third Pillar activities in JHA (later Justice, Liberty and Security, JLS), rather than the Second Pillar of the CFSP (European Council, 2004, 31). Interior ministers lead responsibility in this area and involve foreign ministries where there are external dimensions to the issue (Keohane, 2005, 9).

Nevertheless, the steady drift of powers to the EU and the increasing number and roles of its internal security agencies attests to its growing importance. Amongst the agencies with explicit competences in counter-terrorism are the European Police Office (Europol), the European Judicial Cooperation Unit (Eurojust), the Police Chiefs' Operational Task Force (PCOTF) and the European Border Agency (Frontex). Many of these agencies have overlapping powers and jurisdictions that are founded on a mix of legal bases. The Union requires extensive coordination to be effective: this, and the fact that member states differ in the extent of the cooperation that they make available to Europol and Eurojust, have proved to be significant obstacles in their own right. The EU has no figure comparable to the US Secretary for Homeland Security but instead appointed in 2004 a counter-terrorism coordinator. A former Dutch interior minister, Gijs de Vries, was the first incumbent, but he possessed no budgetary authority, few staff and was dependent on the priority attached to counter-terrorism by the EU presidency of the day. His sense of frustration with the limitations of the role led him to resign and he was replaced by Gilles de Kerchove, a senior official from within the Council Secretariat.

As well as structures, the EU has developed a range of important policies. The Union arrived at a common definition of terrorism and agreed the European Arrest Warrant (EAW) of 2001–2. The EAW designates thirty-two offences, including terrorism, as punishable by at least three years imprisonment, and speeds up the extradition process between European states. In 2001 it launched an Action Plan with over 200 counter-terrorism measures. Following the Madrid and London bomb attacks in March 2004 and July 2005 respectively, the Action Plan was replaced by a more coherent Counter-Terrorism Strategy (Council of the European Union, 2005). In this Strategy, the EU focused on four priority areas: protecting citizens and critical infrastructure across Europe; disrupting terrorist networks; minimizing the damage from terrorist attacks; and preventing the radicalization of individuals (Nilsson, 2006, 75). It was envisaged that the EU could complement national counter-terrorism capacities, assist in developing new capabilities amongst member states, and help to stimulate international cooperation amongst the Union's allies.

The US has been exasperated by the time it has taken for EU policies to be agreed upon and then implemented (Interview, 2008d). It is accepted that all states have ratification processes that have to be respected, but the procrastination within the EU reflects the complexity of its decision-making processes and the fact that states vary in the priority they attach to terrorism. For example, some states have made little effort to translate EU-wide conventions into national law because they do not perceive themselves to be under immediate threat. There has been no simple split comprising America versus Europe: countries such as the UK, Spain and France tend to share American priorities towards terrorism. US frustration also centres on what it perceives to be the limited opportunity to influence EU decision-making (Interview, 2005). Yet similar complaints are heard in Brussels as Commission officials bemoan that the interagency battle in Washington leaves little room for external influence (Interview, 2004c). This is in some ways a more substantial criticism because the US has tended to be the driving force behind new counter-terrorism policies and the EU has found itself reacting to a US agenda that it has been unable to influence.

Law enforcement and judicial cooperation

Three policy areas have come to dominate the transatlantic internal security relationship: law enforcement and judicial activity; border cooperation; and data sharing. The first of these has required an important cultural change because police and internal security agencies have traditionally worked within their own national jurisdictions. Different types of legal systems (civil and common law) and nationally focused threat assessments meant that in the past there was relatively little police and judicial activity across national borders (Kirchner and Sperling, 2007, 128). In the context of contemporary transnational terrorism, internal security actors have been required to learn the habits of external cooperation and information sharing. The benefit for the US in its relationship with the EU is that it enjoys a single point of contact, rather than interacting with twenty-seven different European legal systems and legislative frameworks.

Institutional cooperation has been relatively straightforward to achieve. Legal attachés and attorneys were already resident in US embassies across Europe, dealing with crime and drug trafficking issues, and counter-terrorism merely added to their number. Innovation has been evident in placing representatives within the government structures of the other side – an FBI officer has been placed in Europol, while Europol has posted two of its officers to Washington DC (Interview, 2004b). An official from the DHS resides in the US Mission to the EU and an American liaison attorney attends weekly meetings of Eurojust (Interview, 2008e). This has facilitated more systematic communication between the two sides as well as a better understanding of the day-to-day problems each confronts.

Less straightforward has been stimulating cooperation in law enforcement and judicial policy. The US and the EU have found this to be a slow and incremental process that has touched upon core areas of sovereignty and confidence in the other sides' judicial systems. The issue of the death penalty in some US states was a significant problem, as the 1998 European Convention on Human Rights prohibited the extradition of an individual from a European country to face execution. It was circumvented by a political understanding provided by the US Department of Justice that they would not press for the ultimate penalty in extradition cases from Europe (Interview, 2004a). In return, the US has been concerned by what it has perceived to be the modest sentences handed down to convicted terrorists in European courts. In the case of the convicted Lockerbie bomber, Abdul Baset al-Megrahi, there was strenuous protest from US senators when he was released early on compassionate grounds. Attempts to smooth the transatlantic relationship achieved a significant milestone with the signing in June 2003 of a Mutual Legal Assistance Treaty between America and the EU, facilitating the sharing of evidence in judicial matters and speeding up the process of extradition.

The US and the EU have cooperated to target the financial lifeblood of terrorist activity. This has been viewed as one of the few areas of terrorist vulnerability, where clandestine activities become visible to national and international monitoring. In line with UNSCR 1373 (2001), both the US and the EU supported the creation of a Counter-Terrorism Committee comprising fifteen members to report on every country's efforts to freeze terrorist assets, prevent travel and share information (Millar and Rosand, 2006). Lists were drawn up under UNSCR 1373 of people and groups that were suspected of involvement in terrorist activities and their assets were frozen. This caused some transatlantic frictions over the designated groups – for instance, the Union resisted American efforts to treat the Lebanese organization Hezbollah in this way, due to its role in domestic politics (Butler, 2007). The EU enhanced its laws against money laundering (de Vries, 2004a), and through its Third Money Directive 2005/60/EC introduced the responsibility amongst financial and legal organizations to report on suspicious money transactions, requiring member states to have appropriate penalties in place.

Yet differing counter-terrorism priorities between the US and the EU have complicated the relationship. First, under a range of legislation including the 2001 PATRIOT Act, the 2004 Intelligence Reform and Terrorism Prevention Act and the 2007 Protect America Act, the US gave extensive new powers to its internal security agencies. These powers included the confidential use of informants and plea bargaining within trials, the confiscation of personal property and powers of intrusion into private bank accounts (United States National Strategy for Homeland Security, 2007, 6;

Schulhofer, 2005). America and Europe differ over electronic surveillance methods and the use of wiretap evidence. This presents a problem as some US material gathered through bank accounts or through electronic surveillance would be inadmissible in a European court (Best, 2001).

Second, the US dismantled the barrier between information gathered for law enforcement purposes and intelligence gathered under the 1978 Foreign Intelligence Surveillance Act. This led to thousands of intelligence files being opened to law enforcement officers with an eye to undertaking criminal prosecutions (Rees, 2006, 83). European countries, in contrast, have preserved the distinction between criminal information gathered for purposes of a trial and intelligence for national security purposes (Muller-Wille, 2008, 52). This has resulted in a divergence of operational cultures between the two sides of the Atlantic. EU states have been fearful of jeopardizing their own legal processes due to relying on material that has been derived from US intelligence sources.

Third, there has been an underlying difference in philosophy between the US and the EU towards the risk of terrorist attacks. American authorities have focused on disrupting terrorist plots at an early stage, through the use of intelligence information. The impact of 9/11 meant that US agencies have been unwilling to take any chances that plots could proceed to fruition and have been eager to intervene at the earliest opportunity. In contrast, some EU countries have been willing to monitor the actions of radicals in order to build up a complete picture of their activities. For example, in the UK and Germany, plots have been allowed to develop to quite an advanced stage before the perpetrators have been arrested, in order to construct the best possible case for prosecution.

Border security cooperation

The issue of border security has brought the two sides of the Atlantic together, albeit unexpectedly, because they are separated by thousands of miles of ocean. Both sides have recognized the vulnerability of their borders. The US has long and permeable land borders to the north and south, whilst the Union has created, through the 1990 Schengen Convention, a common external frontier and then borderless travel throughout the area of the member countries. The transatlantic allies have also come to recognize their interdependence. The EU has been mindful that any US security measures impact directly on its interests, due to the visa-waiver travel agreement for its citizens. America is vulnerable to individuals that are allowed to travel to the US under European regulations. After all, the 9/11 hijackers travelled to America legitimately from Europe. The outgoing Secretary for Homeland Security Michael Chertoff, in a speech in Ireland in January 2008, warned that the future terrorist threat to America would be likely to originate from Europe (Weaver, 2008).

As part of its efforts to enhance the security of its immigration arrangements the US required both national and foreign airlines to improve in-flight precautions against hijacking, through the provision of reinforced cockpit doors, greater oversight of baggage handling and the selective introduction of air marshals. As part of the United States Visitor and Immigrant Status Indicator Technology, the federal authorities requested biometric identifiers to accompany the presentation of travel documents. Visa-waiver countries were given sufficient time to develop a facial image and two fingerprints in travel documents that are compatible with those of the US, after initial concerns about EU states meeting the deadline (Koslowski, 2005, 98). O'Hanlon noted that 'until digitised passports with biometric indicators are widely used by qualifying countries, the visa waiver program will continue to constitute a substantial loophole in US border security' (O'Hanlon, 2006, 98: *Agence Presse*, 2007e).

The US has not only been concerned about passengers entering its territory but also the importation of goods. Approximately 10 million containers arrive in American ports or cross its land borders each year and it is feared that this could be used as a means to smuggle in a weapon – nuclear, radiological, biological or chemical in nature. The US and EU negotiated the Container Security Initiative (CSI) in April 2004 that facilitated the placing of American customs personnel in European ports. These personnel were given the task of monitoring transatlantic cargoes and providing twenty-four-hour advance warning of their contents prior to departure for the US. This was an important agreement as it amounted to voluntary restrictions on sovereign trade powers. The US government had approached individual European governments in 2002 but the European Commission had stepped in when it became clear that there were implications for the European single market. The US has built upon the CSI by designing a Customs–Trade Partnership against Terrorism (2001) that provides a role for private sector shipping companies (Clarke and Beers, 2006, 194). Firms with a proven record of maintaining security provide electronic manifests of containers in return for faster processing in US ports.

All of these measures have followed a similar pattern in which the EU has been forced to react to US initiatives. In some cases, such as US 'smart borders' policies, America has adopted measures with important extra-territorial dimensions (Pawlak, 2010, 139). This has reflected both the power of the US and its ability to act quickly, but it has led to important knock-on effects for its allies. In an attempt to address these issues, America and the EU agreed to establish a policy forum dedicated to internal security issues. The result was the creation of the High Level Policy Dialogue on Borders and Transport Security (PDBTS) in April 2004, involving representatives from the US Departments of State, Justice and Homeland Security with the EU Directorate General for Justice and Home Affairs and the European Commission. The PDBTS was designed to discuss ideas and forewarn the other side of plans before they ever reached the implementation stage. This would enable officials on the other side of the Atlantic to weigh the implications for them of a new policy and put anticipatory measures in place. It was an early attempt in the area of counter-terrorism cooperation to plan together for the future.

Data sharing

Intelligence and criminal data are amongst the most closely guarded secrets by states and the US maintains relationships of varying degrees of intimacy with individual European states. Some of these bilateral relationships are very close, such as with the UK, France and Germany, and these countries are reluctant to put their privileged interaction with the US at risk in order to share more widely. Alliance Base in Paris, an intelligence sharing centre, is illustrative of the way that some of the larger European countries have sought to build upon their special relationship with the world's leading power in intelligence matters (Aldrich, 2009, 130).

Nevertheless, the US has signalled its interest in developing a multilateral sharing relationship with the EU. Pooling information amongst the largest possible number of allies has become an essential element in effective counter-terrorism policy. One element of this has become a regular interchange between the US Department of Justice and Europol, based in the Hague. Europol is the common point of contact for the sharing of criminal data amongst all twenty-seven EU countries, although there are variations amongst European countries over the amounts of information that they share with the agency. Another element is the passing of intelligence between the US and the EU Joint Situation Centre (Sitcen), housed within the Council Secretariat. In the absence of a consensus about an EU intelligence body, Sitcen is the closest thing that the Union possesses to such an organization. It gathers information on both external and internal security issues (Keohane, 2008, 129) and draws on material from the Counter-Terrorism Group, an off-shoot of the long-standing Berne Group. It was expanded in 2005 to include seconded national intelligence officers from seven of the member states. Muller-Wille (2004) advocated expanding Sitcen and enhancing its significance by ensuring that it receives a greater proportion of intelligence derived from the member states.

The principal obstacle to the transatlantic sharing of data has been the appropriate level of individual privacy and the extent of the access granted. Many European governments, the European Commission and Parliament have expressed disquiet at US data protection standards and its absence of legislation. They have not been convinced of the adequacy of US safeguards over the retention of data to meet both stringent EU and national standards of privacy and have feared that information will be released throughout the US legal system. These concerns were evident in the agreements drawn up between Europol and the US Justice Department. An accord was signed to share strategic and technical information with the US in December 2001 but it was a full year later before a complementary arrangement was agreed to share personal data. Similarly, the Society for Worldwide Interbank Financial Telecommunications was criticized by the European Parliament for making financial banking records available to the US (Bilefsky, 2006, 3). The US has responded to European worries by arguing that its procedures are misunderstood and that it holds all information in a secure manner (Interview, 2008e).

The case of Passenger Name Records (PNR) was the most important example of a US–EU dispute over the handling of data. The American government, in its 2001 Aviation and Transport Act, stipulated that airlines flying to its territory would have to send details in advance of the passengers on board each aircraft. The US wanted as much data as possible from the thirty-nine categories of information that are held within the flight booking system of European airlines (Interview, 2008d). It was made clear to these companies that failure to comply would put at risk their landing rights at American airports. A PNR agreement was duly signed in May 2004 but a legal challenge was mounted by the European Parliament. This was based on the concern that private data would be shared too widely within the US judicial system and that it would be held for too long. According to the European Union Committee of the UK House of Lords, there was a fear that the US was engaged in 'data mining programmes to obtain computer-generated risk assessment scores which aim to identify passengers who may pose a risk' (House of Lords, 2007, 10). This legal challenge, through the European Court of Justice, overturned the agreement and forced the European Commission to negotiate a new agreement with the US in 2006 under Third Pillar arrangements (ibid., 22). Members of the Committee on Civil Liberties in the European Parliament were highly critical of the revised agreement with Washington, arguing that it was a capitulation to American pressure.

It is likely that technological advances will increase the amount of data available and add to pressures for transatlantic sharing. The US is interlinking its existing databases; for example, the DHS has joined its immigration system to the criminal database of the Federal Bureau of Investigation (Interview, 2008d). Certain US agencies have expressed a desire to develop new data mining systems that facilitate the exploitation of very large quantities of information (Jenkins, 2005, 137). This trend is reflected in the EU. Second generations of the Europol and Schengen Information System have been developed as well as efforts to improve interoperability between the Visa Information System and the fingerprint database Eurodac. The US has secured access to some of these new EU sources of information (*Agence Presse*, 2007d, 12) but it is less clear to what extent America is willing to reciprocate with European access to its own databases. American agencies are introducing new forms of security classification that render sharing with allies more difficult and the Europeans are wary of feeding information to American databases that they cannot use.

How these new opportunities for future data sharing are managed will go a long way towards deciding whether transatlantic counter-terrorism activity converges or diverges. After experiencing setbacks with the Europol agreement on personal data and the first PNR agreement, the US and EU have taken steps to negotiate broad principles to facilitate and structure their future cooperation. The

High Level Group on Data Protection was set up for this purpose and provided the framework for transatlantic discussions in 2008 on the sharing of data on European citizens (Kanter, 2008, 4). Its final report was submitted to the EU–US summit in 2008 (Council of the European Union, 2008). Such measures are indicative of a desire on the part of the US and the EU to think strategically about the long-term requirements of working together.

Balancing counter-terrorism with preserving civil liberties

Internal security has offered a new sphere in which the US and the EU have recognized their shared interests. Yet underlying differences in their approach to counter-terrorism – a war versus crime approach, at its most simplistic – has resulted in tensions between them. The administration of George W. Bush was strident in its view that it was at war against terror and that it was pursuing fundamental values such as the promotion of freedom and the preservation of democracy. These values were at the heart of the neoconservative vision of exporting democracy and enjoyed support from leading administration officials such as Paul Wolfowitz and John Bolton. The EU found itself in opposition to the US on these matters. Its view was that America's moral outrage towards terrorism was blinding Washington to its own catalogue of human rights violations. Such abuses were, according to the EU, in marked contrast with the lofty rhetoric of the administration. They were undermining the legitimacy of American actions and serving to fuel hatred of the West in the Muslim world.

EU states pointed to a variety of examples of American excesses. The sanctioning of forms of violent interrogation techniques by the Central Intelligence Agency (CIA) was one area of concern. The 'water-boarding', or simulated drowning, of individuals suspected of terrorist activities had been authorized by senior officials within the US government in order to gather the maximum amount of intelligence. The administration of President Barack Obama looked into the issue of pursuing former officials under President Bush who authorized and colluded in torture but found it to be difficult. The abuse of prisoners by US soldiers and civilian contractors at the Abu Ghraib prison caused a major stain on America's role in Iraq. Detainees had been subjected to sexual humiliation and the threat of extreme violence. Such activities demonstrated the risks in a system where individuals perceive that constraints and forms of accountability have been removed. The use of harsh techniques by US personnel contrasted with the tightly controlled culture of European intelligence agencies. Over the last two decades European agencies have been made increasingly accountable to elected officials, placed on a statutory footing and made subject to the European Convention on Human Rights.

The creation of the Guantanamo Bay and Bagram airbase detention facilities to house prisoners captured during American operations in Afghanistan and Iraq was another source of strain between the US and the EU. The Guantanamo Bay facility was deliberately situated on Cuba outside the jurisdiction of US courts and was designed to hold those 'unlawful combatants' who were deemed a risk to the US but against whom there was insufficient evidence to make a criminal case. EU governments found their nationals incarcerated in a US legal limbo and experienced difficulty in obtaining their release. Some European countries found themselves implicated in dubious American practices. For example, Binyam Mohammed, a British national, was moved by the US authorities, over a two-year period, between Pakistan, Morocco and Afghanistan, before he was sent to Guantanamo Bay. Binyam Mohammed claimed that he was tortured in these various locations and that British intelligence officers from MI5 were complicit in providing questions during his interrogation and benefiting from the intelligence that was extracted (Gibb, 2010, 6–7).

An additional factor undermining EU confidence in US policy resulted from revelations of 'extraordinary rendition'. The CIA had been secretly flying terror suspects to other countries so that they could be tortured in ways that were not permissible on US territory. Detention facilities were alleged in a number of third countries, including Syria, Jordan and Egypt as well as in central Europe. EU states expressed outrage that such flights had used their airspace and their airports for the transport of these individuals. The European Parliament supported an inquiry on behalf of the Council of Europe, led by Dick Marty, a Swiss Senator, to look into CIA secret flights. EU counter-terrorism coordinator Gijs de Vries warned that extraordinary rendition was undermining the effectiveness of Western efforts to combat terrorism (*Agence Presse*, 2007d). On the other hand, some European countries were less frank about the fact that they had colluded in these US activities and had accepted the intelligence that had been procured (Geyer, 2007, 145).

As well as discomfort with US domestic policies, there has been

European criticism of the countries with whom America has aligned itself. The desire to universalize the counter-terrorism agenda led policymakers in Washington to choose closer cooperation with authoritarian governments around the world that were willing to contribute to the War on Terror. The George W. Bush administration declared common cause with the Russian and Chinese governments, who both claimed to be fighting terrorism, but used the opportunity to act against internal opposition movements. America overlooked the military coup that had brought Pervez Musharraf to power in Pakistan because of its crucial geostrategic position in relation to Afghanistan and its willingness to confront Islamic extremism. Repressive regimes such as the Islam Karimov government in Uzbekistan were embraced in order to acquire the use of airfields to conduct the war against the Taliban. The EU pointed to the undemocratic nature of these governments and their records of human rights violations, arguing that temporary alliances of convenience could risk undermining the legitimacy of Western actions in the eyes of the world.

After President Bush's re-election in 2004 there was a reappraisal and a tempering of US strategy. This was based on an appreciation that many of its actions had been counter-productive and that the conflict in Iraq had gone badly wrong. The appointment of Condoleezza Rice as Secretary of State and the ultimate removal of Defense Secretary Donald Rumsfeld were important signals of a change of thinking. This was complemented by work that began in 2005 on a new Strategy against Violent Extremism to remove the impression that the US was waging a crusade against Muslims. There was a discernible attempt by the US to restore its tarnished legitimacy and the willingness of its allies to trust its policies. President Bush talked of beginning a 'new era of transatlantic unity' and mending fences with allies (Bush, 2005). However, considerable damage had already been done to EU confidence in American policy. Sir David Omand could still argue at this late stage in the War on Terror that there was no agreement 'on the fundamentals of the strategy to be followed ... and *the limits that should be placed on the means that are acceptable and justifiable*' (Omand, 2005, 110, my emphasis). The excesses of Guantanamo Bay, Abu Ghraib and extraordinary rendition had undermined belief in US adherence to the rule of law.

President Barack Obama signalled his desire to heal the divisions with Europe that had been created by his predecessor and has taken steps to address many of Europe's concerns. He ordered the cessation of torture and of extraordinary rendition and the closure of secret detention facilities abroad. He also announced the end of military tribunals to try terrorist suspects and his intention to close down Guantanamo Bay within a year (*Economist*, 2009d, 54). Jonathan Faull, Director in the Directorate General for JLS in the European Commission, expressed optimism that there would be a convergence of US and EU policy as the Obama administration shared Europe's commitment to the rule of law (*Guardian Unlimited*, 2009). In May 2010 the NSS assured the world that there would be no more attempts to spread democracy by force (United States National Security Strategy, 2010).

Yet even the Obama administration, untainted by the scandals of its predecessor, has found it hard to draw a line under the issues that sapped America's legitimacy. Closing Guantanamo Bay has proved to be more difficult than expected, due to a small number of detainees considered too dangerous to release. It was not until June 2009 that European foreign ministers reached an agreement to receive fifty of their nationals back from that detention facility (*Guardian Unlimited*, 2009). The assumptions implicit in US policy have not changed significantly under the new incumbent. The US is still fearful of a mass casualty attack and is worried that any relaxation in its guard could lead to disaster. Lastly, the President has found that he has limited room for manoeuvre in changing past policies. He is vulnerable to criticism from hawks, such as former Vice President Richard Cheney, that he could pursue policies that would compromise America's domestic security.

Conclusion

Homeland security cooperation is a powerful illustration of how the security agenda between the US and the EU has been changing. In the period since 9/11, when foreign policy issues have been a source of transatlantic tension, a new security relationship has grown behind the scenes. This relationship reflects the linkage between external and internal security and the sense of shared vulnerabilities within an interdependent world. It has demonstrated the resilience of the transatlantic bond and its capacity to adapt to new threats and circumstances.

There can be no doubting the fact that the cultivation of a new and innovative field of security cooperation has presented major

challenges. Fashioning cooperation on matters such as border security, the sharing of highly sensitive data and law enforcement has all
presented significant difficulties and necessitated finding creative
means of cooperation. The absence of a multilateral framework of
counter-terrorism practices has led the US to adopt unilateral solutions that have raised significant implications for European allies
(Pawlak, 2010, 143). It has brought together actors in governments
unused to working together in a manner that has been described by
Anne-Marie Slaughter as 'transgovernmentalism' (Slaughter, 2004).
It has exposed differences and contrasting priorities between the EU
and the US. The former has placed greater emphasis on legitimacy in
countering terrorism, believing that a crucial part of its strength lies
in preserving its values. The latter has been driven by a determination to address its new found vulnerabilities and prevent further,
potentially more destructive, attacks.

Nevertheless, both sides of the Atlantic have recognized the need
to work with the other. For the EU this has meant defining a strategy for the external dimension of its JLS policies. For the US, it has
involved cooperating both with individual states and with the EU as
a whole. 'Despite the EU's complexities ... while the US has many
links with individual member states in the JHA field, it sees considerable added value in the EU's ability to deliver cooperation with all
27 countries' (Faull and Soreca, 2008, 398). The US has been able to
arrive at a legal assistance treaty with the Union that delivers meaningful judicial cooperation, and it has been able to sign airline
passenger agreements that deliver information on people seeking to
set foot on American soil. The two sides must continue to work
together to enhance their police, judicial, intelligence, transport and
financial patterns of cooperation. This field of cooperation has
every prospect of growing more important in the future.

Conclusion

'The central question in the transatlantic relationship today is whether the US and Europe can ... coalesce around a new strategic purpose and paradigm to guide future cooperation across the Atlantic.'   (Asmus and Pollack, 2002)

Since the end of the Cold War, there have been two military security agendas in transatlantic relations. One security agenda has focused on Europe and has involved the adaptation of the roles of security organizations since 1990. The other security agenda has concerned the extent to which the EU and the US have cooperated in the face of growing global challenges such as states of concern, nuclear proliferation and international terrorism. It would be too simplistic to argue that strategic divergence has resulted from Europe concentrating on regional concerns and the US on global issues. Nevertheless, there have been marked tensions between the two sides of the Atlantic in their approach to extra-European security. These have included differences in both threat perception and in the instruments that each side employs. It has illustrated how perceptions of interests have led European states to varying levels of commitment when the threat they perceive is not existential.

The two security agendas reflect the underlying structural changes in the transatlantic security relationship. The US was prioritizing global concerns throughout the 1990s, as demonstrated by its actions towards North Korea and Iraq, whereas for the Europeans this became a more significant consideration after 9/11. Concomitantly, the US was turning away from and downgrading the importance it attached to European security. What has resulted over time has been a rebalancing, rather than a revolution, in the priorities of the two sides. Although the administration of George W. Bush has been portrayed as representing a dramatic change from the era of President Bill Clinton, it is more accurate to see it as the accentuation of post-Cold War trends. Core strategic interests have remained consistent in American foreign policy, regardless of who has occupied the White House. The unipolar hegemony of the US and the deepening of European integration were systematic factors that have remained consistent. President Barack Obama has continued with much of the strategic agenda of his predecessor, including the War on Terror, the conflict in Afghanistan and the focus on Iran. Despite his popularity in Europe, the continuities in President Obama's foreign relations have resulted in disappointed hopes.

For purposes of analytical clarity in this book, these two security agendas have been discussed separately, but in reality they have been interwoven. Europe has assumed growing responsibility for its own security, as demonstrated by EU troops policing the Balkans and the EU enlargement process projecting stability into its neighbourhood. As Keukeleire and MacNaughton (2008, 16) have argued, the post-Cold War order provided more opportunities for the EU's civilian power to be exercised, but at the same time required it to create a military capability of its own. EU states have welcomed a residual security role for the US and have regarded it as an important insurance policy in the event of a significant conflict. The US has wanted to preserve the benefits of leading NATO and was prepared to intervene in Bosnia and Kosovo when it thought that the Alliance was at risk.

European security has been less central to the transatlantic relationship, and provided less of the glue keeping the sides together, but it has not been unimportant. The US has appreciated that there remain security issues to be addressed on the continent. These include the future orientation of countries such as Ukraine and states in the Caucasus: not least because of their proximity to Russia and their potential energy resources. The US needs to encourage the Union to embrace the next stages of its enlargement process and reach out to states like Turkey and to those with an accession perspective in the western Balkans.

This leaves the issue of the new security agenda in relation to global challenges; and here the picture is more uncertain. Whether the EU can be described as a truly global actor in the first place excites considerable debate. It is a major actor in terms of its spending on aid and international development, as well as trade and regulatory policy. Its own assessment of the ESS reports that 'we have worked to build human security, by reducing poverty and inequality, promoting good governance and human rights, assisting development, and addressing the root causes of conflict' (European Council, 2008, 2). Yet the EU obtains relatively little credit for the 'soft power' it exerts around the world. It enjoys influence with individual countries and organizations, but in geopolitical terms its power is limited. This is exemplified by the resources it has expended on the Middle East peace process but the marginal influence that it wields.

Part of the reason for this lack of influence is because the Union is perceived to be unable to project its personality. Due to its difficulties in achieving an internal consensus, the EU has lacked a leadership role in global security. Its members exhibit a predisposition to pursue separate interests and a reluctance to let the EU represent them. They do not agree about the role military power should play outside of Europe and the Union's strategic culture is under-developed. Those countries eager to see it wield more influence argue that closer integration, the greater use of majority voting and the enhancement of the powers of the European Commission are prerequisites for the EU to be able to speak and act with more purpose.

The fears of the early post-Cold War period that the EU would become the rival of the US have not been borne out by experience. Rather, the US has consolidated its position and it has appeared unchallengeable by Europe. The EU's potential as a 'competitor' of the US has been limited. According to Kupchan: 'the main threat to the Atlantic link stems from too little Europe, *not too much*' (Kupchan, 2001, 4, my emphasis).

EU states, eager to curry favour in Washington, have often waited to see how America will react before adopting a position of their own (Espinosa, 2005, 45). At other times, when the EU has failed to come up with policies of its own or adequate resources, it has contented itself with playing the role of America's critic (Kissinger and Summers, 2004, 13). It has offered Washington the benefit of its opinion without making a contribution of its own. This has led to American accusations of European free-riding and a failure to burden-share. It is possible to envisage growing tensions between the US and EU if the perception remains that Europe does too little for itself.

In light of these doubts it is pertinent to ask whether global security issues are likely to promote the convergence of US–EU interests or actually to drive the two sides farther apart. On the basis of recent experience, extra-European security challenges have frequently been the cause of rifts and obstacles within the relationship. Even though the two sides have agreed on broad objectives, they disagreed on how to achieve them – extra-territorial-sanctions policy towards states like Libya and Cuba have exemplified this problem. It has also been possible to discern occasions when the US has sacrificed European interests on the altar of global security priorities. The neglect of European views during the Afghan and Iraqi conflicts was a glaring example, but more recently the Obama administration showed itself willing to cancel its deployment of missile defences in central Europe in order to engage Russia on arms control and imposing sanctions on Iran.

Dissatisfaction on the part of each side of the Atlantic with the other has been exacerbated by the gulf in military capabilities. 'Washington is accustomed to an EU that talks above its weight while punching below it' (Howorth, 2007, 177). The US may become increasingly aggrieved that they themselves provide by far the largest share of the defence burden. One solution that has been mooted is for Europe to focus its efforts on the defence of the continent and leave global security to the US. This would enable each side to play to its strengths and would limit the points of friction between them. Seasoned commentators of the transatlantic relationship, however, warn against such a simplistic division of labour. Hamilton (2003, 544) has cautioned that it would exonerate the Europeans of responsibility, render them dependent on US wider policy and leave Washington bearing most of the risks.

Dwelling on EU frailties, however, can neglect some of the potential strengths it brings to its relationship with America. The EU is only weak in relation to the US, not in absolute terms. Whilst it is true that only a few Union members can muster large-scale forces to fight on a high intensity battlefield, the EU can make other sorts of contributions. It is already taking responsibility for providing peace and security in areas adjacent to west and central Europe and through its enlargement process it is extending stability. The EU can provide considerable expertise and resources in terms of civilian crisis management and post-conflict reconstruction. Its members have valuable experience in conducting policing, border, rule of law and security sector reform missions. These strengths have come to be recognized by the US. Secretary of State Condoleezza Rice (2008, 3) acknowledged them to be a part of US national interests and Secretary of Defense Robert Gates (2010) talked of the importance of the EU and its 'civilian capabilities'.

The EU is also a promoter of security norms and plays a significant role in promulgating and sustaining regimes, such as in the field of arms sales and landmines. The Union itself serves as a role model for a form of global governance constructed around political and economic integration, peaceful negotiation and the transcendence of power politics. In the words of Nicolaidis (2006, 100), the Union's global influence 'lies in its power of attraction more than its projection of power ... it can serve as an inspiration ... as a pioneer'.

Much depends on the predisposition of the US to work with its allies and the framework it uses to operationalize such activity. The US enjoys the luxury of being able to choose whether to work with other countries through established organizational relationships, such as the EU or NATO, through temporary coalitions of states or on a bilateral basis. A similar choice confronts individual European states: whether to invest effort in working through the EU or whether to construct ad hoc coalitions. In recent years Washington has not prioritized working with allies because it has confronted relatively small and unsophisticated military adversaries. The US has regarded permanent alliance relationships as encumbrances that complicate rather than assist its defeat of an opponent. It has wanted to define the threat to its own interests and take the action it has judged to be necessary, without having to compromise with the views of its allies. European states have been unwilling to follow US prescriptions and have wanted a say in interpreting those threats.

In the past, the US exercised its power in ways that served as a source of attraction to others. In the words of Ikenberry (2004, 14), 'American leaders ... realised that to legitimate American power was to turn coercion and domination into authority and consent.' After 2001 the US forgot those precepts and consequently paid a high price for its determination to define the threats and assemble coalitions of countries willing to follow its lead. By demonstrating a proclivity to pursue its own interests, without consideration to those of others, American unilateralism led to a loss of legitimacy (Albright, 2008). America was viewed as undermining the international order by its actions and it suffered condemnation. Only in concert with allies will America possess the legitimacy to act in the wider world (Korski and Gowan, 2009, 24). It is in Europe that the US can find the sort of allies that broadly share its values and are prepared to work alongside it in multilateral frameworks. By joining together they can form the core of coalitions of countries to address security problems. In the words of the former High Representative for the CFSP, 'when the EU and the US work together, they are an engine for positive change in the world' (Solana, 2001).

No one disputes the asymmetries in the relationship and the fact that the EU needs the US more than vice versa. It is the US that leads in global issues and, if it does not, the EU will not fill the vacuum. William Wallace (2001, 20) expressed doubts over whether the US is willing to share leadership with the EU in political and military matters. Steinberg (2003, 115) discussed such a prospect and called it an 'elective partnership': he contended that neither the US nor the EU are compelled to cooperate together by existential threats, but rather choose to do so based on the identification of mutual interests. The extent to which a partnership can be realized will depend both on the EU's capacity to act and the willingness of Washington to treat it as an equal.

Embracing the idea of a partnership will require changes by both sides. First, the US needs to change its attitude towards the EU and resist treating it like a junior lieutenant. This would mean engaging in meaningful consultation about the types of operations they might undertake in different parts of the world and their division of tasks. Instead of expecting the EU to provide the economic reconstruction effort after a US intervention, there would need to be consensus about the need for action in the first place. In return, the EU should focus on a global agenda of security issues in a way that it does not do at present.

Second, the EU would have to be prepared to make more than a token contribution to the full range of potential security tasks, including war-fighting. Developing capabilities beyond the important area of post-conflict reconstruction would require wiser spending on defence, ceasing the duplication of defence resources amongst countries and concentration on efforts to make forces interoperable with the US. The EU needs to develop a rationalized defence market that produces equipment efficiently, standardized amongst the members, even though this may mean compromises over some specifications. Furthermore, the Union would have to revisit the Berlin Plus arrangements so as to ensure that it could contribute to operations alongside the US and be less dependent on the provision of American assets. All of this will have to occur against a backcloth of relative financial austerity. Defence will not be exempt from the squeeze on the budgets of public spending programmes and hence more will have to be achieved with less resources.

My argument is that the security challenges confronting the US and the EU are multifaceted and require a mixture of military and civilian capabilities. Such complex challenges are driving the two sides of the Atlantic towards increased cooperation. The US has found to its cost that the threats it faces are not susceptible to resolution by the application of its overwhelming coercive strength. American military might has offered limited traction in trying to contain states of concern and has struggled to counter the Sunni insurgency in Iraq and the Taliban in Afghanistan. Even America's enormous military strength has been liable to overstretch when confronting a myriad range of threats. It has discovered to its cost that it must enlist the help of allies, particularly when it attempts the complex task of nation-building and reconstruction.

This is not to say that US 'hard power' has become irrelevant. There are still scenarios in which its preponderance is vital, such as in deterring (and if necessary conducting) interstate wars. But the evolving security challenges have resulted in interdependence and necessitate countries finding new ways of working together (Rubin, 2008, 102). Preventing nuclear proliferation in the case of Iran has required the US to convince a host of countries, including Russia and China, to impose economic sanctions. Even terrorism is not something that can be addressed comprehensively by hard power. Ensuring the integrity of EU territory and the US homeland from terrorist attack, for example, depends upon measures that are taken by both sides. A closely interconnected world requires the US and the EU to cooperate in order to counter threats from both state and substate actors.

For the Union, with its relatively modest capabilities, acknowledging interdependence has not been too difficult. The ESS pointed out that contemporary security threats required international cooperation and that no country could cope with the problems alone (European Council, 2003b, 12). For the US, however, as a state that sees itself as sustaining the international security order, this is a harder prospect. Accepting that both new security threats and its own changing strategic needs have increased America's connectedness with the EU will not come easily (Asmus, 2006, 28). However, the long term security challenges posed by non-state actors such as al-Qaeda point in this direction. By accepting that the transatlantic relationship needs to change to take account of this interdependence may help to answer the question posed by the US Secretary of Defense, Robert Gates, at the 2007 Munich Security Conference. He asked 'how a partnership originally formed to defend fixed borders should adapt to an era of unconventional and global threats' (quoted in Brimmer, 2007, 13).

The two sides of the Atlantic need to think about how they can best combine their respective threat perceptions and strategic policies (Everts, 2001, 14). The US has tended to concentrate on military problems that are amenable to technical solutions, whilst Europe has tended to devote its energies to sustaining the broadest possible dialogue with other countries. Both the US and the EU will need to reflect on whether security regimes, such as that governing nuclear non-proliferation, need to be overhauled and whether the NPT should remain the backbone of that system. Similarly, both sides will have to consider whether a new regime, such as in the field of international counter-terrorism cooperation, needs to be constructed. If they fail to undertake such fundamental policy thinking, the risk is that they may diverge in their priorities.

The US and the EU must enter into a more sustained and systematic dialogue on security matters. They need to cultivate an understanding of each other's point of view (Daalder and Goldgeier, 2001, 72) and be capable of influencing it before their respective positions have hardened. The ad hoc frameworks that have characterized approaches to dealing with issues, such as nuclear proliferation, need to be replaced by more permanent arrangements. In order to achieve this they must develop an institutional dialogue that goes beyond the NTA. Such a framework must be capable of ranging seamlessly across both European and global security issues. It should accommodate concerns that are currently discussed bilaterally, as well as within the US–EU relationship (Balladur, 2008). It must be complemented by a much more open relationship between the EU and NATO.

This is not to presume that the two sides of the Atlantic will always overcome their differences, as such an assumption would be naïve. The EU and the US will have different perspectives on some issues and no amount of dialogue will make it possible to draw them into alignment. On the Middle East, for example, they are likely to hold contrasting opinions and sympathies. Yet, it is not too much to hope that consultation will help to narrow the divide and prevent disagreement from one area spilling over into a general malaise in transatlantic relations. 'They must learn how to disagree more agreeably', in that they must find ways to take different positions without opposing each other (Kupchan, 2008, 126).

There is evidence of change in US attitudes. In spite of having few links to Europe prior to becoming President, Barack Obama has signalled his desire to work to restore America's relationship with

Europe. Even a benign hegemon needs to have friends and to lead a group of like-minded countries. He has recognized that America's power is not limitless and that transatlantic institutions are an important element in America's strength. In the words of Secretary of State Hillary Clinton (2009, 5), 'we have started by reinvigorating our bedrock alliances ... in Europe, that means improved bilateral relations [and] ... a more productive partnership with the European Union'. By doing so, the administration has demonstrated its determination to restore a more consensual US leadership. Obama has engaged with European leaders and shown a willingness to listen and to try to convince other leaders to follow America's example. The coming years in transatlantic security relations will reveal whether the two sides can consolidate this process of convergence.

In the short to medium term Afghanistan will prove to be the test case. Even though it is not strictly a US–EU issue, it is the largest NATO military operation, and as such will have important ramifications for all aspects of the transatlantic security relationship. An optimistic scenario is that Western forces will be able to contain the insurgency and gradually hand over security functions to the Afghan army and police. This would facilitate withdrawal in relatively good order, with a functioning government in Kabul able to impose its will on the rest of the country. A pessimistic scenario involves the haemorrhaging of European military forces from the country – the Netherlands left in August 2010 – and the narrowing of support for the US. The result could engender a sense of panic and the transfer of the situation to an Afghan government on the brink of collapse, with the subsequent return of the Taliban to power. Whilst the former scenario would accord the US and its European allies a sense of achievement on which they can build, the latter would lead to mutual recriminations. It would make it harder for the EU and the US to cooperate together in future conflicts.

The experiences of fighting bitter and costly insurgencies in Iraq and Afghanistan may deter the US from the conduct of future expeditionary operations. America will approach nation-building tasks with extreme caution and may be reluctant to act at all. Rather than actually intervene on the ground, the US may use its long-range military power to strike at targets that it deems to be a threat to its interests without taking the risk of placing its personnel on the ground. This may be a change in tactics that results from recent chastening experiences. What is more important in the long run is that the US continues to perform its role in supporting the global security order.

No other country is in the position of being able to supplant the vital part played by America in international security.

The transatlantic security agenda is in a constant state of evolution. The range of issues changes over time and new security challenges, such as cyber security, environmental degradation, access to energy and pandemic diseases, are likely to preoccupy attention in the future. The rise of international terrorism has demonstrated how a relatively peripheral issue can suddenly come to dominate the international agenda. The task for the EU and the US is to preserve the vitality and trust within their relationship that will enable them to adapt to new demands. Failure to do so will allow security threats to grow and nullify the ability of the US and EU to tackle them. It will also limit the ability of the transatlantic allies to demonstrate the leadership in security matters that the rest of the world has come to expect.

Bibliography

Books

Albright, M. (2008) *Memo to the President Elect*, HarperCollins, New York.

Alcaro, R. (ed.) (2008) *Re-launching the Transatlantic Security Relationship*, Instituto Affari Internazionali, Rome.

Anderson, J., Ikenberry, J. and Risse, T. (eds) (2008) *The End of the West? Crisis and Change in the Atlantic Order*, Cornell University Press, Ithaca and London.

Andrews, D. (ed.) (2005) *The Atlantic Alliance Under Stress: US-European Relations after Iraq*, Cambridge University Press, Cambridge.

Ash, T. G. (2005) *Free World: America, Europe and the Surprising Future of the West*, Vintage Books, New York.

Ashdown, P. (2007) *Swords and Ploughshares. Bringing Peace to the 21st Century*, Weidenfeld & Nicolson, London.

Bartlett, C. (1992) *'The Special Relationship': A Political History of Anglo-American Relations Since 1945*, Longman, London.

Baylis, J. and Roper, J. (eds) (2006) *The United States and Europe. Beyond the Neo-Conservative Divide?* Routledge, London.

Biscop, S. (2005) *The European Security Strategy: A Global Agenda for Positive Power*, Ashgate, Aldershot.

Biscop, S. and Lembke, J. (eds) (2008) *EU Enlargement and the Transatlantic Alliance: A Security Relationship in Flux*, Lynne Rienner, Boulder.

Bobbitt, P. (2008b) *Terror and Consent: The Wars for the Twenty-First Century*, A. Knopf, New York.

Bosch, O. and Ham, P. van (eds) (2007) *Global Non-Proliferation and Counter-Terrorism: The Impact of UNSCR 1540*, Royal Institute for International Affairs, London.

Bowker, M. and Williams, P. (1988) *Superpower Détente: A Reappraisal*, Sage, London.

Brimmer, E. (ed.) (2006) *Transforming Homeland Security: US and European Approaches*, John Hopkins University, Washington, DC.

Brzezinski, Z. (2007) *Second Chance*, Basic Books, New York.

Byman, D. (2005) *Deadly Connections: States that Sponsor Terrorism*, Cambridge University Press, Cambridge.

Calleo, D. (1987) *Beyond American Hegemony: The Future of the Western Alliance*, Basic Books, New York.

Chandrasekaran, R. (2006) *Imperial Life in the Emerald City: Inside Iraq's Green Zone*, Vintage, New York.

Chomsky, N. (1994) *World Orders, Old and New*, Columbia University Press, New York.

Clark, I. (2001) *Post-Cold War Order*, Oxford University Press, Oxford.

Clark, W. (2001) *Waging Modern War*, Public Affairs, New York.

Cooper, R. (2003) *The Breaking of Nations: Order and Chaos in the Twenty-First Century*, Atlantic Books, London.

Cottey, A. (2007) *Security in the New Europe*, Palgrave Macmillan, Basingstoke.

Croci, O. and Verdun, A. (eds) (2006) *The Transatlantic Divide: Foreign and Security Policies in the Atlantic Alliance from Kosovo to Iraq*, Manchester University Press, Manchester.

Croft, S., Redmond, J., Rees, W. and Webber, M. (1999) *The Enlargement of Europe*, Manchester University Press, Manchester.

Cronin, P. (ed.) (2008) *Double Trouble. Iran and North Korea as Challenges to International Security*, Praeger Security International, Westport, Connecticut.

Daalder, I., Gnesotto, N. and Gordon, P. (eds) (2006) *Crescent of Crisis: US–European Strategy for the Greater Middle East*, Brookings Institution Press, Washington, DC.

Daalder, I. and Lindsay, J. (2003) *America Unbound: The Bush Revolution in Foreign Policy*, Brookings Institution Press, Washington, DC.

Daalder, I and O'Hanlon, M. (2001) *Winning Ugly: NATO's Wars to Save Kosovo*, Brookings Institution Press, Washington, DC.

Dalgaard-Nielsen, A. and Hamilton, D. (eds) (2005) *Transatlantic Homeland Security: Protecting Society in the Age of Catastrophic Terrorism*, Routledge, London.

Dannreuther, R. and Peterson, J. (eds) (2006) *Security Strategy and Transatlantic Relations*, Routledge, London and New York.

De Porte, A. (1979) *Europe Between the Superpowers: The Enduring Balance*, Yale University Press, New Haven.

Deutsch, K. (1957) *Political Community and the North Atlantic Area: International Organization in the Light of Historical Experience*, Princeton University Press, Princeton.

Dockrill, S. (1991) *Britain's Policy for West German Rearmament 1950–1955*, Cambridge University Press, Cambridge.

Duffield, M. (2002) *Global Governance and the New Wars*, Zed Books, London.

Edwards, G. and Pijpers, A. (eds) (1997) *The Politics of European Treaty Reform*, Pinter, London.

Ferguson, N. (2004) *Colossus: The Price of America's Empire*, Penguin, New York.

Forsberg, T. and Herd, G. (2006) *Divided West. European Security and the Transatlantic Relationship*, Chatham House Papers, Royal Institute of International Affairs and Blackwell Publishing, Oxford.

Gardner, A. (1996) *A New Era in US–EU Relations? The Clinton Administration and the New Transatlantic Agenda*, Avebury Press, Aldershot.

Giegerich, B. (2006) *European Security and Strategic Culture. National Responses to the EU's Security and Defence Policy*, Nomos, Baden-Baden.

Goldgeier, J. (1999) *Not Whether but When: The US Decision to Enlarge NATO*, Brookings Institution Press, Washington, DC.

Gompert, D. and Larabee, S. (1997) *America and Europe: A Partnership for a New Era*, Cambridge University Press and RAND, Cambridge.

Gordon, P. and Shapiro, J. (2004) *Allies at War: America, Europe, and the Crisis over Iraq*, McGraw-Hill and the Brookings Institution Press, New York.

Grabbe, H. (2006) *The EU's Transformative Power*, Palgrave Macmillan, London and Basingstoke.

Greco, E., Gasparini, G. and Alcaro, R. (eds) (2006) *Nuclear Non-Proliferation: The Transatlantic Debate*, Insituto Affari Internazionali, Rome.

Haglund, D. (1991) *An Alliance Within the Alliance? Franco-German Military Cooperation and the European Pillar of Defense*, Westview Press, Boulder, CO.

Hall, J. and Paul, T.V. (eds) (1999) *International Order and the Future of World Politics*, Cambridge University Press, Cambridge.

Hallenberg, J. and Karlsson, H. (eds) (2006) *Changing Transatlantic Security Relations. Do the US, the EU and Russia Form a New Strategic Triangle?* Routledge, London.

Haass, R. (1996) *The Reluctant Sheriff: The United States after the Cold War*, Council on Foreign Relations, Washington, DC.

Haass, R. (ed.) (1999) *Transatlantic Tensions: The United States, Europe, and Problem Countries*, Brookings Institution Press, Washington, DC.

Ham, P. van (2004) *WMD Proliferation and Transatlantic Relations: Is a Joint Western Strategy Possible?* Clingendael Institute, The Hague.

Hodgson, G. (2009) *The Myth of American Exceptionalism*, Yale University Press, New Haven and London.

Hoffman, B. (1998) *Inside Terrorism*, Columbia University Press, New York.

Howorth, J. (2007) *Security and Defence Policy in the European Union*, Palgrave Macmillan, Basingstoke and New York.

Howorth, J. and Keeler, J. (eds) (2003) *Defending Europe: NATO and the Quest for European Autonomy*, Palgrave Macmillan, London and New York.

Hunter, R. (2001) *The European Security and Defense Policy: NATO's Companion – or Competitor?* RAND Publications, Brussels.

Huntington, S. (1997) *The Clash of Civilizations and the Remaking of World Order*, Touchstone, New York.

Hyde-Price, A. (2000) *Germany and European Order: Enlarging NATO and the EU*, Issues in German Politics, Manchester University Press, Manchester.

Ignatieff, M. (ed.) (2005) *American Exceptionalism and Human Rights*, Princeton University Press, Princeton, NJ.

Ikenberry, G. J. (2001) *After Victory: Institutions, Strategic Restraint and the Rebuilding of Order after Major Wars*, Princeton University Press, Princeton, NJ.

Ilgren, T. (ed.) (2006) *Hard Power, Soft Power and the Future of Transatlantic Relations*, Ashgate, Aldershot.

Jackson, M. (2007) *Soldier: The Autobiography of General Sir Mike Jackson*, Bantam Press, London.

Jones, S. (2007) *The Rise of European Security Cooperation*, Cambridge University Press, Cambridge.

Kagan, R. (2003) *Of Paradise and Power: America and Europe in the New World Order*, Alfred Knopf, New York

Kellman, B. (2007) *Bioviolence: Preventing Biological Terror and Crime*, Cambridge University Press, Cambridge.

Kennedy, P. (1989) *The Rise and Fall of the Great Powers: Economic Change and Military Conflict from 1500–2000*, Fontana, London.

Keohane, R. and Nye, J. (2001) *Power and Interdependence*, 3rd edn, Longman, New York.

Keukeleire, S. and MacNaughton, J. (2008) *The Foreign Policy of the European Union*, Palgrave Macmillan, Basingstoke.

Kirchner, E. and Sperling, J. (2007) *EU Security Governance*, Manchester University Press, Manchester and New York.

Kopstein, J. and Steinmo, S. (ed.) (2008) *Growing Apart? America and Europe in the Twenty-First Century*, Cambridge University Press, Cambridge.

Kotzias, N. and Liacouras, P. (eds) (2006) *EU–US Relations: Repairing the Transatlantic Rift*, Palgrave Macmillan, Basingstoke.

Lansford, T. (2002) *All for One: Terrorism, NATO and the United States*, Ashgate, Aldershot.

Lindberg, T. (ed.) (2005) *Beyond Paradise and Power. Europe, America and the Future of a Troubled Partnership*, Routledge, London and New York.

Litwak, R. (1999) *Rogue States and US Foreign Policy: Containment after the Cold War*, Woodrow Wilson Center Press, Washington, DC.

Longhurst, K. (2004) *Germany and the Use of Force. The Evolution of German Security Policy 1990–2003*, Manchester University Press, Manchester and New York.

Lundestad, G. (2003) *The United States and Western Europe Since 1945: From 'Empire' by Invitation to Transatlantic Drift*, Oxford University Press, Oxford.

Mahncke, D., Rees, W. and Thompson, W. (2004) *Redefining Transatlantic Security Relations: The Challenge of Change*, Manchester University Press, Manchester and New York.

Mann, J. (2004) *Rise of the Vulcans: The History of Bush's War Cabinet*, Viking Press, New York

Manners, I. and Whitman, R. (eds) (1998) *From Civilian Power to Superpower?* Macmillan, Basingstoke.

McCormick, J. (2007) *The European Superpower*, Palgrave Macmillan, Basingstoke.

McGuire, S. and Smith, M. (2008) *The European Union and the United States: Competition and Convergence in the Global Arena*, Palgrave Macmillan, Basingstoke.

Mead, W. R. (2001) *Special Providence. American Foreign Policy and How it Changed the World*, Alfred Knopf, New York.

Menon, A. (2000) *France, NATO and the Limits of Independence 1981–97: The Politics of Ambivalence*, Palgrave Macmillan, Basingstoke.

Meyer, C. (2006a) *DC Confidential*, Phoenix, London.

Meyer, C. (2006b) *The Quest for a European Strategic Culture: Changing Norms on Security and Defence in the European Union*, Palgrave Macmillan, Basingstoke.

Muller-Brandeck-Boucquet, G. (ed.) (2006) *The Future of European Foreign, Security and Defence Policy after Enlargement*, Nomos, Baden-Baden.

Nadelmann, E. (1993) *Cops across Borders: The Internationalization of US Criminal Law Enforcement*, Pennsylvania State University Press, PA.

Nadelmann, E. and Andreas, P. (2006) *Policing the Globe: Criminalization and Crime Control in International Relations*, Oxford University Press, Oxford.

Nuttall, S. (2000) *European Foreign Policy*, Oxford University Press, Oxford.

Nye, J. (2002) *The Paradox of American Power: Why the World's Only Superpower Can't Go It Alone*, Oxford University Press, New York.

Orbie, J. (ed.) (2008) *Europe's Global Role: External Policies of the European Union*, Ashgate, Aldershot.

Owen, D. (1995) *Balkan Odyssey*, Gollancz, London.

Pauly, R. and Lansford, T. (2005) *Strategic Preemption: US Foreign Policy and the Second Iraq War*, Ashgate, Aldershot.

Philippart, E. and Winand, P. (eds) (2001) *Ever Closer Partnership: Policy-Making in US–EU Relations*, Peter Lang, Brussels.

Pillar, P. (2001) *Terrorism and US Foreign Policy*, Brookings Institution Press, Washington, DC.

Pond, E. (2004) *Friendly Fire, The Near Death of the Transatlantic Alliance*, Brookings Institution Press, Washington, DC.

Riddell, P. (2003) *Hug Them Close, Blair, Clinton, Bush and the 'Special Relationship'*, Politico's, London.

Riker, W. (1962) *The Theory of Political Coalitions*, Yale University Press, New Haven, CT.

Risse-Kappen, T. (1995) *Cooperation Among Democracies: The European Influence on US Foreign Policy*, Princeton University Press, Princeton, NJ.

Rees, W. (1998) *The Western European Union at the Crossroads: Between Trans-atlantic Solidarity and European Integration*, Westview Press, Boulder, CO.

Rees, W. (2006) *Transatlantic Counter-terrorism Cooperation: The New Imperative*, Routledge, London and New York.

Salmon, T. and Shepherd (2003) *Toward a European Army: A Military Power in the Making?* Lynne Rienner Publishers, Boulder and London.

Schimmelfenig, F. and Sedelmeier, U. (2005) (eds) *The Politics of European Union Enlargement*, Routledge, London.

Schulhofer, S. (2005) *Rethinking the Patriot Act: Keeping America Safe and Free*, Century Foundation, New York.

Serfaty, S. (1997) *Stay the Course: European Unity and Atlantic Solidarity*, Praeger in conjunction with the Center for Strategic and International Studies, Westport.

Serfaty, S. (ed.) (2005) *Visions of the Atlantic Alliance: The United States, the European Union and NATO*, Significant Issues Series, Volume 27, Number 8, Center for Strategic and International Studies, Washington, DC.

Singer, M. and Wildavsky, A. (1993) *The Real World Order: Zones of Peace, Zones of Turmoil*, Chatham House Publishers, New Jersey.

Slaughter, A.-M. (2004) *A New World Order: Whither Thou Pollyanna?* Princeton University Press, Princeton, NJ.

Sloan, S. (2005) *NATO, the European Union and the Atlantic Community. The Transatlantic Bargain Reconsidered*, 2nd edn, Rowman & Littlefield, Lanham, MD.

Smith, K. (2003) *European Union Foreign Policy in a Changing World*, Polity, Cambridge.

Smith, M. and Timmins, G. (2000) *Building a Bigger Europe: EU and NATO Enlargement in Comparative Perspective*, Ashgate, Aldershot.

Smith, R. (2007) *The Utility of Force: The Art of War in the Modern World*, Alfred Knopf, New York.

Solomon, G. (1998) *The NATO Enlargement Debate, 1990–1997: The Blessings of Liberty*, Praeger in conjunction with the Center for Strategic and International Studies, Westport.

Sperling, J. (ed.) (1999) *Two Tiers or Two Speeds? The European Security Order and the Enlargement of the European Union and NATO*, Europe in Change Series, Manchester University Press, Manchester.

Stares, P. (ed.) (1992) *The New Germany and the New Europe*, The Brookings Institution, Washington, DC.

Steffenson, R. (2005) *Managing EU–US Relations: Actors, Institutions and the New Transatlantic Agenda*, Manchester University Press, Manchester.

Stetter, S. (2007) *EU Foreign and Interior Policies: Cross-pillar Politics and the Social Construction of Sovereignty*, Routledge, London and New York.

Tanter, R. (1999) *Rogue Regimes: Terrorism and Proliferation*, St Martin's Press, New York.

Telo, M. (2006) *Europe: A Civil Power? European Union, Global Governance, World Order*, Palgrave Macmillan, Basingstoke.

Toje, A. (2008) *America, the EU and Strategic Culture: Renegotiating the Transatlantic Bargain*, Routledge, London.

Wallace, H. and Wallace, W. (eds) (2000) *Policy Making in the European Union*, 4th edn, Oxford University Press, Oxford.

Walt, S. (1987) *The Origins of Alliances*, Cornell University Press, Ithaca and London.

Winand, P. (1993) *Eisenhower, Kennedy and the United States of Europe*, St Martin's Press, New York.

Wit, J., Poneman, B. and Gallucci, R. (2004) *Going Critical: The First North Korean Nuclear Crisis*, Brookings Institution, Washington, DC.

Wright, L. (2006) *The Looming Tower: Al-Qaeda's Road to 9/11*, Allen Lane, London and New York.

Zakaria, F. (2008) *The Post-American World*, W.W. Norton & Company, London and New York.

Articles and chapters in books

Aggestam, L. (2008) 'Introduction: Ethical power Europe?' *International Affairs*, 84, 1, pp. 1–11.

Aldrich, R. (2009) 'US–European intelligence co-operation on counter-terrorism: Low politics and compulsion', *British Journal of Politics and International Relations*, 11, 1, pp. 122–39.

Allen, D. (1998) ' "Who speaks for Europe?" The search for an effective and coherent external policy', in J. Peterson and H. Sjursen (eds) *A Common Foreign and Security Policy for Europe?* Routledge, London, pp. 41–58.

Allin, D., Andreani, G., Errera, P. and Samore, G. (2007) 'Repairing the damage: Possibilities and limits of transatlantic consensus', Adelphi Paper 389, Routledge for the International Institute for Strategic Studies, Abingdon.

Allison, G. (2005) 'Nuclear terrorism and the transatlantic community' in S. Serfaty (ed.) *Visions of the Atlantic Alliance: The United States, the European Union and NATO*, Significant Issues Series, Volume 27, No.

8, Center for Strategic and International Studies, Washington, DC, pp. 212–26.

Alvarez-Verdugo, M. (2006) 'Mixing tools against proliferation: The EU's strategy for dealing with weapons of mass destruction', *European Foreign Affairs Review*, 11, 3, pp. 417–38.

Andreani, G. (1999) 'The disarray of US non-proliferation policy', *Survival*, 41, 4, pp. 42–59.

Andreani, G. (2000) 'Why institutions matter', *Survival*, 42, 2, pp. 81–95.

Aoun, E. (2003) 'European foreign policy and the Arab–Israeli dispute: Much ado about nothing', *European Foreign Affairs Review*, 8, 3, pp. 289–312.

Arbatov, G. (2008) 'The inexorable momentum of escalation', in P. Cronin (ed.) *Double Trouble: Iran and North Korea as Challenges to International Security*, Praeger Security International, Westport, CT.

Asmus, R. (2003) 'Rebuilding the Atlantic Alliance', *Foreign Affairs*, September/October, pp. 20–31.

Asmus, R. (2005) 'Rethinking the EU: Why Washington needs to support European integration', *Survival*, 47, 3, pp. 93–102.

Asmus, R. (2006) 'The European Security Strategy: An American view', in R. Danreuther and J. Peterson (eds) *Security Strategy and Transatlantic Relations*, Routledge, London and New York.

Asmus, R. and Pollack, K. (2002) 'The new transatlantic project', *Policy Review*, No. 115, Hoover Institution, October and November.

Asmus, R., Kugler, R. and Larrabee, S. (1996) 'What will NATO enlargement cost?' *Survival*, 38, 3, pp. 5–26.

Baghat, G. (2006) 'Europe's energy security: challenges and opportunities', *International Affairs*, 82, 5, pp. 961–75.

Bailes A. (2005a) 'The price of survival: Shared objectives, different approaches', in S. Serfaty (ed.) *Visions of the Atlantic Alliance: The United States, the European Union and NATO*, Significant Issues Series, Volume 27, No. 8, Center for Strategic and International Studies, Washington, DC, pp. 173–92.

Bailes, A. (2005b) 'The European Security Strategy: An Evolutionary History', SIPRI Paper 10, February, http://sipri.org.

Bailes, A. (2008) 'The EU and a "better world": What role for the European Security and Defence Policy?' *International Affairs*, 84, 1, pp. 115–30.

Barbe, E. and Kienzle, B. (2007) 'Security provider or security consumer? The European Union and conflict management', *European Foreign Affairs Review*, 12, 4, pp. 517–36.

Barbe, E. and Johansson-Nogues, E. (2008) 'The EU as a modest "force for good": The European Neighbourhood Policy', *International Affairs*, 84, 1, pp. 81–96.

Bertram, C. (2006) 'The EU and the Future of Transatlantic Relations' in N. Kotzias and P. Liacouras (eds) *EU–US Relations: Repairing the Transatlantic Rift*, Palgrave, Macmillan, Basingstoke, pp. 41–2.

Bertram, C. (2008) 'Rethinking Iran: From confrontation to cooperation', Chaillot Paper 110, EU Institute for Security Studies, Paris, August.

Binnendijk H. and Kugler, R. (2002) 'Transforming European forces', *Survival*, 44, 3, pp. 117–32.

Biscop, S. (2008) 'NATO and the ESDP: Complementing or Competing?' in S. Biscop and J. Lembke (eds) *EU Enlargement and the Transatlantic Alliance: A Security Relationship in Flux*, Lynne Rienner, Boulder, CO.

Boswell, C. (2003)'The "External Dimension" of EU immigration and asylum policy', *International Affairs*, 79, 3, pp. 619–38.

Bowen, W. (2001) 'Missile defence and the transatlantic security relationship', *International Affairs*, 77, 3, pp. 485–507.

Brimmer, E. (2007) 'Seeing blue: American visions of the European Union', Chaillot Paper 105, EU Institute for Security Studies, Paris, September.

Brown, M. (1995) 'The flawed logic of NATO expansion', *Survival*, 37, 1, pp. 34–52.

Bull, H. (1982) 'Civilian Power Europe: A contradiction in terms?' *Journal of Common Market Studies*, 12, 2, pp. 149–64.

Copeland, T. (2001) 'Is the "New Terrorism" really new? An analysis of the new paradigm for terrorism', *Journal of Conflict Studies*, 21, 2, pp. 7–27.

Cornish, P. and Edwards, G. (2005) 'The strategic culture of the European Union: A progress report', *International Affairs*, 81, 4, pp. 801–20.

Coulon, J. (2003) 'How unipolarism died in Baghdad', *European Foreign Affairs Review*, 8, 4, pp. 537–41.

Cox, M. (2007) 'The Imperial Republic in an Age of War: The United States from September 11 to Iraq', in C. Ankersen (ed.) *Understanding Global Terror*, Polity, Cambridge.

Croci, O. (2003) 'A closer look at the changing transatlantic relationship', *European Foreign Affairs Review*, 8, 4, pp. 469–91.

Cronin, P. (2008) 'The trouble with Iran', in P. Cronin (ed.) *Double Trouble: Iran and North Korea as Challenges to International Security*, Praeger Security International, Westport, CT.

Daalder, I. (2003) 'The end of Atlanticism', *Survival*, 45, 2, pp. 147–66.

Daalder, I. and Goldgeier, J. (2001) 'Putting Europe first', *Survival*, 43, 1, pp. 71–92.

Daalder, I. and Goldgeier, J. (2006) 'Global NATO', *Foreign Affairs*, September– October, pp. 105–13.

Den Boer, M. (2003) 'The EU counter-terrorism wave: Window of opportunity or profound policy transformation?' in M. van Leeuwen (ed.) *Confronting Terrorism: European Experiences, Threat Perceptions and Policies*, Kluwer Law International, The Hague, pp. 185–206.

Denza, E. (2005) 'Non-proliferation of nuclear weapons: The European Union and Iran', *European Foreign Affairs Review*, 10, pp. 289–311.

Deudney, D. and Ikenberry, G. J. (1999) 'The nature and sources of liberal international order', *Review of International Studies*, 25, pp. 179–96.

Dobbins, J. (2005) 'What the wise men might say', in S. Serfaty (ed.) *Visions of the Atlantic Alliance. The United States, the European Union and NATO*, Significant Issues Series, Volume 27, No. 8, Center for Strategic and International Studies, Washington, DC, pp. 229–44.

Dobbins, J. (2008) 'European and American roles in nation-building', in R. Alcaro (ed.) *Re-launching the Transatlantic Security Relationship*, Instituto Affari Internazionali, Rome.

Drezner, D. (2008) 'The transatlantic divide over diplomacy', in J. Kopstein and S. Steinmo (ed.) *Growing Apart? America and Europe in the Twenty-First Century*, Cambridge University Press, Cambridge.

Duchene, F. (1972) 'Europe's role in a world of peace', in R. Mayne (ed.) *Europe Tomorrow: Sixteen Nations Look Ahead*, Fontana, London, pp. 32–47.

Dumbrell, J. (2009) 'The US–UK relationship: Taking the 21st century temperature', *British Journal of Politics and International Relations*, 11, 1, pp. 64–78.

Dunn, D. H. (2007) ' "Real men want to go to Tehran": Bush, pre-emption and the Iranian nuclear challenge', *International Affairs*, 83, 1, pp. 19–38.

Ekengren, M. and Engelbrekt, K. (2006) 'The impact of enlargement on EU actorness: Enhanced capacity, weakened cohesiveness', in J. Hallenberg and H. Karlsson (eds) *Changing Transatlantic Security Relations. Do the US, the EU and Russia Form a New Strategic Triangle?* Routledge, London.

Errera, P. (2005) 'Three Circles of Threat', *Survival*, 47, 1, pp. 71–88.

Espinosa, E. L. de (2005) 'Differences that make a difference', in S. Serfaty (ed.) *Visions of the Atlantic Alliance: The United States, the European Union and NATO*, Significant Issues Series, Volume 27, No. 8, Center for Strategic and International Studies, Washington, DC, pp. 31–52.

Falke, A. (2000) 'The EU–US conflict over sanctions policy: Confronting the hegemon', *European Foreign Affairs Review*, 5, 2, pp. 139–63.

Faull, J. and Soreca, L. (2008) 'EU–US relations in Justice and Home Affairs', in B. Martenczuk and S. van Thiel (eds) *Justice, Liberty and Security: New Challenges for EU External Relations*, Brussels University Press, Brussels.

Fitzpatrick, M. (2009) 'Stopping nuclear North Korea', *Survival*, 51, 4, pp. 5–12.

Fohrenbach, G. (2006) 'Transatlantic homeland security and the challenge of diverging risk perceptions', in E. Brimmer (ed.) *Transforming Homeland Security: US and European Approaches*, Johns Hopkins University, Washington, DC.

Freedman, L. (2003) 'Prevention, not Pre-emption', *The Washington Quarterly*, 26, 2, pp. 105–14.

Geipel, G. (1999) 'The cost of enlarging NATO', in J. Sperling (ed.) *Two Tiers or Two Speeds? The European Security Order and the Enlargement of the European Union and NATO*, Europe in Change Series, Manchester University Press, Manchester.

Geyer, F. (2007) 'Human rights, intelligence cooperation and the EU Counter-Terrorism Strategy', in D. Spence (ed.) *The European Union and Terrorism*, John Harper Publishing, London.

Giegerich, B. and Wallace, W. (2004) 'Not such a soft power: The external deployment of European forces', *Survival*, 46, 2, pp. 163–82.

Gordon, P. (1997–98) 'Europe's uncommon foreign policy', *International Security*, 22, 3, pp. 74–100.

Gordon, P. (2003) 'Bridging the Atlantic divide', *Foreign Affairs*, 82, 1, pp. 70–83.

Haas, P. (1997) 'Epistemic communities and the dynamics of international environmental cooperation' in V. Rittberger (ed.) *Regime Theory and International Relations*, Clarendon Press, Oxford.

Haass, R. (2008) 'The age of nonpolarity. What will follow US dominance', *Foreign Affairs*, May–June, pp. 44–56.

Hagman, H-C. (2002) 'European crisis management and defence: The search for capabilities', Adelphi Paper 353, Routledge for the International Institute for Strategic Studies, Abingdon.

Hamilton, D. (2003) 'Three strategic challenges for a global transatlantic partnership', *European Foreign Affairs Review*, 8, 4, pp. 543–55.

Hamilton, D. (2008) 'The United States: A normative power? in N. Tocci (ed.) *Who is a Normative Foreign Policy Actor? The European Union and its Global Partners*, Centre for European Policy Studies, Brussels.

Hanggi, H. and Tanner, F. (2005) 'Promoting security sector governance in the EU's neighbourhood', Chaillot Paper 80, EU Institute for Security Studies, Paris, September.

Harries, O. (1993) 'Collapse of the West', *Foreign Affairs,* 72, 4, pp. 41–53.

Heisbourg, F. (2000a) 'Europe's strategic ambitions: The limits of ambiguity', *Survival*, 42, 2, pp. 5–15.

Heisbourg, F. (2000b) 'Brussel's burden', *The Washington Quarterly*, 23, 3, pp. 127–33.

Higgot, R. (2005) 'The theory and practice of global governance. Accommodating American exceptionalism and European pluralism', *European Foreign Affairs Review*, 10, 4, pp. 575–94.

Hill, C. (1993) 'The Capability–Expectations Gap, or conceptualising Europe's international role', *Journal of Common Market Studies*, 31, 3, pp. 305–28.

Holbrooke, R. (1995) 'America, a European power', *Foreign Affairs*, 74, 2, pp. 38–51.

Howorth, J. (2003) 'France, Britain and the Euro-Atlantic crisis', *Survival*, 45, 4, pp. 173–92.

Hunter, R. (2005) 'NATO and the European Union: Inevitable partners', in S. Serfaty (ed.) *Visions of the Atlantic Alliance: The United States, the European Union and NATO*, Significant Issues Series, Volume 27, No. 8, Center for Strategic and International Studies, Washington, DC, pp. 55–72.

Ikenberry, G. J. (2004) 'The end of the neo-conservative moment', *Survival*, 46, 1, pp. 7–22.

International Affairs (2009) 'War over Kosovo: Ten Years on', Special Edition, 85, 3, May.

Jenkins, B. (2005) 'Intelligence and homeland security', in A. Dalgaard-Nielsen and D. Hamilton (eds) *Transatlantic Homeland Security: Protecting Society in the Age of Catastrophic Terrorism*, Routledge, London, pp. 126–46.

Joffe, J. (1984) 'Europe's American Pacifier', *Foreign Policy*, Spring, pp. 64–82.

Kagan, R. (2004) 'America's Crisis of Legitimacy', *Foreign Affairs*, 83, 2, pp. 65–87.

Kagan, R. (2008) 'The September 12 paradigm: America, the world and George W. Bush', *Foreign Affairs*, 87, 5, pp. 25–39.

Kemp, G. (1999) 'The challenge of Iran for US and European policy', in R. Haass (ed.) *Transatlantic Tensions. The United States, Europe, and Problem Countries*, Brookings Institution Press, Washington, DC.

Keohane, D. (2008) 'The absent friend: EU foreign policy and counter-terrorism', *Journal of Common Market Studies*, 46, 1, pp. 125–46.

Keukeleire, S. (2001) 'Directorates in the CFSP/CESDP of the European Union: A plea for "Restricted Crisis Management Groups"', *European Foreign Affairs Review*, 6, 1, pp. 75–101.

Khasson, V., Vasilyan, S. and Vos, H. (2008) ' "Everbody needs good neighbours": The EU and its neighbourhood', in J. Orbie (ed.) *Europe's Global Role. External Policies of the European Union*, Ashgate, Aldershot.

Koslowski, R. (2005) 'Border and transportation security in the transatlantic relationship' in A. Dalgaard-Nielsen and D. Hamilton (eds) *Transatlantic Homeland Security: Protecting Society in the Age of Catastrophic Terrorism*, Routledge, London, pp. 89–106.

Krauthammer, C. (1990) 'America and the world', *Foreign Affairs*, 70, 1, pp. 23–33.

Kupchan, C. (2003) 'The end of the West', *Atlantic Monthly*, 291, November.

Kupchan, C. (2005) 'The legitimacy of American power in question' in S. Serfaty (ed.) *Visions of the Atlantic Alliance: The United States, the European Union and NATO*, Significant Issues Series, Volume 27, No. 8, Center for Strategic and International Studies, Washington, DC, pp. 245–59.

Kupchan, C. (2008) 'The Atlantic order in transition: The nature of change in US–European relations', in J. Anderson, J. Ikenberry, and T. Risse (eds) *The End of the West? Crisis and Change in the Atlantic Order*, Cornell University Press, Ithaca and London.

Lake, A. (1994) 'Confronting backlash states', *Foreign Affairs*, 73, 2, pp. 45–59.

Lavenex, S. (2004) 'EU external governance in "wider Europe"', *Journal of European Public Policy*, 11, 4, pp. 680–700.

Lindstrom, G. (2007) 'Enter the Battlegroups', Chaillot Paper 97, EU Institute for Security Studies, Brussels, February.

Lindstrom, G. and Schmitt, B. (2003) (eds) 'Fighting proliferation: European perspectives', Chaillot Paper 66, EU Institute for Security Studies, Paris, December.

Litwak, R. (2002) 'The new calculus of pre-emption', *Survival*, 44, 4, pp. 53–80.

Luck, E. (2004) 'The US, counterterrorism, and the prospects for a multi-lateral alternative', in J. Boulden and T. Weiss (eds) *Terrorism and the UN: Before and after September 11*, Indiana University Press, Bloomington and Indianapolis.

Mandelbaum, M. (1996) 'Foreign policy as social work', *Foreign Affairs*, 75, 1, pp. 16–32.

Mandelbaum, M. (1999) 'A perfect failure: NATO's war against Yugoslavia', *Foreign Affairs*, 78, 5, pp. 2–8.

Manners, I. (2002) 'Normative power Europe: A contradiction in terms?' *Journal of Common Market Studies*, 40, 2, pp. 234–58.

Marsh, S. (2006) 'The United States and the Common European Security and Defence Policy: No end to drift?' in J. Baylis and J. Roper (eds) *The United States and Europe: Beyond the Neo-Conservative Divide?* Routledge, London.

Matlary, J. (2008) 'Much ado about little: The EU and human security', *International Affairs*, 84, 1, pp. 131–43.

Mead, W. R. (2004) 'America's sticky power', *Foreign Policy*, 141, March–April, pp. 46–53.

Mearsheimer, J. (1990) 'Back to the future: Instability in Europe after the Cold War', *International Security*, 15, 1, pp. 5–56.

Mearsheimer, J. (1993) 'The case for a Ukrainian nuclear deterrent', *Foreign Affairs*, 72, 3, pp. 50–66.

Menon, A. (2003) 'Why ESDP is misguided and dangerous for the Alliance', in J. Howorth and J. Keeler (eds) *Defending Europe: NATO and the Quest for European Autonomy*, Palgrave Macmillan, London and New York, pp. 203–18.

Menon, A. (2004) 'From crisis to catharsis: ESDP after Iraq', *International Affairs*, 80, 4, pp. 660–48.

Menon, A. (2009) 'Empowering paradise? ESDP at ten', *International Affairs*, 85, 2, pp. 211–26.

Moens, A. (2003) 'ESDP, the United States and the Atlantic Alliance', in J. Howorth and J. Keeler (eds) *Defending Europe: NATO and the Quest for European Autonomy*, Palgrave Macmillan, London and New York, pp. 25–38.

Moisi, D. (1999) 'Iraq', in R. Haass (ed.) *Transatlantic Tensions. The United States, Europe, and Problem Countries*, Brookings Institution Press, Washington, DC.

Monar, J. (2003) The challenges of eastern enlargement' in V. Mitsilegas, J. Monar and W. Rees (eds) *The European Union and Internal Security: Guardian of the People?* Palgrave Macmillan, Basingstoke.

Moravcsik, A. (2003) 'Striking a new transatlantic bargain', *Foreign Affairs*, 82, 4, pp. 74–89.

Muller, H. (2003) 'Terrorism, proliferation: A European threat assessment', Chaillot Paper 58, EU Institute for Security Studies, Paris, December.

Muller-Wille, B. (2004) 'For our eyes only? Shaping an intelligence community within the EU', Occasional Paper No. 50, EU Institute for Security Studies, Paris, January.

Muller-Wille, B. (2008) 'The effect of international terrorism on EU intelligence cooperation', *Journal of Common Market Studies*, 46, 1, pp. 49–73.

Nasr, V. and Takeyh, R. (2008) 'The costs of containing Iran', *Foreign Affairs*, January–February, pp. 85–94.

Nau, H. (2008) 'Iraq and previous transatlantic crises: Divided by threat not institutions or values', in J. Anderson, J. Ikenberry and T. Risse (eds) *The End of the West? Crisis and Change in the Atlantic Order*, Cornell University Press, Ithaca and London.

Neuss, B. (2009) 'Asymmetric Interdependence: Do America and Europe need each other?' *Strategic Studies Quarterly*, Winter, pp. 110–24.

Niblett, R. (2005) 'Europe inside out', *The Washington Quarterly*, 29, 1, pp. 41–59.

Nicolaidis, K. (2005) 'The power of the superpowerless', in T. Lindberg (ed.) *Beyond Paradise and Power: Europe, America and the Future of a Troubled Partnership*, Routledge, London and New York, pp. 93–120.

Nicolaidis, K. (2006) 'Living with our differences' in N. Kotzias and P. Liacouras (eds) *EU–US Relations: Repairing the Transatlantic Rift*, Palgrave Macmillan, Basingstoke.

Nilsson, H. G. (2006) 'The EU Action Plan on Combating Terrorism: Assessment and Perspectives', in D. Mahncke and J. Monar (eds) *International Terrorism: A European Response to a Global Threat?* College of Europe Studies No. 3, PIE Peter Lang, Germany.

Noi, A. U. (2005) 'Iran's nuclear programme: The EU approach to Iran in comparison to the US' approach', *Perceptions*, Spring, pp. 79–95.

Nye, J. (2000) 'The US and Europe: Continental drift?' *International Affairs*, 76, 1, pp. 51–61.

Nye, J. (2003) 'US power and strategy after Iraq', *Foreign Affairs*, 82, 4, pp. 60–73.

Nye, J. (2006) 'Soft power and European–American affairs', in T. Ilgren (ed.) *Hard Power, Soft Power and the Future of Transatlantic Relations*, Ashgate, Aldershot.

Obama, B. (2007) 'Renewing American leadership', *Foreign Affairs*, 86, 4, pp. 2–16.

O'Hanlon, M. (2006) 'Border protection', in M. d'Arcy, M. O'Hanlon, P. Orszag, J. Shapiro and J. Steinberg, *Protecting the Homeland 2006/2007*, Brookings Institution Press, Washington, DC.

Omand, D. (2005) 'Countering International Terrorism: The Use of Strategy', *Survival*, 47, 4, pp. 107–16.

Orbie, J. (2008) 'A civilian power in the world? Instruments and objectives in European Union external policies', in J. Orbie (ed.) *Europe's Global Role. External Policies of the European Union*, Ashgate, Aldershot.

Ortega, M. (2007) 'Building the Future: The EU's contribution to global governance', Chaillot Paper 100, EU Institute for Security Studies, Paris, April.

Oudenaren, J. van (2004) 'US reactions to the EU Security Strategy', *Oxford Journal of Good Governance*, 1, 1, pp. 43–7.

Parachini, J. (2003) 'Putting WMD terrorism into perspective', *The Washington Quarterly*, 26, 4, pp. 37–50.

Pawlak, P. (2010) 'Transatlantic homeland security cooperation: The promise of new modes of governance in global affairs', *Journal of Transatlantic Studies*, 8, 2, pp. 139–57.

Perkovich, G. (2003) 'Bush's nuclear revolution: A regime change in non-proliferation', *Foreign Affairs*, 82, 2, pp. 2–8.

Perkovich, G. (2005) 'Transatlantic cooperation for nuclear nonproliferation', in S. Serfaty (ed.) *Visions of the Atlantic Alliance: The United States, the European Union and NATO*, Significant Issues Series, Volume 27, No. 8, Center for Strategic and International Studies, Washington, DC, pp. 193–211.

Peterson, J. (2004) 'America as a European power: The end of empire by integration?' *International Affairs*, 80, 4, pp. 613–29.

Peterson, J. and Steffenson, R. (2009) 'Transatlantic institutions: Can partnership be engineered?' *British Journal of Politics and International Relations*, 11, 1, pp. 25–45.

Pfaff, S. (2008) 'The religious divide: Why religion seems to be thriving in the United States and waning in Europe', in J. Kopstein and S. Steinmo (ed.) *Growing Apart? America and Europe in the Twenty-First Century*, Cambridge University Press, Cambridge.

Pollack, K. (2006) 'A common approach to Iran', in I. Daalder, N. Gnesotto and P. Gordon (eds) *Crescent of Crisis: US–European Strategy for the Greater Middle East*, Brookings Institution Press, Washington, DC.

Pollack, M. (2005) 'The new transatlantic agenda at ten: Reflections on an experiment in international governance', *Journal of Common Market Studies*, 43, 5, pp. 899–919.

Pond, E. (2005) 'The dynamics of the feud over Iraq' in D. Andrews (ed.) *The Atlantic Alliance Under Stress: US–European Relations after Iraq*, Cambridge University Press, Cambridge.

Quille, G. (2006) 'Prospects for a common transatlantic nuclear non-proliferation strategy' in E. Greco, G. Gasparini and R. Alcaro (eds) *Nuclear Non-Proliferation: The Transatlantic Debate*, Insituto Affari Internazionali, Rome, February.

Rees, W. (2009) 'Securing the homelands: Transatlantic cooperation after Bush', *British Journal of Politics and International Relations*, 11, 1, pp. 108–21.

Rees, W. and Aldrich, R. (2005) 'Contending cultures of counterterrorism: Transatlantic divergence or convergence?' *International Affairs*, 81, 5, pp. 905–24.

Rice, C. (2008) 'Rethinking the national interest: American realism for a new world', *Foreign Affairs*, July–August, pp. 2–26.

Ridder, E. de, Schrijvers, A. and Vos, H. (2008) 'Civilian power Europe and eastern enlargement: The more the merrier?' in J. Orbie (ed.) *Europe's Global Role. External Policies of the European Union*, Ashgate, Aldershot.

Roberts, B. and Muller, H. (1999) 'Proliferation', in F. Burwell and I. Daalder (eds) *The US and Europe in the Global Arena*, Macmillan, Basingstoke.

Roy, O. (2003) 'Euro-Islam: The Jihad within', *The National Interest*, Spring, pp. 63–73.

Rubin, J. (2008) 'Building a new atlantic alliance: Restoring America's partnership with Europe', *Foreign Affairs*, July–August, pp. 99–110.

Rudolf, P. (1999) 'Critical engagement: The European Union and Iran', in R. Haass (ed.) *Transatlantic Tensions: The United States, Europe, and Problem Countries*, Brookings Institution Press, Washington, DC.

Rynning, S. (1999) 'French defence reforms and European security: Tensions and intersections', *European Foreign Affairs Review*, 4, 1, pp. 99–119.

Sangiovanni, M. E. (2003) 'Why a Common Security and Defence Policy is bad for Europe', *Survival*, 45, 3, pp. 193–206.

Sauer, T. (2004) 'The Americanization of EU nuclear non-proliferation policy', *Defense and Security Analysis*, 20, 2, pp. 113–31.

Schake, K. (2000) 'NATO's fundamental divergence over proliferation', *Journal of Strategic Studies*, 23, 3, pp. 111–28.

Schake, K. (2003) 'The United States, ESDP and constructive duplication', in J. Howorth and J. Keeler (eds) *Defending Europe: NATO and the Quest for European Autonomy*, Palgrave Macmillan, London and New York, pp. 107–34.

Schake, K., Bloch-Laine, A. and Grant, C. (1999) 'Building a European defence capability', *Survival*, 41, 1, pp. 20–40.

Schmitt, B. (2005) (ed.) 'Effective non-proliferation: The European Union and the 2005 NPT Review Conference', Chaillot Paper 77, EU Institute for Security Studies, Paris, April.

Shapiro, J. and Byman, D. (2006) 'Bridging the Transatlantic Counterterrorism Gap', *The Washington Quarterly*, 29, 4, pp. 33–50.

Simon, S. and Benjamin, D. (2000) 'America and the New Terrorism', *Survival*, 42, 1, pp. 59–75.

Smith, K. (2005) 'Beyond the civilian power EU debate', *Politique Europeenne*, 17, pp. 63–82.

Smith, M. (1996) 'The European Union and a changing Europe: Establishing the boundaries of order', *Journal of Common Market Studies*, 34, 1, pp. 5–28.

Smith, M. (2009) 'Transatlantic economic relations in a changing global political economy', *British Journal of Politics and International Relations*, 11, 1, pp. 94–107.

Solana, J. (2001) 'Destined to cooperate' *Financial Times*, 14 June.

Solana, J. (2002) 'Europe's place in the world', 23 May, http://ue.eu.int/ueDocs/cms.

Specter, A. with Bradish, C. (2006–07) 'Dialogue with adversaries', *The Washington Quarterly*, 30, 1, pp. 9–25.

Sperling, J. (1999) 'Enlarging the EU and NATO', in J. Sperling (ed.) *Two Tiers or Two Speeds? The European Security Order and the Enlargement of the European Union and NATO*, Europe in Change Series, Manchester University Press, Manchester.

Stanzel, V. (1999) 'Dealing with the backwoods: New challenges for transatlantic relations', *The Washington Quarterly*, 22, 2, pp. 17–23.

Steinberg, J. (2003) 'An elective partnership: Salvaging transatlantic relations', *Survival*, 45, 2, pp. 113–46.

Steinberg, J. (2008) 'Real leaders do soft power: Learning the lessons of Iraq', *The Washington Quarterly*, 31, 2, pp. 155–64.

Stevenson, J. (2003) 'How Europe and America defend themselves', *Foreign Affairs*, 82, 2, pp. 75–90.

Sur, S. (2006) 'The Non-Proliferation Treaty and the Review Conferences', in E. Greco, G. Gasparini and R. Alcaro (eds) *Nuclear Non-Proliferation: The Transatlantic Debate*, Insituto Affari Internazionali, Rome, February.

Takeyh, R. (2001) 'The rogue who came in from the cold', *Foreign Affairs*, 80, 3, pp. 62–73.

Takeyh, R. (2004) 'Iran builds the bomb', *Survival*, 46, 4, pp. 51–63.

Tetrais, B. (1999) 'Nuclear policies in Europe', Adelphi Paper 327, Oxford University Press for the International Institute for Strategic Studies, London.

Tetrais, B. (2006a) 'A common approach to Iran', in I. Daalder, N. Gnesotto and P. Gordon (eds) *Crescent of Crisis: US–European Strategy for the Greater Middle East*, Brookings Institution Press, Washington, DC.

Tetrais, B. (2006b) 'A European perspective: The EU and nuclear non-proliferation: Does soft power work?' in E. Greco, G. Gasparini and R. Alcaro (eds) *Nuclear Non-Proliferation: The Transatlantic Debate*, Insituto Affari Internazionali, Rome, February.

Tetrais, B. (2008) 'The transatlantic strategic debate: Deterrence, non-proliferation and missile defense', in R. Alcaro (ed.) *Re-launching the Transatlantic Security Relationship*, Instituto Affari Internazionali, Rome.

Tocci, N. (2008) 'Profiling normative foreign policy: The European Union and its global partners', in N. Tocci (ed.) *Who is a Normative Foreign Policy Actor? The European Union and its Global Partners*, Centre for European Policy Studies, Brussels.

Treverton, G. (2006) 'A post-modern transatlantic Alliance', in T. Ilgren (ed.) *Hard Power, Soft Power and the Future of Transatlantic Relations*, Ashgate, Aldershot.

Valencia, M. (2005) 'The Proliferation Security Initiative: Making waves in Asia', Adelphi Paper 376, Routledge for the International Institute for Strategic Studies, London.

Walker, W. (2007) 'Nuclear enlightenment and counter-enlightenment', *International Affairs*, 83, 3, pp. 431–53.

Wallace, W. (1997) 'On the move: Destination unknown', *The World Today*, 53, 4, pp. 99–102.

Wallace, W. (2001) 'Europe, the necessary partner', *Foreign Affairs*, 80, 3, pp. 16–34.

Walt, S. (1991) 'The renaissance of security studies', *International Studies Quarterly*, 35, 2, pp. 211–39.

Walt, S. (1998–99) 'The ties that fray: Why Europe and America are drifting apart', *The National Interest*, 54, Winter, pp. 3–11.

Waltz, K. (1981) 'The spread of nuclear weapons: More may be better', Adelphi Paper 353, International Institute for Strategic Studies, London.

Webber, M. (2009) 'NATO: The United States, transformation and the war in Afghanistan', *British Journal of Politics and International Relations*, 11, 1, pp. 46–63.

Whitman, R. (2006) 'Road map for a route march? (De-)civilianizing through the EU's Security Strategy', *European Foreign Affairs Review*, 11, pp. 1–15.

Winer, J. (2005) 'Cops across borders. The evolution of transatlantic law enforcement and judicial cooperation', in A. Dalgaard-Nielsen and D. Hamilton (eds) *Transatlantic Homeland Security: Protecting Society in the Age of Catastrophic Terrorism*, Routledge, London.

Witney, N. (2008) 'The European Defence Agency' in S. Biscop and J. Lembke (eds) *EU Enlargement and the Transatlantic Alliance: A Security Relationship in Flux*, Lynne Rienner, Boulder, CO.

Ziemke, C. (2000) 'The national myth and strategic personality of Iran: A counterproliferation perspective', in V. Utgoff (ed.), *The Coming Crisis: Nuclear Proliferation, U.S. Interests, and World Order*, MIT Press, Cambridge, MA.

Other documents, newspapers and speeches

Afghanistan Study Group Report (2008) 'Revitalizing our efforts and rethinking our strategies', Center for the Study of the Presidency, Washington, DC, 30 January.

Agence Presse (1999) 'EU/south-eastern Europe', No. 7472, 27 May.

Agence Presse (2000) 'Turkey is not pleased with arrangement decided in Feira for European but non-EU NATO allies', No.7744, 24 June.

Agence Presse (2003a) 'Agreement on permanent units for planning EU's military and civil operations', No. 8605, 13 December.

Agence Presse (2003b) 'Structured cooperation in defence possible if open to all member states', No. 8566, 18 October.

Agence Presse (2004a) 'EU expected to have three battle groups by 2005 and thirteen by 2007, to conduct two military operations simultaneously', No. 8832, 23 November.

Agence Presse (2004b) 'Europeans and Americans want to work together', No. 8789, 21 September.

Agence Presse (2007a) 'EU/Neighbourhood Policy: Resolved to join EU one day', No. 9493, 4 September.

Agence Presse (2007b) 'Darfur/Chad', No. 9465, 2 October.

Agence Presse (2007c) 'EU/ Neighbourhood', No. 9558, 6 December.

Agence Presse (2007d) 'EU and US wish to place their databases in network', No. 9568, 19 December.

Agence Presse (2007e) 'US extends visa waiver to 12 but new legislation increases the bar' No. 9480, 1 August.

Agence Presse (2008) 'European Parliament/Enlargement', No. 9577, 11 January.

Albright, M. (1998) 'The right balance will secure NATO's future', *The Financial Times*, 7 December.

Annan, K. (1999) 'Two concepts of sovereignty', *The Economist*, 18 September, pp. 81–82.

Archik, K. and Gallis, P. (2004) 'NATO and the European Union', Congressional Research Service Report for Congress, Washington, DC, 6 April.

Asmus, R. and Pollack, K. (2002) 'The new transatlantic project', Policy Review, The Hoover Institution, October and November.

Baker, J. (1989) 'A New Atlanticism', Speech of US Secretary of State James Baker, Berlin Press Club, November.

Balladur, E. (2008) 'For a Union of the West', Speech by former Prime Minister Edouard Balladur at Johns Hopkins School of Advanced International Studies, 11 September, *Policy World*, February 2009.

Barnier Report (2003) European Convention Working Group VIII on Defence, Brussels.

Best, R. (2001) 'Intelligence and law enforcement: Countering transnational threats to the US', Congressional Research Service Report for Congress, Washington, DC, 16 January.

Bilefsky, D. (2006) 'EU lawmakers assail Swift over data sharing', *The International Herald Tribune*, 5 October, p. 3.

Binnendijk, H. (2005) 'A trans-Atlantic storm over arms for China', *The International Herald Tribune*, 9 February, p. 6.

Blair, T. (2000) Speech by Prime Minister Tony Blair in Warsaw, Poland, 6 October.

Blix, H. (2010) Oral evidence from Dr Hans Blix to the Iraq Inquiry, 27 July, http://www.iraqinquiry.org.transcripts/oralevidence-bydate/100727.aspx (uncorrected transcript: accessed 9 August 2010).

Bobbitt, P. (2008a) ' "Terror" is the enemy', *The New York Times*, 14 December, p. 10.

Bosworth, S. (2009) Testimony of Ambassador Stephen Bosworth, Special Representative for North Korea Policy, US Department of State, before the Senate Foreign Relations Committee, 11 June, Washington, DC.

Boyes, R. (2010) 'Germany in crisis after surprise resignation of President Horst Kohler', *Times Online*, 1 June.

Burwell, F. (2006) 'Transatlantic transformation: Building a NATO–EU security architecture', Atlantic Council Policy Paper, February, www.acus.org.

Bush, G. W. (2002a) President George W. Bush delivers the graduation speech at West Point, The White House, 1 June, http.www.whitehouse.gov/news/releases/2002/06 (accessed 21 August 2002).

Bush, G. W. (2002b) State of the Union Speech by President George W. Bush to both Houses of Congress, January, Washington, DC.

Bush, G. W. (2005) Remarks by President George W. Bush at Concert Noble, Brussels, 21 February, courtesy of the Embassy of the United States to Belgium, http://www.uspolicy.be/Article.asp?ID=2A17CEE7-C702-45A8-8579-203A49485E4C (accessed 2 September 2009).

Butler, D. (2007) 'US lawmakers pressuring EU on Hezbollah designation', Associated Press Worldstream, 20 June, (accessed 10 July 2009).

Cameron, F. and Balfour, R. (2006) 'The European Neighbourhood Policy as a Conflict Prevention Tool', EPC Issue Paper No. 47, European Policy Centre, Brussels.

Charter, D. (2008) 'Royal Navy takes over task force on pirate sea patrols', *The Times*, 9 December, p. 37.

Charter, D., Whittel, G. and Bremner, C. (2010) 'Europe warns Obama: this relationship is not working', *The Times*, 15 July, p. 1.

Clarke, R. and Beers, R. (Chairs) (2006) *The Forgotten Homeland*, A Century Foundation Task Force Report, Century Foundation Press, New York.

Clarke, R. and McCaffrey, B. (Co-chairmen) (2004) 'NATO's role in confronting international terrorism', Atlantic Council Policy Paper, www.acus.org.

Clinton, H. (2009) Speech by Secretary of State Hillary Clinton at the Council on Foreign Relations, Washington, DC, 15 July, pp. 1–10.

Clinton, W. (1996) Speech by President Bill Clinton to the United Nations General Assembly, 24 September.

Cooper, R. (2002) Speech by European Council official Robert Cooper at the Conference of the British International Studies Association, University of Warwick, December.

Council of Ministers (1998) 'Pre-accession pact on organised crime between the member states of the European Union and the applicant countries of central and eastern Europe and Cyprus', 98/C 220/01, 28 May, Brussels.

Council of Ministers (2003) 'Basic principles for an EU strategy against weapons of mass destruction', 10352/03, Brussels, June.

Council of the European Union (2004) 'EU–US declaration on the non-proliferation of weapons of mass destruction', Dromoland Castle, 26 June.

Council of the European Union (2005a) 'Implementation of the Action Plan to Combat Terrorism: Report from the Counter-terrorism Coordinator', 15704/05, 12 December, Brussels.

Council of the European Union (2005b) 'The European Union Counter-terrorism Strategy', 14469/4/05, 30 November.

Council of the European Union (2008) 'Final report by EU–US High Level Contact Group on information sharing and privacy and personal data protection', 9831/08, Brussels, 28 May.

Declaration on Western European Union (1992) Treaty on European Union, Maastricht, Section B, paragraph 4, February.

Dempsey, J. (2008) 'Europe lagging in effort to train Afghan police', *The International Herald Tribune*, 29 May, p. 2.

Dittrich, M. (2006) 'Muslims in Europe: Addressing the challenges of radicalisation', European Policy Centre, Brussels, http://www.epc.eu.

Economist, The (2000) 'A shield in space: Missile defences', 3 June, pp. 23–5.

Economist, The (2001) 'Keeping friends', 10 February, pp. 27–30.

Economist, The (2004) 'The weapons that weren't: Special Report: Intelligence failures', 17 July, pp. 23–25.

Economist, The (2006a) 'Special Report: North Korea: The nightmare comes to pass', 14 October, pp. 25–7.

Economist, The (2006b) 'Predictions of its death were premature: Special Report: NATO's Future', 25 November, pp. 22–5.

Economist, The (2006c) 'Joining the nuclear family', 4 March, pp. 65–6.

Economist, The (2007) 'Charlemagne: Berlin minus', 10 February, p. 44.

Economist, The (2008a) 'A ray of light in the dark defile: The state of NATO', 29 March, pp. 31–3.

Economist, The (2008b) 'Redrawing the MAP in Europe', 12 April, p. 41.

Economist, The (2008c) 'Charlemagne: Balkan exceptionalism', 17 May, p. 54.

Economist, The (2008d) 'In the nick of time: A special report on EU enlargement', 31 May, pp. 3–16.

Economist, The (2008e) 'A hero at home, a villain abroad', 21 June, pp. 85–6.

Economist, The (2008f) 'Behind America's shield', 23 August, pp. 32–3.

Economist, The (2008g) 'When nuclear sheriffs quarrel', 1 November, pp. 73–4.

Economist, The (2008h) 'A damp squib', 22 November, p. 48.

Economist, The (2008i) 'Iran's nuclear programme: As the enrichment machines spin on', 2 February, pp. 29–32.

Economist, The (2009a) 'Have combat experience, will travel', 28 March, pp. 70–1.

Economist, The (2009b) 'Charlemagne: A surfeit of leaders', 11 April, p. 41.

Economist, The (2009c) 'Talking Turkey', 11 April, p. 16.

Economist, The (2009d) 'Lexington: After the dark side', 25 April, p. 54.

Economist, The (2009e) 'Giving a shunt towards Europe', 23 May, pp. 39–40.

Economist, The (2009f) 'Charlemagne: Turkey's circular worries', 5 September, p. 48.

Economist, The (2009g) 'America and eastern Europe: End of an affair?' 12 September, pp. 47–8.

Economist, The (2009h) 'An Iranian nuclear bomb, or the bombing of Iran?' 5 December, pp. 27–30.

Economist, The (2010a) 'And the price of nuclear power?' 27 February, pp. 65–6.

Economist, The (2010b) 'Chain reaction', 17 April, p. 13.

Economist, The (2010c) 'Not just any deal will do', 22 May, p. 67.

Economist, The (2010d) 'Consensus costs', 5 June, p. 74.

Economist, The (2010e) 'Is Turkey turning?' 12 June, pp. 51–2.

Economist, The (2010f) 'Charlemagne: Shrinking the job to fit the woman?' 13 February, p. 46.

European Commission (1997) 'Agenda 2000. Summary and Conclusions of the Opinions of the Commission Concerning the Applications for Membership to the European Union Presented by the Candidate Countries', July, Strasbourg.

European Commission (2004) 'European Neighbourhood Policy strategy paper', COM(2004) 373 final, Brussels, 12 May.

European Commission (2006) 'Enlargement strategy and main challenges 2006–2007', COM (2006) 649, Brussels, 8 November.

European Council (1992) Treaty on European Union, Maastricht, 7 February.

European Council (1999a) Presidency Conclusions, Helsinki, 10–11 December.

European Council, (1999b) Presidency Conclusions, Special European Council Tampere, Finland, October.

European Council, (1999c) Presidency Conclusions, Cologne, 4–5 June.

European Council (2000) Presidency Conclusions, Santa Maria da Feira, 19–20 June.

European Council (2003a) Presidency Conclusions, Brussels, 12 December.

European Council, (2003b) 'The European Security Strategy: A Secure Europe in a Better World', Brussels, 12 December.

European Council (2003c) 'EU Strategy against Proliferation of Weapons of Mass Destruction', Thessaloniki, Greece, December, http://www.consilium.europa.eu/uedocs/cmsUpload/st15708.en03.pdf.

European Council (2004) Presidency Conclusions, Brussels, 4–5 November.

European Council (2008) 'Report on the Implementation of the European Security Strategy: Providing Security in a Changing World', S407/08, 11 December, Brussels.

Evans, M. (2001) 'Guthrie seeks to ease US tension over Euro force', *The Times*, 9 February, p. 2.

Evans, M. (2008) 'Summit setback for NATO expansion plan', *The Times*, 4 April, p. 40.

Everts, S. (2001) 'Unilateral America, lightweight Europe: Managing divergence in transatlantic foreign policy', Centre for European Reform, London.

Financial Times, The (2003) Open Letter of the Group of Eight, 8 January.

Finkelstein, D. (2009) 'Let us reach for a better future', Speech of the President of the United States, Barak Obama, *The Times*, 6 April, p. 9.

Frankel, G. (2004) 'Europe, US diverge over how to fight terrorism', *The Washington Post*, 28 March, A15.

Gallis, P. (2006) 'NATO in Afghanistan: A Test of the Transatlantic Alliance' Congressional Research Service Report for Congress, Washington, DC, 22 August.

Gates, R. (2010) Speech by Secretary of Defense Robert Gates at the NATO Strategic Concept Seminar, National Defense University, Washington, 23 February.

Gibb, F. (2010) 'They say that they were tortured, now tell us the truth, urges watchdog', *The Times*, 20 February, pp. 6–7.

Gordon, P. (2009) 'The Lisbon Treaty: Implications for future relations between the European Union and the United States', Testimony of Philip Gordon, Assistant Secretary for European and Eurasian Affairs, to the House Committee on Foreign Affairs, Subcommittee for Europe, 15 December.

Grant, C. (2003) 'Transatlantic rift: How to bring the two sides together', Centre for European Reform, July, www.cer.org.

Guardian, The (2009) 'President Obama pledges a new beginning between the US and Muslims around the world', 4 June.

Guardian Unlimited (2009) 'EU and US draw up plans for new counter-terrorism regime', 15 June (accessed 10 July 2009).

Haass, R. (2002) 'Charting a New Course in the Transatlantic Relationship', Remarks to the Centre for European Reform, London, 10 June.

Hamilton, D. (2004) 'American perspectives on the European Security and Defence Policy', Danish Institute for International Studies, http://www.esdp-course.ethz.ch/content.

High Level Panel on Threats for the Twenty-first Century (2007) 'A More Secure World: Our Shared Responsibility', United Nations, New York, December.

House of Lords (2007) 'The EU/US Passenger Name Record (PNR) Agreement', European Union Committee, HL Paper 108, The Stationery Office, London.

Irish Chair (2010) 'The NPT Review Conference 2010', Institute of International and European Affairs, 15 June.

Kanter, J. (2008) 'EU seeks to allay privacy concerns: Data-sharing talks with US draw fire', *The International Herald Tribune*, 3 July, p. 4.

Katzman, K. (2006) 'The Iran–Libya Sanctions Act (ILSA)', Congressional Research Service Report for Congress, Washington, DC, 3 April.

Katzman, K. (2008) 'Iran: US concerns and policy responses', Congressional Research Service Report for Congress, Washington, DC, 4 September.

Kennedy, J. F. (1962) Presidential address on the goal of an Atlantic partnership, Philadelphia, 4 July.

Keohane, D. (2005) 'The EU and International Terrorism' in "Securing the European Homeland: The EU, Terrorism and Homeland Security", Bertelsmann Stiftung, Gutersloh, August.

Kidd, J. (2009) 'Turkey's participation in the European Union's Common European Security and Defence Policy, 1998–2003', unpublished doctoral thesis, King's College, London.

Kissinger, H. (1973) 'The Year of Europe', Speech to the Associated Press Annual Luncheon, New York, 23 April.

Kissinger, H. and Summers, L. (Co-chairs) (2004) 'Renewing the Atlantic Partnership', Report of an Independent Task Force Sponsored by the Council on Foreign Relations, New York.

Korski, D. and Gowan, R. (2009) 'Can the EU rebuild failing states? A review of Europe's civilian capabilities', European Council on Foreign Relations, London, October, http://www.ecfr.eu/page/documents.pdf (accessed 21 June 2010).

Kupchan, C. (2001) 'The US–European relationship: Opportunities and challenges', Evidence before the Senate Foreign Relations Subcommittee, Washington, DC, 25 April.

Kutchesfahani, S. (2006) 'Iran's nuclear challenge and European diplomacy', European Policy Centre Paper 46, Brussels, March.

Lebl, L. (2007) 'Advancing US interests with the EU', The Atlantic Council, January.

Leeuwen, M. (1999) 'EU and US: Security relations and the New Transatlantic Agenda', Netherlands Institute for International Affairs 'Clingendael', The Hague.

Lloyd Parry, R. (2010) 'Weakness at heart of mission to put fear of God into North', *The Times*, 28 July, pp. 26–27.

Lugar, R. (2002) 'NATO's role in the war on terrorism', Speech to US–NATO Missions Annual Conference, Brussels, reported in *Washington File*, US Embassy in London, 18 January.

Maddox, B. (2008) 'Iran's nuclear threat will be first test for new president', *The Times*, 30 May, p. 42.

Meetings of the Heads of State (2003) Summit on Defence between France, Germany, Belgium and Luxembourg, Brussels, 29 April.

Meyer, C. (2009) Oral evidence from Sir Christopher Meyer to the Iraq Inquiry, 26 November, http://www.iraqinquiry.org.transcripts/oral evidence-bydate/091126.aspx (final transcript: accessed 9 August 2010).

Millar, A. and Rosand, E. (2006) 'Allied against terrorism: What's needed to strengthen worldwide commitment', A Century Foundation Report, New York.

Missiroli, A. (2008) 'Policy Brief. Revisiting the European Security Strategy – Beyond 2008', European Policy Centre, Brussels, April.

National Commission on Terrorist Attacks upon the United States (2004) The 9/11 Commission Report, W.W. Norton, New York.

National Intelligence Estimate (2007) 'Iran: Nuclear intentions and capabilities', National Intelligence Council, Washington, DC, November.

NATO (1995) 'Study on NATO Enlargement', Brussels.

NATO (2010) 'NATO 2020: Assured security; dynamic engagement. Analysis and recommendations of the group of experts on a New Strategic Concept for NATO', Brussels, 17 May.

Niblett, R. and Mix, D. (2006) 'Transatlantic approaches to sanctions: Principles and recommendations for action', CSIS Europe Program Report, 10 October.

Niksch, L. (2002) 'North Korea's nuclear weapons program', Congressional Research Service Report for Congress, Washington, DC, 22 January.

North Atlantic Council (1994) 'Declaration of the Heads of State and Government', NATO Headquarters, Brussels, 10–11 January.

North Atlantic Council (1999) 'Washington Summit Communique', Washington, DC, 24 April.

North Atlantic Council (2002) 'Declaration by the Heads of State and Government participating in the North Atlantic Council', Prague, 21–22 November.

North Atlantic Council (2009) 'Declaration by the Heads of State and Government participating in the North Atlantic Council', Strasbourg/Kehl, 4 April.

Nuland, V. (2008a) Speech at the London School of Economics, London, 25 February.

Nuland, V. (2008b) Speech to the Press Club and American Chamber of Commerce, Paris, 22 February.

Nunn, S. and Lellouche, P. (2005) 'Now in rehearsal, the unthinkable: NATO's Black Dawn', *The International Herald Tribune*, 31 May, p. 8.

Obama, B. (2009a) Speech to the United Nations, New York, September.

Obama, B. (2009b) Speech given at the University of Cairo, June.

Pank, P. (2009) 'Patrolling the sea for piracy is like policing America's East coast with five police cars', *The Times*, 1 December, p. 37.

Patten, C. and Lamy, P. (2003) 'Let's put away the megaphones: A trans-Atlantic appeal', *The International Herald Tribune*, 9 April, p. 8.

Petersberg Declaration (1992) Council of Ministers, Western European Union, Bonn, 19 June.

Peterson, J. (2005) (Chairman) 'Review of the framework for relations between the European Union and the United States', Commissioned by the European Commission, Directorate General External Relations, Unit C1, Final Report.

Pew Survey (2009) 'US seen as less important, China as more powerful', *Press Report*, 3 December, http://people-press.org/report/?pageid=1622 (accessed 8 August 2010).

Philip, C. (2009a) 'Secret document exposes Iran's nuclear trigger', *The Times*, 14 December, pp. 1, 7.

Philip, C. (2009b) 'Tehran feels heat as world leaders declare war on the threat of nuclear weapons', *The Times*, 25 September, pp. 42–43.

Portela, C. (2004) 'The Role of the EU in the non-proliferation of nuclear weapons: The way to Thessaloniki and beyond', PRIF Reports 65, Frankfurt Peace Research Institute, Frankfurt.

Prodi, R. and Verhofstadt, G. (co-chairs) (2010) 'Reshaping EU–US relations: A concept paper', A Reflection Group consisting of Romano Prodi, Guy Verhofstadt, Jerry Buzek, Etienne Davignon, Jacques Delors,

Joschka Fischer, Paavo Lipponen and Tommaso Padoa-Schioppa, Notre Europe, Paris, March.

Reid, T. (2009) 'Poles feel exposed as Obama's missile shield heads south', *The Times*, 18 September, pp. 6–7.

Reid. T. and Whittell, G. (2009) 'Huge deployment of extra troops is Obama's vision for quick end to the war', *The Times*, 2 December, pp. 6–7.

Rice, C. (2003) Speech at the International Institute for Strategic Studies, London, Office of the Press Secretary, The White House, 26 June.

Rumsfeld, D. (2001) 'A new kind of war', *The New York Times*, 27 September.

Scheffer, J. de Hoop (2007) 'NATO and the EU: Time for a new chapter', Keynote Speech by the NATO Secretary General, Berlin, 29 January.

Schroeder, G. (2005) Speech of German Chancellor Gerhard Schroeder at the 41st Munich Security Conference, 12 February.

Solana, J. (2001) 'Destined to Cooperate', *The Financial Times*, 14 June.

Solana, J. (2003) 'Europe and America: Partners of choice', Speech by the EU High Representative to the Foreign Policy Association, New York, 7 May.

Stelzenmüller, C. (2008) 'Transatlantic power failures: America and Europe, seven years after 9/11: Hard power humbled, soft power exposed, and a looser, more pragmatic relationship', Brussels Forum Series, German Marshall Fund.

Talbott, S. (1999) 'America's stake in a strong Europe', Speech by the Deputy Secretary of State, Strobe Talbott, at the Royal Institute for International Affairs, London, October.

Transatlantic Trends (2004) German Marshall Fund of the United States, http://www.gmfus.org/trends/doc/2004_english_key.pdf (accessed 8 August 2010).

Transatlantic Trends (2009) 'Survey: support for US leadership skyrockets in Europe', Press Information, German Marshall Fund of the United States, http://www.gmfus.org/trends/pressinfo.html (accessed 8 August 2010).

United Nations High Level Panel on Threats (2004) 'A more secure world: Our shared responsibility', The Secretary General's High Level Panel on Threats, Challenges and Change, December.

United States National Security Strategy (2002) The White House, Washington, DC.

United States National Security Strategy to Combat Weapons of Mass Destruction (2003) The White House, Washington, DC, December.

United States National Security Strategy (2006) The White House, Washington, DC, March.

United States National Security Strategy (2010) Overview of the National Security Strategy, The White House, 27 May, www.America.gov.

United States National Strategy for Combating Terrorism (2003) The White House, Washington, DC, February.

United States National Strategy for Homeland Security (2002) The White House, Washington, DC.

United States National Strategy for Homeland Security (2007) The White House, Washington, DC, October.

Vershbow, A. (2000) Speech at the Transatlantic Forum, Paris, 22 May.

Vershbow, A. (2001) Speech at the Netherlands Institute for International Relations, Clingendael, 23 March.

Volker, K. (2006) Remarks at Media Roundtable, Brussels, 6 February, http://www.state.gov/.

Vries, G. de (2004a) Speech to the CSIS, Washington, DC, 13 May, http://ue.eu.int/uedocs/cmsUpload/CSIS_Washington.13_May_2004. pdf.

Vries, G. de (2004b) Address at the Seminar on EU cooperation in preparing for attacks with CBRN-agents, Ministry of Foreign Affairs, The Hague, 7 July.

Weaver, M. (2008) 'US considers tighter travel rules for European visitors', *Guardian Unlimited*, 16 January, www.guardian.co.uk/print. 332086192-332106710.html (accessed 21 January 2008).

Witney, N. and Shapiro, J. (2009) 'Towards a post-American Europe: A power audit of EU–US relations', European Council on Foreign Relations, London, 2 November, http://wwwecfr.eu/page/-/documents/ towards_a_post_American_Europe.pdf (accessed 21 June 2010).

Woolf, A. (2010) 'The New START Treaty: Central limits and key provisions', Congressional Research Service Report for Congress, Washington, DC, 18 June.

Wright, R. (2008) 'Major powers discuss Iran strategy', *The Washington Post*, 26 February, A12.

Zoellick, R. (1990) 'The new Europe in a new age: Insular, itinerant or international? Prospects for an alliance of values', US Department of State Despatch, 24 September.

Interviews

Interview (1999) conducted by the author, US Department of Defense, Washington, DC, November.

Interview (2004a) conducted by the author with an official from the Counter-terrorism Section, US Department of Justice, Washington, DC, September.

Interview (2004b) conducted by the author with representatives of the European Police Office, Offices of the European Commission, Washington, DC, September.

Interview (2004c) conducted by the author with an official from the European Commission Mission to the US, Washington, DC, September.

Interview (2005) conducted by the author with an official from the Department of State, US Mission to the EU, Brussels, February.

Interview (2006) conducted by the author with Major General Tim Cross, British Deputy to General Jay Garner, Office for Reconstruction and Humanitarian Assistance, Nottingham, October.

Interview (2008a) conducted by the author with an official from the European Commission Mission to the US, Washington, DC, February.

Interview (2008b) conducted by the author with an official from the Office for Europe and Regional Affairs, US Department of State, Washington, DC, February.

Interview (2008c) conducted by the author with an official from the Office for Civil Reconstruction and Development, US Department of State, Washington, DC, March.

Interview (2008d) conducted by the author with an official from the US Department of Homeland Security, Washington, DC, March.

Interview (2008e) conducted by the author with an official from the Department of Justice, US Mission to the European Union, Brussels, April.

Interview (2008f) conducted by the author with an official from the Department of Homeland Security, US Mission to the European Union, Brussels, April.

Index

Note: **bold** = extended discussion.